THE HISTORY OF MUSIC
TO THE DEATH OF SCHUBERT

Da Capo Press Music Reprint Series

GENERAL EDITOR

FREDERICK FREEDMAN

VASSAR COLLEGE

THE
HISTORY OF MUSIC
TO THE DEATH OF
SCHUBERT

By John Knowles Paine

DA CAPO PRESS · NEW YORK · 1971

A Da Capo Press Reprint Edition

This Da Capo Press edition of
The History of Music to the Death of Schubert
is an unabridged republication of the first
edition published in Boston and London in 1907.

Library of Congress Catalog Card Number 78-127280
SBN 306-70038-7

Published by Da Capo Press
A Division of Plenum Publishing Corporation
227 West 17th Street, New York, N.Y. 10011
All Rights Reserved

Manufactured in the United States of America

THE HISTORY OF MUSIC
TO THE DEATH OF SCHUBERT

THE HISTORY OF MUSIC
TO THE DEATH OF
SCHUBERT

BY

JOHN K. PAINE, Mus.D.

LATE PROFESSOR OF MUSIC IN HARVARD UNIVERSITY

BOSTON AND LONDON
GINN AND COMPANY, PUBLISHERS

The Athenæum Press

GINN & COMPANY · PRO-
PRIETORS · BOSTON · U.S.A.

PREFACE

During the last few years of his life Professor Paine frequently expressed the wish that his lectures on the History of Music, to which he had devoted much care and thought, might be published, and with a view to the fulfillment of this wish, he had had the lectures covering the period to the death of Schubert typewritten and had begun the revision of this material for the printer. The remainder of the work existed only in the form of manuscript notes and had not received the same careful treatment which had been given to the earlier portion. It was therefore decided to omit the later lectures in accordance with what it was thought would have been the desire of Professor Paine himself. The title has been made to fit the abbreviated form in which the book appears.

The editor, whose chief qualification for his task is a deep love for Professor Paine and a slight knowledge of ancient musical instruments, consented, only with reluctance, to the request of Mrs. Paine that he should see the book through the press. His work has consisted largely in verifying names and dates, and in making such changes in form and style as he could feel reasonably sure Professor Paine would himself have made. The editor is also responsible for the form in which the title appears and for most of the marginal notes. He wishes to acknowledge his indebtedness to Professor J. D. M. Ford and to Professor G. L. Kittredge of Harvard University, who have assisted him in reading the proof and have aided him with many important suggestions, and particularly to the latter, whose invaluable advice has been as generously given as it was freely asked.

ALBERT A. HOWARD

CONTENTS

PART I—ANCIENT AND MEDIÆVAL MUSIC

PART II—ORIGIN OF DRAMATIC MUSIC
OPERA AND ORATORIO

THE HISTORY OF MUSIC

PART I

ANCIENT AND MEDIÆVAL MUSIC

CHAPTER I

THE MUSIC OF THE GREEKS AND ROMANS

The history of music presents to the student peculiar difficulties in the way of tracing the gradual development of the art from its obscure beginnings in remote antiquity to its culmination in our own time. The monuments of ancient architecture and sculpture and the books of early poetry, which have so long outlived the nations that produced them, are fit memorials of the rise and progress of these arts; but we are unable to reproduce ancient music from the few reputed specimens at hand, or the theoretical treatises of ancient authors. It is easy to account for this want of knowledge concerning the music of primitive times.

Music, as compared with poetry, requires a far more complex system of written signs in order to note faithfully every phase of thought and emotion as expressed through the manifold combinations of musical tone. Ages must have passed away before even the rudest notation could be invented. This tardy development of the art also corresponds, historically, with the growth of our moral and spiritual nature, and as music is the most emotional and mystical of the fine arts, so it stands out prominently in history as identified with Christianity. Yet music, apparently, is as old as the world, and must have been born with speech itself. If we turn to wholly uncivilized men, we observe a natural love of music, as exhibited in their rude songs and dances.

3

Earliest
music vocal

The earliest music was undoubtedly vocal, and long preceded the invention of musical instruments. There is reason
to believe that the rhythmical element in music soon aroused
the attention of primitive men, and led to the invention of
the lowest class of instruments, like the drum, tambour, and
castanets, which served merely to intensify the rhythmical
effect in dancing and singing. This may be considered as the
first decided step in musical progress; for the invention of
such instruments was the result of reflection; whereas the first
rude unaccompanied singing was as spontaneous as speech.

The next step would naturally lead to the invention of
certain wind instruments, suggested possibly by the singing
of the birds, the sound of falling water, or the whistling wind,
or by experiments in blowing on the crooked horn of an
animal. This may have been the origin of the flute, Pan's
pipe, and the horn. The imitation of sounds in nature may
likewise have given rise to stringed instruments like the harp,
lyre, and cithara. A Greek myth relates that while Mercury
was walking for pleasure on the banks of the Nile, his foot
accidentally struck against a tortoise shell, across which some
dried tendons were stretched. This blow produced a musical
sound which suggested to him the idea of the lyre.

Music in
Greece

It would far exceed the limits set for these lectures to
attempt to give an account of the music of uncivilized races
of men; neither have we the time to examine the musical
record of old nations like the Chinese, Indians, Arabians, and
Persians. We find these more or less civilized people in the
possession of a variety of musical instruments, of a tonal system
of scales and keys, and of a kind of notation. These characteristics are likewise true of the ancient Egyptians, Hebrews, and
other people of pre-Hellenic culture. Classical Greece was
the first land where music was cultivated for its own sake.
Hitherto it had held a subordinate rank, and was used chiefly
to regulate the steps of the dance, to heighten the joys of the
festival, and to aid the rites of religion; it was also practised

for its supposed medicinal qualities. But the Greeks, with their wonderful love and appreciation of the beautiful, honored music as one of the highest arts.

Apollo, the god of light and inspiration, who announced to men the infallible will of Zeus, was not only a prophetic but a musical god. As the leader of the Muses he was represented in human form, — the embodied ideal of young Greece, and the model of singers and musicians.

The world of the gods resounded with divine music, and it was the gift of the gods to men. Orpheus, the heroic son of the Muses, charmed with his song the rocks, the trees, and wild animals, and moved even the merciless gods of Hades with the power of his lyre. Among the ancient Greeks music for the first time in history attained a complete artistic development. It is evident, from the attention devoted to the subject by the greatest philosophers of antiquity, that this art acted powerfully on the Greeks, and that its external position was higher even than that of architecture or of sculpture. Music was regarded by them as of the utmost importance to the state. They gave the word the most extended significance: the name "music" comprehended not only the art of sounds, but also poetry, dancing, oratory, philosophy, astronomy, and grammar.

The history of Greek music may be divided into three great periods. The first embraces the obscure, half-mythological age; the second commences with the Dorian migration about a thousand years before Christ, and closes about the time of the Peloponnesian War, four centuries before Christ. This long epoch witnessed the development and culmination of Greek music, and the names of the great musicians, Terpander, Sappho, Arion, Pythagoras, Pindar, Simonides, Phrynis, Timotheus, and others, testify to the high state of excellence which the Greeks had attained in the lyric, heroic, and dramatic styles.

The third and last period, from the time of the Peloponnesian War till about the beginning of the Christian era, was

Periods of development

rich in musical theorists like Aristoxenus, Didymus, Euclid, Ptolemy, Plato, Aristotle, and Plutarch. The music of this epoch, however, lost its former simple and noble characteristics. The mere technics of the art gained the ascendency; instrumental music was practised separately from poetry; brilliant virtuosos, singers, and performers on the cithara, flute, and lyre became common. In this manner the true aim of Greek music was lost, and its glory was destined to fade away. The various forms of Greek music may be classified according to the chronological order of their development. In the earliest times were sung the religious hymns of the priests; the Homeric age abounded in epic ballads and recitals of the rhapsodists; this was succeeded by the age of the lyrists and great musicians; and finally came the culminating epoch of the drama, in which all styles of music — recitative, lyric, and dramatic — reached their full and harmonious development.

The wonderful euphony and flexibility of the Greek language generated music spontaneously, and poetry and music sprang from the same source — poet and musician were one. These two arts were so interwoven that the history of the one cannot be pursued satisfactorily without intimate reference to the other.

Styles of singing

The Greeks had two styles of singing, *recitative* and *arioso*. The former was a kind of chant or recital used chiefly in the declamation of epic poetry. This recitative was limited to a few tones, and was held strictly subordinate to the quantity of the syllables and the rhetorical accent of the words. The other, more melodious style, was likewise dependent on the rhythmical and metrical structure of the verse, but greater freedom characterized it in the movement and modulation of the tones; in this respect it approached more nearly to modern melody.

The simple, recitative style was the more ancient; its particular class of melodies was the so-called nomes, which are supposed to have been formerly hymns to Apollo. In earlier times the nomes were of great simplicity; they probably held the same relation to later Greek melodies that the old church chorals do to modern airs. Subsequently the nomes became more varied and numerous. They had certain peculiarities of rhythmical and tonal treatment which expressed particular national or individual characteristics of style. These strongly marked features may have given rise to the name, — from νόμος (law), — thus designating the strict rule of melodic treatment required of the artist.

The chorus of the drama was sung to the various nomes which had been handed down from earlier times. This explains how it was that the great dramatists were able to set music to their own poetry; for as the dialogue was simply recited, they had only to give instructions what nomes or well-known melodies were to be sung in the chorus. The singing of the chorus was accompanied by dancing and instrumental playing; the rhythm was marked by the stamping of heavy wooden soles worn by the coryphæus, or chorus leader.

Instrumental music was an important auxiliary of singing, *Instrumental music* but with the Greeks it never gained a worthy independence, as in modern times. Pure instrumental music was confined to feats of skill in solo playing, and though the expertness which a performer might show was oftentimes a matter of astonishment, this branch of ancient music did not meet with favor from the most cultivated minds. Plato denounces such instrumental music as inartistic and mere legerdemain. Our chief sources of knowledge concerning ancient music are the theoretical writings of Aristoxenus, Euclid, Bacchus, Aristides, Didymus, Ptolemy, Plato, Aristotle, Plutarch, and others. These writings do not aim to give descriptions or analyses of musical compositions, neither do they enter into the doctrine of musical theory, but are devoted principally to the discussion of general musical subjects, which the ancients sought to justify and establish on philosophical grounds. I shall not attempt to enter into the details of the ancient theory of music, for it is a subject requiring so much time and study that we can only dwell for a moment on its general features.

The foundation of the Greek scale was the tetrachord, a series of four tones comprised within the limits of the interval of a *perfect fourth*. The tetrachord was diatonic, chromatic, or enharmonic, according to the disposition of its intermediate intervals. It was diatonic when it consisted of two whole tones and one half tone, bc−d−e or d−ef−g; it was chromatic when it contained two half tones and a minor third ascending, bcc♯−e or eff♯−a; and it was enharmonic when two quarter tones rested on the fundamental note followed by a major third, bb+c−e, ee+f−a. This quarter tone, which I have indicated by +, could have been nothing more than a mere sliding of the voice, or manner of singing. There is no reason for believing that the Greeks had more delicate organs of hearing or a more sensitive appreciation of musical intonation than we possess, and the ear does not seem to be endowed with the faculty of recognizing in practical music any finer distinction of sound than the half tone. This Greek enharmonic order, with its quarter tones, was derived from the old Dorian scale of Olympus, in which the third and seventh were wanting:

The new scale was produced by a simple sliding of the voice between e and f and b and c, — a manner of singing which every good judge will pronounce bad.

The *pentatonic* scale of Olympus was formed from the same intervals as the primitive Chinese and Gaelic minor scale, in which the fourth and seventh are wanting:

It was probably introduced into Greece from Western Asia before the Dorian invasion or together with it.

The diatonic scale was probably built up from this Dorian scale of Olympus. The introduction of one tone is attributed to Terpander, who added a seventh string to the lyre. The Dorian scale in his day was —

The scale was rendered a complete octachord by Pythagoras, who supplied the fifth, or missing tone, as follows :

Hypate	Parhy-pate	Lichanos	Mese	Paramese	Trite	Paranete	Nete
Lowest tone	Next lowest	Index tone	Middle	Next to middle	3d tone	Next to last	Last tone

The diatonic tetrachords were of three kinds, — Dorian, Lydian, and Phrygian, called after the several divisions of the Greek people. The Dorian tetrachord has the semitone at the beginning of the group; for example, ef–g–a or bc–d–e. The Lydian tetrachord has the semitone at the end ; as, c–d–ef or g–a–bc. The Phrygian tetrachord has the semitone in the middle ; as, d–ef–g or a–bc–d.

From these three ancient diatonic tetrachords sprang the whole system of Greek scales. They were combined in an ascending or descending order, and were either conjunct or disjunct as they were required to complete the octachord :

1. Conjunct   2. Disjunct

There were nine octave groups, or diatonic scales, formed in Scales this manner, each one being composed of five whole tones and two half tones, as in our modern scales, which were taken from the Greek system. Each octave group differed from the others in the disposition or order of the half tones. The Dorian octave group extended from E to e, the Phrygian from D to d, and the Lydian from C to c; each was attended by two relative scales whose keynotes were placed a fourth below or a fifth above the keynote of the principal scale. The Dorian, Phrygian, and Lydian scales were generally composed of two disjunct tetrachords, as follows:

Their relative scales were composed of conjunct tetrachords, making but seven tones, which left one tone over, called the diazeuctic (dividing tone), as follows:

When this dividing tone appears as the highest tone, the scale is called *hyper;* when the dividing tone appears as the lowest tone, the scale is called *hypo.* Hyperdorian is, therefore, the scale a fifth above the Dorian; hypodorian, the scale a fourth below the Dorian, thus:

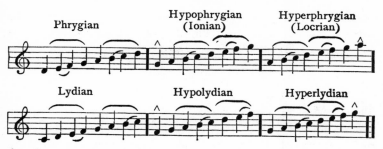

As the octave contains only seven different tones, there
can be only seven different octave groups in reality, instead
of the nine which are given in the table. It will be seen that
the hyperphrygian corresponds with the hypodorian, and the
hyperlydian with the hypophrygian.

Extension of the scale

Until the time of Aristoxenus (c. 350 B.C.) the scale confined itself to eight tones of two disjunct tetrachords, called
the octachordum Pythagorae, as before described. From this
octachord sprang the more extended system, with a compass
of two octaves from A to a′, and consisting of five conjunct
Dorian tetrachords, with a fundamental preparatory tone,
called the proslambanomenos (additional tone) as follows :

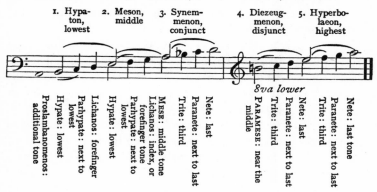

It will be seen from this table that in order to preserve
the intervals of the Dorian tetrachord, which has a semitone

between the first two tones, it was necessary to repeat two tones, c and d, in the tetrachords 3 and 4, as follows :

Thus it will be observed that two of the apparent eighteen tones appear twice, so that there are, in reality, but sixteen different tones in this double octave scale. This was called the *perfect, immutable* system. It resembles closely our modern minor scale. We find it in use in the time of Euclid (300 B.C.). This system includes all the sounds within the ordinary compass of men's voices.

The Greeks transposed this system through all the semitones, so that there were twelve different keys, as in modern music, but there appeared to be fifteen, three being repeated. Of these, five were principal keys, having their stations, that is, their fundamental tones, in the middle of the compass, each within a semitone of the other : they were the Dorian, D ; the Ionian, D♯; the Phrygian, E ; the Æolian, F ; the Lydian, F♯. The different character of the modes and the pitch of key at which a melody was sung had an ethical meaning to the Greeks, which is difficult for us to appreciate.

Knowledge of harmony   There is no convincing proof that the Greeks had any practical knowledge of harmony, or music in different parts, beyond the most limited meaning of the term ; for the ratios of the intervals of musical sound made by Pythagoras, through the divisions of the monochord — an instrument which he invented for this purpose — did not distinguish the difference existing between a large and a small whole tone, as the modern system does ; accordingly, the major third was too large, and the minor third was too small, to be in good tune. This was likewise the case with the major and minor sixths ; the result was that the third and sixth were classed among the dissonant intervals. As no satisfactory harmony can exist without the use of the major and minor thirds and sixths, all dissonant intervals such as the second, seventh, etc., were of no practical value in Greek music, except as the successive tones of a melody.

It remained for modern Europeans to discover the hidden beauty of discords, when used in combination with concords according to rules founded on acoustical principles. This definition of dissonant intervals reduced Greek music to the narrow limits of the consonance of the unison and octave; probably no other intervals were used except the fourth and fifth, touched sparingly in the instrumental accompaniment.

The word "harmony," however, was used by the Greeks to designate the congruity or harmonious relation of the parts of a thing to its whole, or even the harmonious relation of two distinct things one to the other, as we sometimes use the expression. The special application of the word which they made to music was to indicate every melodious order of tones, whether of the most limited or the most extended form; the name "harmony" comprised even the various single parts, or elements, which severally contributed to the total effect of their music. Thus it signified the arioso style; tonal modulations; the diatonic, chromatic, and harmonic elements; the various keys and octave groups; in short, everything that held the legitimate relation of the parts of a thing to the whole.

Greek definition of harmony

Unison music, if prolonged, grows very monotonous and tiresome to modern ears. We crave the rich effects of harmony, and the superiority we claim for our music on this score may stand in the way of our just estimation of the worth of ancient unison singing. We may well believe that the chorus of the Greek tragedy must have exercised a wonderful power over its hearers through the absolutely correct manner in which it was performed; a unison of which we have no conception, for it is only possible under similar conditions. The Hebrews and other old nations must likewise have known something of such a pure unison. In the fifth chapter of Second Chronicles we read : " The trumpeters and singers were as one, to make one sound to be heard in praising and thanking the Lord." Perhaps the mere physical effect of massive unison singing may be imagined from the account given by Josephus of a performance before King Solomon of a band of two hundred thousand singers accompanied by forty thousand harps, forty thousand sistra, and two hundred thousand trumpets, making four hundred and eighty thousand musicians in all !

Melody

We are sure that the Greeks had no melody in the modern sense of the term, for in their so-called melopœia, or art of melody, the strains were held subservient to the rhythm and meter of the word ; whereas in the case of the modern canti-lena, or air, the syllables are made to conform in a large measure to the free movement of the tones and to equal divisions of time.

" Even though single melodies of the Greeks," says Ambros, " were called by particular names, there is no good reason for believing that as music they had any stamp of individuality to distinguish them one from another, or to give them any great variety. It was not so much the flow of melody which won the admiration of the auditors as the refinement of expression in the declamation of the same. When the singer appeared before the public it did not weigh so much *what* he sang as *how* he sang. He was a musical declamator, and what he executed appeared almost like an effusion of sudden inspiration, or a free improvisation."

Extant Greek music

The oldest specimen of Greek music extant is the melody of a part of the first Pythian ode of Pindar. It was alleged to have been discovered by Kircher (1650) in the library of a monastery near Messina. Since his day, search has been made for the original manuscript, but with no success, and doubt has been thrown on the genuineness of the melody. Other specimens of ancient music are three hymns — to Calliope,

Nemesis, and Apollo. The hymn to Nemesis is by Mesomedes, who lived in the time of Hadrian, in the second century. The other two hymns were written by Dionysius, who is supposed to have lived in the time of the Emperor Constantine, in the fourth century. Consequently these specimens are not relics of the classical period of Greek music, like the Pindaric ode, but were written when the old music had died out. They were brought to light by Vincenzo Galilei, father of the celebrated astronomer. He discovered them in a library at Rome, and first made them known in 1581, but was unable to decipher them. Burette, the French academician, was more successful. Subsequently a number of critics and scholars, including Father Martini, Marpurg, Forkel, Burney, Fétis, and Friedrich Bellermann, have given their own versions of the music of these relics. As important variations in the rhythm and measure characterize these attempts to reproduce, or at least to approximate the original music, considerable doubt is thrown over the whole matter. Bellermann, however, is now generally accepted as the most reliable authority on the subject.

It is difficult to form even a feeble idea of the effect of Greek music from these decipherments, for in the transposition into our modern tonal system they must have been greatly modified and modernized. However, the Greek notation, or semeiography, answered the purposes of their music. It consisted of over a hundred characters, — letters of the alphabet in various positions, — which represented the pitch but not the length of the tones.

MUSICAL INSTRUMENTS OF THE GREEKS

The most prominent stringed instrument of the Greeks was the lyre. Other names given to this class of instruments were phorminx, cithara, magadis, sambyke, chelys (Latin *testudo*), barbiton, psalterion, simicon, epigonion, etc. Some of these instruments were of Egyptian and Chaldean origin. The lyre

Stringed instruments

class of instruments and the aulos (flute) were the chief instruments employed by the Greeks in their classical declamatory music. The lyre was one of the most ancient instruments. Apollo is represented in plastic art holding the lyre in his hands. The word "lyre" (λύρα) does not occur in Homer; whereas the cithara (κίθαρις) and the phorminx (φόρμιγξ) are mentioned by him. The lyre had only four strings originally. Terpander (700 B.C.) increased the number of strings to seven. The scale consisted of two conjunct Dorian tetrachords :

Development of the lyre

In the time of Pythagoras (600 B.C.) an eighth string was added to the lyre, thus completing the octave. We owe this eight-stringed lyre to the Egyptians. Its scale consisted of two disjunct Dorian tetrachords :

Several centuries later a third conjunct tetrachord was added, making the ten-stringed lyre.

The cithara differed from the open-stringed lyre in having a wooden body which served as a resonator, whereby the tone was enriched. This and the other lyre instruments were often played with a short staff made of ivory, quill, or metal, held in the right hand, and used in plucking the strings. One of the most prominent of the lyre class was the magadis, which had twenty strings, enabling the performer to play in octaves ; this was called *magadizing*. The sambyke was very much like the magadis. The epigonion had forty strings, —a doubling of the twenty-stringed magadis. Its tone, therefore, was much stronger. Chelys and testudo are merely the Greek and Latin names of the tortoise, used to designate the lyre with reference to its origin.

The chief wind instrument of the Greeks was the aulos (αὐλός), — a name applied to a variety of tubes, or pipes, in which the air column vibrated by means of the breath of the player. There were three types : (1) the pipe which was sounded by blowing across the open end, or an open hole in its side ; (2) the pipe which had a reed mouthpiece inserted at one end ; (3) the kind in which the sound was produced by pressing the lips against the open end of the tube, thus forming a natural reed without a mouthpiece. These instruments had finger holes, in order to produce the diatonic and chromatic scales. The first type may be termed a flute ; the second, a kind of oboe, inasmuch as it employs a double reed. All of these instruments, however, had a tube of cylindrical bore, like the modern clarinet. Some of them may have employed the single reed, like the clarinet, but most of them had the double-reed (oboe) mouthpiece. Both single and double pipes were used, though with few exceptions the works of ancient art show a pair of pipes. Assyrian and Egyptian reliefs also show the double pipe almost exclusively. " In deciding how the musician performed on his two pipes at once there are three possibilities to be considered : he may have produced the same tone simultaneously on both pipes in unison ; he may have produced tones separated by an octave ; or he may have played the melody on one pipe and an accompaniment in accord, with smaller intervals than the octave, on the second." It is probable that this last method of playing on the two pipes by one performer was the one practised, for it was a wholly useless difference for one pipe to be longer than the other in case the pipes were to be sounded in unison. Moreover, it would be very difficult to keep the pipes in perfect tune with each other in unison playing. In performing on double pipes the longer, Phrygian, pipe was held in the left hand, and played the melody. The shorter pipe was held in the right hand, and played the accompanying harmonic intervals, — probably the fourth and fifth. But possibly in the

Wind instruments

The double pipe

music of the orgiastic worship of Cybele and of Bacchus, the Phrygian pipe, held in the left hand, played the accompanying part above the melody of the shorter pipe, and sometimes droned below it. " In performing on the double pipe a great deal of pressure was exerted by the breath on the cheeks and lips, and to relieve this pressure the performer made use of a bandage, passing over the mouth and cheeks, and provided with holes through which the mouthpieces of the instruments could be passed." [1]

Pitch and range of the pipe

Aristoxenus (350 B.C.) enumerates five classes of pipes, short and long, with reference to the pitch of each instrument. He gives the range of a single pipe as two octaves and a fifth. The entire range of these five classes was more than three octaves, corresponding closely with the compass of the human voice — from bass to soprano. Greek writers state that three different kinds of pipes were used for the three different scales, — Dorian, Phrygian, and Lydian, — until Pronomus improved the instruments so that all three scales could be played on the same pair of pipes. His achievement was so much admired by his countrymen that a statue was raised in his honor beside that of their great Epaminondas. This perfect aulos was used in the Pythian contests. The ancient pipe, held horizontally in playing, with the lips applied to an embouchure, was of Libyan origin. It is the prototype of the modern flute.[2]

Though the lyre, in all its varieties, was the ideal instrument for the service of the Greek drama and all forms of poetry, yet the aulos, or flute, held the next position in the estimation of the people. It was played on various public occasions, — at festivals, funerals, banquets, and at the

[1] This account of the aulos is cited from Professor A. A. Howard's article in the Harvard Studies, Vol. IV.

[2] Musical writers generally apply the name " flute " to all kinds of ancient pipes indiscriminately. The proper designation for pipes with oboe-reed or clarinet-reed mouthpieces is aulos; to those blown through the open end of the tube or through an embouchure on the side, the name " flute " applies.

Pythian games, — also as an accompaniment in the chorus of the drama and other declamatory vocal music. A number of flute virtuosos arose who were highly honored. The instruments were greatly improved in the course of time. The famous flute player Ismenias of Thebes is said to have paid no less than fifteen hundred dollars for a pair of flutes. In the time of the Persian War (fifth century before Christ) flute playing became a part of the training of boys. Bœotia was the land of flutes. Athens, in the time of Pericles, cultivated flute playing. The Spartans employed the flute to lead chorus singing, and it was the instrument of the battlefield. But Plato and Aristotle held flute music in contempt, as less suited than that of the lyre to accompany the words.

Other wind instruments of the Greeks were the trumpet, horn, and syrinx, or Pan's pipe. The syrinx was formed of seven, eight, or nine short hollow reeds fixed together in graduated lengths by wax, so as to produce the scale. The lower ends of the reeds were either closed or open; the upper ends were open, and were played on by the mouth. It was used by shepherds. The Greek hydraulos, or water organ, was suggested by the syrinx. The Greeks had also a number of instruments of percussion, — cymbals, drums, sistrum, and the like. These had a prominent place in the music at the festivals of Dionysus.

Pure instrumental music did not stand high in the estimation of Greek philosophers, yet certain descriptive, or "programme," forms of music were popular two or three centuries before the Christian era, at the time when Greek art was in its decline. Strabo and Pollux describe a Pythian instrumental nomos in five divisions, or movements, which aimed to represent the contest of Apollo with the dragon. After a prelude, or introduction, Apollo chooses the place of battle; in the next movement he calls the dragon to the fight; then the battle is represented by trumpets, flutes, etc., in iambics, with the gnashing of the monster's teeth in his death agony

Descriptive instrumental music

—a realistic effect produced by the shrill syrinx and short runs of the flutes. In the final movement Apollo celebrates his victory by a godlike dance. The orchestra consisted of flutes, citharas, trumpets, drums, and the syrinx. This first symphony, or symphonic poem, was composed by Timosthenes, a ship captain, who lived nearly three hundred years before Christ. He may be dubbed the Berlioz or Richard Strauss in the field of Greek programme music. Plato said of mere instrumental music that one can find no definite meaning in it; but that was before the time of the Pythian symphonic poem of Timosthenes.

Music highly esteemed by the Greeks

Music among the Greeks held not only an exalted position as compared with the other arts, but assumed a political and ethical significance, and, moreover, was considered to be of great symbolic importance to astronomy. The Pythagoreans believed that God regulated all things according to harmony. The seven planets of ancient astronomy were supposed to give out in sublime harmony the tones of the seven-stringed lyre, which was tuned to the seven degrees of the Dorian scale, as follows :

Moon	Mercury	Venus	Sun	Mars	Jupiter	Saturn
E	F	G	A	B	C	D

Plato and other philosophers gave earnest attention to this subject, and the speculations of the early Christian, mediæval, and modern writers with regard to the so-called music of the spheres testify to the fascination which this grand conception has for the mind, and would almost justify belief in its existence to-day.

The remarkable political and ethical significance attached by the Greeks to music is shown in the statements of her great philosophers. It is related that in primitive times the laws of state were sung to music. Plato declared that the introduction of new keys would be attended with great danger to the whole state, for the keys could not be changed without affecting the fundamental laws of the country. This influence of their music for good or evil can readily be accounted for by the fact that Greece was never the centralized state of a united nation, and that the several branches of the people had their individual, peculiar customs and tastes, as well as their own characteristic melodies and keys. Such marked contrasts of tribal music would naturally awaken the most powerful associations in the minds of the refined and sensitive Greeks.

We read in Plato that "the mixed Lydian and the hyper-lydian melodies are plaintive and wailing compositions, and must be discarded, as they are unfit even for virtuous women, much more for men. Lydian and Ionian melodies are effeminate and convivial. These are called 'lax modes,' and therefore should not be employed in the training of soldiers. The best music is not that which gives the most pleasure, but that which is acceptable to the noblest. Music should ever hold to the principle that its true object is to represent or imitate the good, the noble, and the worthy. We should, therefore, not judge of music merely as to its agreeableness, but seek that music which has a likeness to the goodness it represents." Character attributed to different modes

Similar opinions as to the moral worth of music were held by Aristotle, who says that its highest calling is to exert a good influence on the character. The Greeks united with instruction in religion instruction in poetry, music, and dancing, under the general name of the art of the Muses, or music; and gymnastics held the next place to music in the education of the young. "Many hold the opinion," says Plato, "that gymnastics is merely for the education of the body, and music for the education of the soul. Those who devote themselves exclusively to gymnastics become too rough and hard, and those who devote themselves exclusively to music become too soft and mild. Therefore music and gymnastics are not for the soul and body respectively, but for the soul, — for the two virtues of Wisdom and Courage, — to put them in harmony."

Music at
Sparta
Even the Spartans, who were more warlike and patriotic than art-loving, did not neglect music : the intellectual side of their education was represented wholly by musical training. The Spartan youth learned to sing, and play the cithara, not for the sake of the music itself, but for its educating influence upon mind and character. The Spartan warriors were led to battle to the sound of flutes and citharas. Terpander quelled a sedition in Sparta by the power of his singing. He raised the patriotic ardor of his hearers to such a pitch that they forgot their quarrel and were eager to march to battle against their common enemy.

These few extracts from the musical opinions of the greatest philosophers of antiquity show that the ancient estimation of music, as an indispensable means of moral and mental education, has never been surpassed in modern times. In fact, there is no modern people, with the exception perhaps of the Germans, who have shown an *equal* appreciation of the true significance of this art. It is true that Greek music included several arts under the name, yet the music of the modern mass, oratorio, and opera is associated with noble poetry. If we are behind the Greeks in our estimation of the ethical worth of music, the art of sounds itself has reached a development in the modern world of which the Greeks had no conception. With us it has become an independent art. It matters not how intimate its modern alliance with poetry may be, the chief interest of a mass, oratorio, or opera centers in the music. Moreover, modern instrumental music has attained, in the symphony, a height which may be called the climax of the art when considered according to its strict æsthetic significance.

But while we do justice to the greatness of our music, we must not fall into the error of underrating the excellence of ancient music, as have many writers and musicians. The few fragments at hand may not give us an exalted idea of its merits, neither can we reproduce Greek music from the scanty accounts of ancient theorists. We may be sure, at all events, that Greek music, like Greek sculpture, was distinguished by its clear and harmonious beauty of form; and so far as music can be called plastic, the term may be applied to that of the Greeks. It was the growth of centuries of cultivated civilization, during which the sensuous and intellectual sides of the art were developed into a complete, organic whole.

About a century and a half before the birth of Christ, Greece became a Roman province, and all the treasures of art, even its artists, musicians, and scholars, were drawn toward Rome, the capital of the world. Before this period Roman music must have been very simple in character. We read of singing at religious ceremonies, at funerals, and at banquets, and the words of an old song of the Arval Brothers are preserved in an inscription. The songs were usually accompanied on the double pipe, which was also used at sacrifices. The trumpet under various names was used for military signals. It is a significant fact that while Roman names are known for the different wind instruments, no such names for stringed instruments, if we except testudo, — an obvious translation from the Greek, — are known to us, while the name for music itself is of Greek origin. With the influx of Greek musicians a new era was introduced. But although the Romans patronized and encouraged art and artists, they remained mere imitators of the Greeks, and the splendor of Greek music, art, and learning was already fading away. The love of the Roman people for the cruel and brutal shows of the amphitheater incapacitated them for appreciating fully the religious character and poetical beauty of the classical Greek tragedy, as embodied in the great dramas of Æschylus, Sophocles, and Euripides. The dramatic interest of the Romans centered in the comedy, in which authors like

Music at Rome

Plautus and Terence showed great talent. They were also passionately fond of choral pantomimes, often wanton and lascivious spectacles with licentious dances. Both vocal and instrumental music were prominent in these performances.

Greek musicians at Rome Greek musicians in Rome devoted themselves to solo instrumental playing, and singing with cithara accompaniment. This citharodic style prevailed under the Empire until the sixth century of our era, and held a prominence in the private life of the Romans analogous to that of the song (*Lied*) with piano accompaniment in modern times. Its most brilliant period was during the time of the emperors, and terminated with the reign of Marcus Aurelius. Among the noted Græco-Roman musicians were Tigellius, protégé of Augustus and Nero, Dionysius, and Mesomedes, friend of Hadrian, whose hymn to Nemesis has already been mentioned. Until the third century citharodic singing was purely Hellenic; in the fourth century it was grafted on the Christian church, but without instrumental accompaniment.

CHAPTER II

EARLY CHURCH MUSIC

There can be no doubt that the early church borrowed most of its music from the East. The sacred music of the Hebrews gave to the music of the new era its holiness, while the superior art of the Greeks bestowed upon it form and beauty. The Greek scales were the foundation of the mediæval and modern scales. The spiritual life born of Christianity led ultimately to the development of a more profound, more inward, musical experience. It is reasonable to suppose that the old music haunted the minds of those men whose faith was superior to suffering and death, and who were exhorted by St. Paul to sing psalms and spiritual songs, making melody in their hearts to the Lord. The first Christians found safe hiding places from persecution in the catacombs and other dark underground rooms, where they could pursue their religious worship unmolested. These gloomy halls of the dead were made bright with the music of the era. It was probably simple unison song in the style of the ancient Jewish and Grecian melody, but pervaded and elevated by the intense fervor of Christian belief.

During the reign of Emperor Constantine, in the fourth century, absolute toleration was granted to the Christians, and at the Council of Nice (325) the Christian was declared to be the official church of the Empire. Splendid basilicas and churches rose up like magic : in the East, at Bethlehem, Jerusalem, and Constantinople; in Rome, over the grave of Peter. It was not long before music, as well as all the fine arts, found encouragement within the church. As in the ancient theater all the arts were combined harmoniously, so likewise in the church they were united to serve the high purposes

25

of religion.   Even at an earlier period *antiphonal* singing had
been introduced.   It owed its origin undoubtedly to the
responsive singing of Jewish temple music, though it is
attributed to Ignatius, bishop of Antioch (d. A.D. 107), who,
according to the legend, heard with rapt delight choirs of
angels answering each other in song.   And this suggested
to him the idea of having this wonderful celestial music imitated by the congregation of worshipers.   The early Church
Fathers, Clemens, Tertullian, Origen, and others, felt special
interest in the cultivation of church music.   The first important step for its advancement was taken in the Council of
Laodicea about 365 ; previously, music had been unwritten ;
there were no definite rules to guide the singers, and the
rapidly increasing number of worshipers found it more and
more difficult to unite their voices melodiously.   The Council
ordered that no person should sing in the church but the
authorized singers from their tribune.   Early in the fourth
century Pope Sylvester is supposed to have established a
school of singing which was soon followed by others.   Flavian,
bishop of Antioch, Diodorus, bishop of Tarsus, St. Basil,
archbishop of Cæsarea, and Damasus, bishop of Rome,
were identified with antiphonal singing.

Our knowledge of this early church music is not accurate,
but we know, at least, that it was derived from Jewish
temple music and other Oriental sources, as well as from
Greek melody.   In general the style was ornate ; it was not
limited to the Greek practice of allotting only one tone to a
syllable, but made free use of melismas (roulades), in which a
whole group of notes were sung to one division of a word in
the Oriental style, and which stood in marked contrast to the
simple word music of the Greeks.   This ornate style characterized the church music of Jerusalem, Antioch, Constantinople, and Armenia.   In the course of centuries it was
simplified in the Roman Church, and with the adoption of
the official antiphonary, or collection of standard melodies, in

the seventh century, the cantus planus (plain chant) became the standard. Meanwhile the Ambrosian hymn arose, which followed the simple and metrical form of Greek song.

St. Ambrose (c. 340–397), bishop of Milan, was the founder **Ambrosian** of Christian hymnody as well as the promoter of church music **hymns** in general. He is known to have written a number of hymns, ten of which are preserved. It is not probable, however, that he composed the melodies of these hymns. There is positive proof that he wrote the words of these six hymns : "Veni redemptor gentium," "Aeterne rerum conditor," "Deus creator omnium," "Illuxit orbi," "Iam surgit hora tertia," "Bis ternas horas explicans." Internal evidence shows that the remaining four are probably authentic : "Aeterna Christi munera," "O lux beata trinitas," "Splendor paternae gloriae," "Hic est dies verus Dei." These hymns are distinguished for their noble simplicity and religious feeling, both in the words and music. In metrical and musical form they are closely related to the contemporary Græco-Roman citharodic songs.

The verse employed by Ambrose is the iambic dimeter (♩ | ♩ ♩ | ♩ ♩ | ♩ ♩ | ♩). Each group of four verses forms a strophe, as in the odes of Horace. They are composed in the Dorian (E), Ionian (G), and Æolian (A) modes. The following Dorian hymn will serve as an example; it shows a decided affinity with the "Hymn to Apollo" by Dionysius, especially in the final cadence :

Ae - ter - na Chris - ti mu - ne - ra Et
mar - ty - rum vic - to - ri - as Lau - des fe - ren - tes
de - bi - tas Lae - tis ca - na - mus men - ti - bus.

The rhythm of these original hymns rested on the quantity of the syllables, as in Greek music. Later hymnodists, Prudentius, Mamertus, Sedulius, etc., used other meters, such as iambic trimeter and trochaic tetrameter. These imitations are as a rule inferior to the original hymns. Sixty of them at most have come down to us, of which not more than twenty are worthy of our interest. Ambrosian song spread rapidly throughout the Empire, and was cultivated for centuries, almost to the present day.

Besides these beautiful hymns there are the Ambrosian chants, in which the recitative style prevails, as in the modern chant. The voice held to one tone mostly, and took a melodious turn only at the end of a sentence or verse. They were sung usually to the psalms of the ritual, and were derived from ancient Jewish temple music. The " Te Deum laudamus " has been attributed to St. Ambrose, but neither the words nor the music were written by him. Recent investigations prove that the hymn is of Oriental origin.[1]

The hymns of Milan had a sphere outside the Roman office. It is true that many churches and monasteries included Ambrosian hymns in the office of the Hours, but their adoption in the Roman Church was far from being universal. The Council of Braga (563) excluded from the sacred office songs in verse and all texts not taken from the Scriptures. The local rites of Rome did not receive the Ambrosian hymns until the commencement of the eleventh century. Some authorities maintain the opinion that Ambrosian church music in general cannot be distinguished from Gregorian music, except so far as the hymns and chants which we have described are concerned.

Gregorian church music
The Ambrosian hymns were based on the versification and poetical meter of the words, like Greek music, whereas the Roman style was unmetrical and made free use of melismas (roulades), or melodic ornaments. This florid style

[1] See Riemann, History of Music, II, 14.

characterized the music of the Eastern churches, but, in the Roman Church, as we have seen, the cantus planus had become the standard. This Gregorian song, or chant, consists of slow, simple, unison tones of nearly equal length, like the modern choral; however, some use is made of musical rhythm. Its distinguishing feature, as compared with Greek metrical music, is the grouping together of tones to one syllable. Even a whole passage is often sung to one division of a word. This is particularly the custom with respect to the singing of some important word, like " Kyrie " or " alleluia." This idea was derived from Asiatic music, which has always stood in strong contrast to the word " music " of the Greeks.

Villateau, in his celebrated description of Egypt, gives an example of curious music sung by the Copts, descendants of the ancient Egyptians. They sometimes prolong a syllable to an inordinate length, " gargling " the tones of an alleluia for a full quarter of an hour. The same practice exists in Judea and other Eastern countries. This florid coloring of the tone, except when carried to a fantastic extreme, as in the East, is a very important element in music, and, through the Gregorian song, laid the foundation for the modern art of figuration and counterpoint ; for by giving the tones sufficient duration and independence, — which could not take place so long as they were tied down to prosody, — it became possible to sound notes of different pitch simultaneously; finally whole melodies could be sung in harmonic relation to each other, and this, under certain conditions, is nothing else than modern counterpoint.

Gregory the Great, who occupied the pontifical throne from 590 to 604, has been called from time immemorial the founder and promoter of Roman Church music. It is said that he had all the good melodies and chants, collected and arranged in the order of the church calendar, written down on parchment ; and that this antiphonary, as it was called, was laid on the altar at St. Peter's and fastened

Influence of Gregory the Great on Roman Church music

by a chain, to serve as a standard for all time, from which no
deviations were to be permitted, and that from this fact the
name cantus firmus (firm song) was derived. Musical historians
have also held that he founded a school of music at Rome,
invented or arranged a system of liturgical music, introduced
a system of notation by means of Roman letters, and increased
the number of modes or scales to eight. But Gevaert and
other recent investigators give strong reasons for believing
that "the tradition which makes St. Gregory the legislator
of the liturgical music and the composer of the melodies of
the antiphonary has no historical basis or probability. It is
a legend which originated in the time of Charlemagne or
later, and which, amplified in the course of the ninth century,
received its definite form in the celebrated writing of
Johannes Diaconus (John the Deacon). It was not generally
accepted until during the eleventh century." John the Deacon
flourished about two hundred and eighty-six years after the
death of Gregory the Great, so that his statements on the subject must be taken with more than a grain of salt, as he is
the only ancient writer who considers Gregory to be author

Authorship
of the an-
tiphonary

of the antiphonary. According to Hope, in the writings of
Gregory "there is not a single line, allusion, or hint of any
kind respecting the chant of the Church or of any antiphonary." Gevaert asserts that the melodies of the antiphonal
mass received their definite form between the accession of
Leo II (682) and that of Gregory II (715). Pope Sergius I
(687–701) was the principal inspirer of that work. The official
antiphonary had been previously adopted under the pontifi-
cate of Agathon (678–682). This question is still the subject of controversy among various musical and ecclesiastical
writers. Though we may concede that the antiphonary did
not receive its definite form before the time of Gregory II, in
the eighth century, this does not preclude the possibility that
the foundation was laid by the first Gregory, or in his time.
We may well believe that he gave his attention to church

music and founded a school, inasmuch as Pope Sylvester
(fourth century) preceded him in this field. Undoubtedly the
so-called Gregorian music was not created by any one man,
but grew up gradually in the course of several centuries as
the "use of Rome." In modern times it has been modified,
and what is now called the Gregorian chant is a hybrid, and
has little resemblance to the old music.

The antiphonary was the liturgical choir book of the Roman
mass, which consisted of the Kyrie, Gloria, Credo, Sanctus,
Benedictus, and Agnus Dei. It also contained antiphons,
graduals, hymns, tracts (sung during Lent), and offertories
(sung during the collection of alms in the holy communion).
The choir books, used in the Seven-Hours services, were the
"Psalter," the "Hymnal," the "Collect," the "Lectionary,"
and the "Nocturns" (used at vespers on Sundays and certain
other days).

I have already stated that the early ornate style of singing was gradually simplified in the Roman Church until the
adoption of the antiphonary in the seventh century. Henceforth the Gregorian cantus planus was the standard for many
centuries. This Gregorian chant consisted of slow, simple
unison tones of nearly equal length, like the modern choral.
It was unlike Greek music or the Ambrosian hymn, inasmuch
as it was not sung to versified words. It was unmetrical and
unphrased, usually, but in many cases the monotonous and
heavy whole notes were relieved by half-note and quarter-
note rhythm. The following citation will exhibit the character
of Gregorian music :

*The
Gregorian
chant*

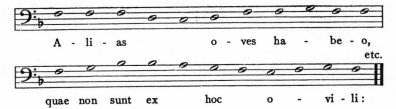

A - li - as   o - ves ha - be - o,
                                        etc.

quae non sunt ex   hoc   o - vi - li :

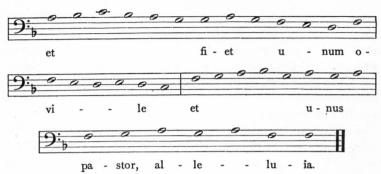

et   fi - et   u - num o -

vi - - le   et   u - nus

pa - stor, al - le - - lu - ia.

The early and mediæval church music was based on the Greek diatonic-scale system. Before the time of St. Ambrose the musical sounds were systematized under the name of " authentic " (genuine). They were thus designated by the church to sanction their use. These four authentic modes, together with the four plagal modes introduced later, were the foundation of all church composition till the seventeenth century.

The authentic modes were at first arranged as follows :

```
        G A B c d e f
      F G A B c d e
    E F G A B c d
  D E F G A B c
```

(Beginning at D these are no other than the Greek octave modes, Phrygian, Dorian, hypolydian, and hypophrygian.) These four modes are miscalled the Ambrosian modes. To them were added later the four plagal modes, erroneously ascribed to St. Gregory. Plagal means " slanting," and is used to designate such modes as were derived or borrowed from the authentic by simply beginning the order of the notes a fourth below, as follows : A to A, B to B, C to c, D to d. The authentic modes were distinguished from the plagal modes by having their keynotes on the first of the scale, as in modern music. Melodies of the authentic modes, therefore, were of a complete, strong, and firm character, whereas the

plagal melodies sought to rise or fall into the authentic keynote, and were softer and more dependent. The authentic
music proceeded from the keynote to the fifth, or from rest
to motion ;

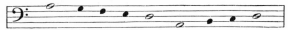

while plagal music sought rest in the authentic keynote, a
fifth below, or a fourth above :

This intimate relation existing between the keynote and the
fifth is in obedience to a natural law, and plays an important
part in every form of music.

Until the chromatic organ came into general use in the
church, these modes were not transposed from key to key.
Gregorian chants were necessarily composed according to
the limited scale and compass just given. The first writer
who treats of the church modes systematically is Flaccus
Albinus — Alcuin of York (d. 804). He directed the educa-
tional reforms of Charlemagne. It is said that Alcuin was
the founder of the University of Paris (790). His system
was to place the eight octave groups in the following order :

*Alcuin's
system*

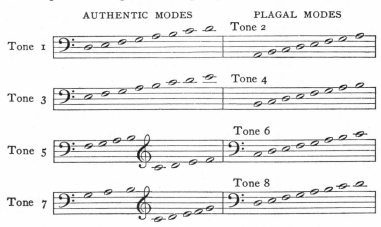

These modes were transposed into other keys, and until the eleventh century, church music was composed in them, but some secular melodies were not restricted to them.

The mediæval church musicians named these modes after the Greek modes, but misapplied the names entirely, as the following comparison will show :

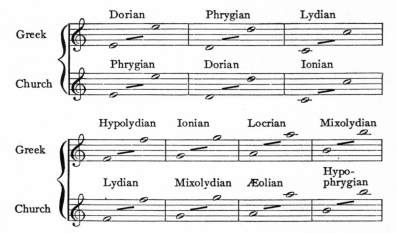

The harsh effect of the tritone, — the three whole tones between F and B, — in the church modes was ultimately forbidden, and, in order to avoid it, one of these two tones was altered chromatically, either by putting B♭ before B, or by raising the F to F♯. The so-called "lyric B♭" was applied to the keyboard of the organ at Winchester, built in the tenth century.

Musical notation

The Greeks used a notation called semeiography, which gave the pitch of the tones accurately but did not indicate their value in time. It comprised more than a hundred characters, — letters of the alphabet erect, inverted, or inclined. In the church this complicated and insufficient system was ultimately abandoned. The first seven letters of the alphabet were substituted for the troublesome Greek names of the tones. The lowest octave was designated by capital letters, A, B, C, D, E, F, G; the next octave by small letters, a, b, c, d, e, f, g, and the eleventh century Guido of Arezzo added double letters for the third octave, aa, bb, cc, etc.

Before Gregory's time a kind of notation was in vogue, Neuma notation quite different from semeiography. It was called neuma notation, the name being derived from the Greek word πνεῦμα (breath). It is not known when this notation was first introduced, but it was probably during the period between Ambrose and Gregory. The only extant copy of the antiphonary of Gregory is written in the neuma notation, a system which the great reformer may have improved. From his day until the fourteenth century it remained in use in church music with few modifications. At the outset it was a simple device to aid the singers, but gradually the number of characters increased to about thirty. They were horizontal or oblique lines and points, resembling the circumflex, acute, and grave accent marks of Greek writing of Alexandrian times, which period may have given rise to them.

These characters may be divided into four classes: first, signs that denote single tones, of which I shall call attention only to the *punctum* ● and *virga* ♩ ♪, the origin of our modern notes, which in the Middle Ages were called points (thus the word "counterpoint" is derived from *punctum contra punctum*, or point against point, — note against note); second, single signs representing two or more tones, —

third, signs denoting a certain manner of singing, or turns, of the voice, —

and fourth, signs that represent a whole phrase or formula of
notes, —

This handwriting did not point out, nor give, the exact value
of the notes, a, b, c, etc. ; it could only indicate in a general
way to the musical sense the raising, lowering, sliding, and
holding of the sounds.

Such a system could be no sure guide to the singers, and
many inaccuracies arose to perplex them. Complaints and
criticisms were made on every side. John Cotton declared
that when one singer sang the third or fifth, another tried
the fourth, or some other interval ; and when one said in
dispute, " Master Trudo taught me to sing it thus," another
replied, " My teacher Salomon sings it quite differently."
" It is a wonder," says Cotton, " if their voices ever happen
to unite agreeably, as each one calls on the name of his
master." He concludes from this clashing of opinion that
there must be as many ways of singing as there are masters
— which, unfortunately, might be said with some degree of
truth nowadays. The singers in the time of Pope Gregory
were not certain how to begin a note, or in what key to sing,
and only by good luck could they strike the right interval.

Improve-
ments in
notation.
Lines

An improvement in the neuma notation was made in the
eighth century by Romanus, a singer of St. Gall, who added
small letters to the characters, which aided the singers to
execute their notes more accurately, and superseded in some
degree oral teaching. But as the intervals were indicated
only approximately, the singers labored on nearly as much in
the dark as before. The chief advantage of this improvement
was to indicate the effects of loud and soft, and the quicker
and slower performance of single tones and groups of tones.
But all of these unsatisfactory devices were set aside by a
happy invention of an unknown person, — an invention simpler and more capable of improvement. It was, to draw a

horizontal line over the text. This line represented f, and was the origin of the modern F clef. All that was written above this line indicated higher tones than f. In the course of time a second line was added to represent c, which was the origin of the modern C clef. The f line was colored red, and the c line, green or yellow. Between the two lines the characters for g, a, and b were inserted. Subsequently, in Hucbald's time, two parallel black lines were substituted, on which these intermediate notes were henceforth written. These four lines were the origin of the modern staff. At a later period a number of lines were added to the four until as many as fifteen were not uncommon. The notes were not written between the lines at this period, but when this improvement was made the number of lines decreased, and was usually four or six up to the time when the staff assumed its present form.

By command of the church the Gregorian song was introduced into distant countries. Pope Gregory I sent to England the Benedictine monk Augustine with forty colleagues, among whom were a number of singers. Schools of singing were founded by them in monasteries at York, Glasgow, and other towns. The Roman style was taught in these schools. Subsequently Boniface and others went from England into Germany and introduced the Roman style there. In the seventh century Pope Vitalian sent two Roman singers, John and Theodore, into Gaul and Britain to turn the fast-languishing song in the monasteries of those countries back to its genuine source. In Britain, especially, their efforts were crowned with success, for it was not long after their advent that the Gregorian song reached a high state of cultivation in that land. In the eighth century twelve singers were sent to King Pepin in France, and also to Germany, where heathenism still prevailed.

The church found arduous work in training the rough and untutored natives of western Europe to sing. The forcible

Gregorian song introduced into other countries

words of John the Deacon, the biographer of **Gregory the Great**, well describe the uncultivated music of that age:

> Among all the people of Europe, the Gauls and Germans are the least capable of comprehending the Gregorian song in its purity. It may be due to their native wildness or because, out of frivolity, they always insert something of their own invention. Their rough, bellowing voices are incapable of modulation, and their intemperate habits render it impossible for their hoarse throats to sing delicate melodies properly. Their voices produce tones only fit to be compared to the clatter of a heavy wagon, and instead of touching the feelings of the hearer, only fill him with disgust.

Charlemagne gave his powerful encouragement to the cultivation of music as well as to all art and learning. During his reign organs were introduced into western Europe from the East. He founded schools of singing at Metz and Soissons, and sacred music was taught under his personal direction. By his command the songs of the old bards were collected by Einhard.

Peter and Romanus

In 790 Pope Hadrian, at the emperor's request, sent two Roman singers, Peter and Romanus, to Metz with a correct copy of the official antiphonary. One of the singers reached Metz, but Romanus, who was in possession of the antiphonary, fell ill on the way, and remained at the monastery of St. Gall, near the boundary line of Switzerland and Italy. He founded there a school of singing which became the most famous of that age. For centuries the superiority of this school was universally celebrated. The antiphonary is still preserved there. Noted masters of this school were Romanus, the founder, Ratpert, Salomo, Tutilo, Ekkehard, Labeo, and

Notker

others. But the most gifted of them all was Notker Balbulus, who was distinguished as a composer, poet, and teacher, and more than all, was one of the most exemplary Christians of his time. He developed a simple, popular song, called the sequence, or prosa, which was a kind of hymn. His sequence, " Media Vita," became famous all over Europe, and has found a permanent place in German church music, under the name of " Mitten wir im Leben sind."

In the Gregorian age it was demanded of every priest that he should understand the art of singing. It was the opinion that no one could teach philosophy or religion without possessing a knowledge of music. This, however, too often signified the absorption of the entire life of the scholastic monk in the groundless theories of music, which may have been profoundly symbolical, but were hardly useful, except, perhaps, to prepare European society for a higher, more modern discipline of the mind. *Knowledge of music required of priests*

No one will deny that the Roman Catholic Church has been the means of preserving many precious relics of ancient art and learning. It is through her agency chiefly that Greece as well as Judea has exerted a great influence in molding the character of modern civilization. The prominence given to music in the church from its very foundation has rendered this art, perhaps, even more than philosophy the handmaid of religion. Although the ancient scales lie at the foundation of the mediæval and modern tonal system, the principal characteristics of modern music are chiefly due to the genius of the mediæval musicians of the Roman Church.

CHAPTER III

POLYPHONIC MUSIC: ORGANUM, DISCANT, AND FAUXBOURDON

Ancients ignorant of counterpoint

During the Middle Ages the learned world was much puzzled by the question whether the ancients were acquainted with what we call counterpoint. Eminent scholars and musical theorists ranged themselves on opposite sides, and the controversy was carried on for centuries. The affirmative opinion was maintained by some of the most learned minds of those years and outweighed, by far, all contemporary opposition. In more enlightened times the negative opinion has prevailed, although it is not shared by certain eminent scholars, like Böckh and Casimir Richter. A majority of the best musical critics and historians, Padre Martini, Forkel, Fétis, Kiesewetter, Marx, Ambros, Gevaert, Riemann, and others, have proved beyond doubt that the ancients were profoundly ignorant of counterpoint, which is the sounding together of two or more different and well-defined voices, or melodies, in harmonic relation to each other. This chief characteristic of modern music has been the means of the gradual development of the present tonal system of scales, keys, and musical measure; and harmony has become so important to our sense and understanding that any composition existing without it, at least in the form of accompaniment, we can hardly tolerate.

But while we are so well satisfied with our music, the Asiatic finds it disagreeable and barbarous. He has no comprehension of any other than unison music, and the sound of two or more simultaneous parts appears to him as mere noise. Fétis tells the story of an Arabian who, listening to a Frenchman playing the " Marseillaise " on the piano, suddenly seized the left hand of the player with the exclamation, " No, first play that melody, then you may play these others." Niebuhr, on asking an Arabian how he liked European music, received the answer, " Your music is a wild, unpleasant shouting, in which no earnest man can find any pleasure." Could a refined Greek musician, Terpander, or Arion, have listened to a modern symphony, he would probably have recognized nothing more than a confusion of sounds, void of all meaning.

We have no knowledge of any attempts to use harmonic intervals in singing during the first eight hundred years of the Christian era. The chief progress made in this long period was in simplifying musical meter by making it more independent of the words, in arranging the compass of the musical sounds into different scales, and in adopting a kind of notation. It was truly a marked epoch in musical history when the first attempts, however feeble and erroneous, were made at harmony. But it is wholly unknown to whom the honor of making these first experiments belongs. The earliest notices of such harmonic singing, under the name of "organum," are by the monk of Angoulême (ninth century) and Scotus Erigena (about the middle of the ninth century) ; and the latter describes such part music as already in general use.

The oldest examples known of any such music are contained in the treatises of Isidor, a learned monk, Otger, or Odo, of Provence, and Hucbald, or Hucbaldus, of St. Amand in Flanders, who lived between the years 840 and 930 and was an earnest student of Greek music. In examples they give, the cantus firmus or principal voice was placed in the tenor, above which was added a second-voice part, singing the same melody throughout, four or five notes higher ; sometimes there was added a third voice, which ran with the upper melody in the octave beneath ; or again, by doubling the parallel fourths or fifths in the octave, four voices were used.

First attempts in harmony

Hucbald

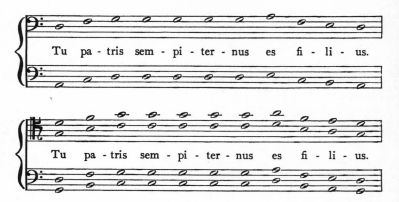

Tu pa - tris sem - pi - ter - nus es fi - li - us.

Tu pa - tris sem - pi - ter - nus es fi - li - us.

Organum   This invention was called the organum, also by the ancient names, diaphonia — different sounds, and symphonia — union of sounds. The least objectionable kind of organum to modern ears was the so-called "roaming" or "wandering" organum. It was composed in two voices of parallel fourths, with a refreshing admixture of thirds, seconds, and unisons in oblique and contrary motion. The fourth was the prominent interval. It is remarkable that the dissonant interval of the second should have been introduced.

Rex cœ - li Do - mi - ne ma - ris un - di - so - ni.
Ti - ta - nis ni - ti - di squa - li - di - que so - li.

Te hu - mi - les fa - mu - li mo - du - lis ve - ne-ran-do pi - is.

Tu pa - tris sem - pi - ter - nus es fi - li - us.

In this example the fifth appears only once. These parallel fifths and octaves produce such a frightful effect that we can hardly conceive it possible that they were ever used in this manner. Kiesewetter, on hearing them tried, declared it impossible; but Ambros holds that the organum was practised by the monks as a penance to the ear, to counteract the sensuous charm of secular music by something utterly antagonistic. We can hardly believe that the singers generally followed out this idea to the bitter end, but prefer to think that, in the improvisations which had now become the fashion, they were very economical in the use of parallel fifths; otherwise Hucbald could not have recommended the organum so heartily, saying, " If two or more of you sing this together with measured gravity, you will find the combination of intervals produces a very sweet and agreeable harmony."

The name "organum" naturally suggests the belief that the first experiments in combining different intervals of sound were made by means of the organ. In that age organs were of the most clumsy construction. The keys were so wide that the organist used his fists or elbows in playing. Under such circumstances not more than two notes could be held down simultaneously. It may have been the practice, for want of skill, to hold down a key while the melody was being sung, — thus producing an harmonic effect something like the droning of a bagpipe. At all events it was by such rude and almost accidental beginnings that the way was opened for subsequent speculations.

Hucbald made improvements in notation in the following manner : between the spaces of a number of parallel lines he inserted the words in a higher or lower position, to indicate the pitch of the tones, aided by the letters T and S (tonus and semitonus) placed in the margin to show whether the steps were tones or half tones.[1] Hucbald applied the names of

Improvements in notation

---

[1] Kiesewetter, Beilagen der Niederländischen Musik, Ex. A.

the Greek scales to the church modes, but in a new order: the scale D . . . d was called Dorian instead of Phrygian; E . . . e was called Phrygian instead of Dorian; F was Lydian; G, mixolydian; A, Æolian; B, hypophrygian; and C, Ionian. These have remained in use ever since as church modes.

The speculations on music of Hucbald and other learned ecclesiastics of his time did not produce any immediate effect or lead to reforms which extended much beyond the walls of the few monasteries where they passed their lives. The practice of church music was not much influenced by the abstruse theories of scholars. Nearly a century elapsed before there appeared in music any new discovery which was worthy of mention. What may have taken place within the monasteries during that time is unknown.

Guido of Arezzo

Music was promoted in the eleventh century by Guido of Arezzo (995 ?–1050 ?), a Benedictine monk of the convent Pomposa, near Ravenna, whose name subsequently attained a higher fame than that of any musician of mediæval times, lasting almost to the present day. Guido's achievements were the improvement of notation and the simplification of the method of teaching singing. According to his own words he had invented "a new method of teaching music by which a boy might make greater progress in a few months than a man of intelligence formerly could in years." He made this the aim of his life, and he succeeded so well in teaching the youth to read music at sight that his reputation was spread abroad, reaching, at last, the ears of Pope John XIX, who sent for him in order to make himself acquainted with his system. The Pope treated Guido with kind attention, turned over the leaves of his antiphonary attentively and with wonder, and did not rise from his seat until he could correctly sing a verse that he had never before seen; thus accomplishing what he had not believed possible when it was reported to him as having been done by others.

The method of instruction pursued by Guido has not been ascertained, except in its general outlines. He taught his pupils the tones and syllables from Pythagoras' monochord, which played a great rôle with mediæval musicians. Guido divided the monochord into a scale of twenty tones, five more than had hitherto been employed, making use of the following notation to indicate the pitch of the separate tones :

$$\text{ΓA B C D E F G a b c d e f g } \begin{matrix} \text{a b c d e} \\ \text{a b c d e} \end{matrix}$$

The double letters represented higher tones than had previously been in use. The Greek gamma, even before Guido's time, had been placed at the beginning of the compass, evidently to distinguish it from the capital G of the octave above. The name " gamut " for the modern scale is derived from this source. Guido fixed the number of lines on which the notes were written at four, as has been mentioned above. Hitherto they had followed no given number, but varied from two to twenty. He was the first to write the notes in the spaces as well as on the lines. Two lines were colored — one red and one green — and represented the clefs F and C ; the other lines, D and A, were black :

Notwithstanding the great advantage gained by this simplification, the many-lined staff continued in use, both in vocal and instrumental music, until the sixteenth century.

Guido was not the inventor of the modern notes, as some have believed ; neither did he use exclusively the points of the neuma characters, which, as has already been stated, were the foundation of the modern notes. His favorite signs for the tones were the Gregorian letters, but he also used many of the neuma characters, which he gave a definite place on the staff to indicate precisely their pitch. The parallel lines were dispensed with when the Gregorian letters were employed, and were simply written above the text, as will be seen from the following example :

Generally only the simple letters were written above the text without attempting to illustrate the upward or downward movement of the sounds, as follows :

Solmization   Solmization, or the application of the syllables, ut, re, mi, fa, sol, la, to the various notes is attributed to Guido, who may have adopted them, though they were not developed into a well-regulated system before the thirteenth century. These six syllables were taken from the first words of the lines of a favorite Latin hymn :

Ut queant laxis   *Re*sonare fibris
*Mi*ra gestorum   *Fa*muli tuorum,
*Sol*ve polluti   *La*bii reatum,
*S*ancte *I*ohannes.

This served as a supposed protection from hoarseness and colds. Mattheson, the Hamburg kapellmeister, says, " When a monk found himself hoarse he hastened to repeat this hymn, and then the devil and superstition were at hand and helped him in a moment."

Neither Guido nor his immediate followers did much for the advancement of harmony. The examples of Guido's

organum differ from Hucbald's : first, in the occasional passage of the cantus firmus below the counterpoint [1]; and
secondly, in the addition of a type of figured ending to the
cantus firmus, or principal voice, while the counterpart holds
out its last note, making a kind of organ point. Guido has
become a mythical character. He has been credited with far
more honor than belongs to him. Writers, particularly those
of the seventeenth century, have lauded him to the skies.
He has been called the restorer, nay, the inventor of music ;
and his predecessors and contemporaries have been ignored.
He was erroneously deemed the inventor of notation, harmony, the gamut, solmization, the clavichord, the hexachord,
and the harmonic hand, — a practical aid to singers, by means
of which they could count the tones of Guido's scale, with
their solmization, on the fingers of the left hand.

In the history of music the twelfth century is an epoch
without names ; yet during this period we mark the first appearance of varied rhythm and exact measure in music and, consequently, the development of the note. Undoubtedly we owe
this remarkable change to the increasing influence of secular
music under the universal sway of the troubadours, whose
rhythmical and pleasing melodies marked a strong contrast to
the grave, heavy, and nearly equal notes of the Gregorian song.

The further growth of counterpoint was closely connected Discantus,
with the metrical, melodious style, and new intervals came florid coun-
into practice. Besides the major and minor thirds and sixths, terpoint
the dissonant intervals of the second, seventh, and augmented
fourth were introduced ; if not freely, as in modern music,
yet as passing notes. This resulted in a kind of counterpoint
called " florid," because two or more notes were used against
one, as passing notes ; for instance,

[1] Ambros, II, 164, Ex. 4.

Such an effect could not be produced unless the notes were sung in exact measurement of time. This florid counterpoint, or discantus (different voices), as it was called, was used first in secular music, but gradually worked its way into sacred music, in spite of opposition; yet it was not before the thirteenth century that it was admitted to general favor. Before the introduction of exact measurement of time the music of the church was sung without strict regard to the time value of the notes. The melismas, or groups of notes strung together, were called " notae ligatae," or bound notes, and were sung somewhat quickly, the accent falling generally on the highest note. Thus, —

Mensural music. Franco of Cologne

The oldest known writer on this subject of new notation, or mensural music as it is called, was Franco of Cologne, prior of the Benedictine Abbey at Cologne in 1190, whose treatises are supposed to belong to the latter part of the twelfth century or the early part of the thirteenth.[1] Franco treats of the various notes used in mensural music, of which there are four kinds, with corresponding pauses; the duplex longa (or maxima as it was called later), the longa, the brevis, and the semibrevis — our modern whole note. Their appearance and relative value are shown in the following table:

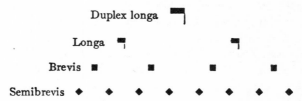

Classification of harmonic intervals

Franco's classification of the different harmonic intervals agrees in the main with that of the present day. He names

---

[1] Theoretical works of Franco of Paris are also preserved.

three kinds of concords: (1) perfect, the unison and octave; (2) middle, the fifth and the fourth; and (3) imperfect, the major and minor thirds. Discords were either perfect — the half tone, the augmented fourth, and the major and minor sevenths; or imperfect — the major and the minor sixths. His only great error was to classify the sixths with the discords.

Franco mentions several kinds of sacred and secular song, — conductus, cantilena, motetus (or motet), hoquetus (ochetus), and rondellus (or rondo). These compositions are generally in three-part counterpoint. The organum, at this time called pure organum (organum purum), used rhythmical counterpoint in the discant, as, for instance:

Tenor

The conductus had no cantus firmus; its three or four parts were free. The rule of three-part composition was that two voices should always form a consonance, the third voice using intervals that would fit with the other two. The following is the opening of a conductus of Franco's time:

Coussemaker mentions several composers of the twelfth and thirteenth centuries — Leoninus, Perotinus, Petrus, and Jean le Grand. Among the contemporaries of Franco were Johannes de Garlandia and the so-called Pseudo-Beda, the unknown author of a treatise on music which appears also under the name of Aristotle.

In England music had long been cultivated. Alfred the Great is supposed to have encouraged both the practice and science of music, and several writers draw the conclusion from this supposition that mensural music flourished earliest in that country. Two of the oldest writers on mensural music, following Franco, were Walter Odington, a Benedictine of Evesham, about 1240, and Hieronymus de Moravia in France, about 1260. Theoretical writings of Marchettus of Padua toward the end of the thirteenth century, and later by Johannes de Muris, Doctor of the Sorbonne, at Paris about 1330, note a decided progress in harmony and measure. Their rules for the use of harmonic intervals show that the feeling for a natural, melodious treatment of the voices had grown more refined, and that they began to comprehend the true nature of combined concords and discords. They established the following rules, which in vocal music have continued to be observed with some modifications almost to the present day. First, two perfect concords — the unison, fifth, and octave — must not succeed each other consecutively in similar motion ; second, a composition must invariably begin and end with a perfect concord ; third, discords can appear only as passing notes and suspensions, always to be resolved, or followed directly by a concord. Contrary motion was recommended as the best.

Rules for use of harmonic intervals

The examples of harmony by Marchettus and De Muris do not lead us to regard them, nor the practical musicians whom they represented, as the founders of modern counterpoint, but rather as guides to the purity and correctness of its elements. De Muris was the first musician, it appears, to adopt the word " counterpoint " as the name for polyphonic music.

Improvised discant

Before these more correct teachings had exerted their full influence, it was the habit with clever singers to improvise parts to accompany the principal melody, or cantus firmus.

This was called *contrapunctum a mente*, or improvised discant, and was the general practice in sacred and secular music. In church music it became so offensive to good taste that finally it had to be abolished by papal decree. Von Nettesheim, a learned writer of the sixteenth century, describes such an extemporary performance as sounding unlike the singing of human voices, but resembling rather the outcries of animals. De Muris condemns unskillful discanters in these words: "If they accord, it is by mere chance; their voices wander about the tenor or plain song without rule, trusting wholly to Providence for their coincidence. They throw sounds about at random, just as awkward people throw stones at a mark, without hitting it once in a hundred times."

The improvised discant was in high favor in France, where it was commonly sung in three parts which proceeded simultaneously in similar motion, note against note, always in the first inversion of the triad, the chord of $\frac{6}{3}$. The cantus firmus was in the highest voice. The two improvised voices were in the interval of the fourth and sixth beneath, except at the close, when the note of the cantus firmus proceeded from the leading note to the eighth of the scale, the middle voice ascended to the fifth, and the lowest voice descended one degree to the keynote; for example,

Among various kinds of improvised discant in later use was the following, in which the tenor voice had the cantus firmus as the lowest part:

Faux-bourdon

This style of music was called the fauxbourdon, or *falso bordone*, because the bass did not consist of the fundamental

notes of the concords, but of inverted thirds, the keynotes being in the upper voice. The fauxbourdon was introduced into the Roman Church from France, about the year 1377, by Gregory XI, and was in favor for a long time. The feeble light that modern historians have been able to throw on the music of the thirteenth and fourteenth centuries — the age of Dante, Chaucer, and Petrarch — seems to have made the darkness of that period more profound.

Examples of early counterpoint

Very few specimens of early contrapuntal music have come down to us unless they still lie buried in monastery libraries. The following examples are extant: first, an old French chanson composed by Adam de la Hale, who was born at Arras in 1240 and died in 1287. He was the author of several little musical plays, from one of which, "Robin and Marion," this three-voiced chanson is taken; second, the fragment of a Gloria, by Guillaume de Machault, which was performed at the coronation of Charles V of France in 1364; third, an Italian canzone in three voices by Francesco Landino, a Florentine organist, in 1360; fourth, an old French chanson in three voices, author unknown. These four specimens were deciphered and printed by Kiesewetter in his valuable history of European music, but several critics have found his decipherments incorrect. Within a few years an important addition has been made to the oldest relics of harmony by the publication of over fifty contrapuntal compositions by Coussemaker, in his work entitled "L'art harmonique aux XIIe et XIIIe siècles."

CHAPTER IV

TROUBADOURS, MINNESINGERS, MINSTRELS, ETC.

Thus far we have devoted our attention almost exclusively Secular music to the history of music in connection with Christian worship; at this point it will be well to glance for a moment at another branch, which played a more important part in the molding and forming of modern music than can be justly estimated. I refer to popular secular music. The first regular attempts in polyphonic music were probably made through the agency of secular melodies as manifested in the discant. At a later period, which we have not yet examined, these secular melodies were interwoven, curiously and ingeniously, into church compositions of the most extended and serious form; even whole masses were built on them. The composers of the Flemish school carried this practice to such an excess that it became a crying evil, finally demanding a reform, which I shall notice later. There is no proper evidence, though good reason for believing, that popular secular music existed in the earliest centuries of the Christian era, just as it did in antiquity; but there are no specimens left to us in writing, and, of course, all oral traditions are completely lost. The spread of Christianity was not favorable to the continuance of the popular music of heathendom, nor did the church encourage original secular poetry and song, seeking rather to draw the minds of its followers away from all earthly things. The great migrations of the fifth and sixth centuries in Europe must have destroyed all remnants of popular song previously existing. It required a new culture of society to bring forth new fruits in verse and song, which, as an essential complement to life, were required to give free play to its joyous and happy moods, just as church music expressed its more solemn and elevated moments.

Melodies lost for lack of system of notation

The history of national popular songs furnishes additional evidence that the music of past ages has been lost simply for want of an accurate system of notation. The poetry of early ages has obtained enduring record and fame in the written words ; and rich treasures of ancient German, French, Scandinavian, and Slavonic folk songs still survive in verse, while the music which gave them soul and fire is lost forever. The reign of Charlemagne was productive of popular poetry and music, as is shown by the variety of songs then in vogue — all the melodies of which, unfortunately, are lost — so that we are unable to decide whether the secular songs were marked with their own peculiar characteristics of popular melody or were similar to the choral songs of church music. But we are led to believe that there was a marked difference, judging from the variety of names given to secular songs at that time. There were love songs and comic songs ; diabolic songs, which were sung at night over the graves of the dead in order to frighten away the devil ; dissolute songs, which were forbidden to be sung in the neighborhood of a church ; songs of victory and of battle, etc. The name " minstrel," or " ménestrel," was a title given by Pepin, father of Charlemagne, to his chapelmaster, and subsequently, during the Middle Ages, the name was applied to traveling players and singers, — a numerous class in Europe from the eighth to the eighteenth century. Prior to the age of the troubadours we are unable to judge of secular music by examples.

Troubadours

Troubadour poetry and song held universal sway in Europe in the eleventh and twelfth centuries. The word " troubadour " is derived from *trobar, trouver*, to find out or devise, and the *art de trobar, gay saber*, or gay science, was practised by kings and princes, who rivaled each other in this profession. The courts of the Dukes of Toulouse, Provence, and

Barcelona were the centers of this poetry and song. Duke William of Poitiers (1087–1127), it is supposed, was the first troubadour. Besides these royal artists there was another class of troubadours, who were held in the service of the princes as court poets.

The troubadours, unlike their contemporaries, the German minnesingers, frequently did not sing their own songs, but held in their employ for this purpose minstrels, or jongleurs, who were persons well skilled in singing and playing. The jongleurs held a subordinate position, and, though here and there individuals were of knightly origin, as a class they belonged to the lower ranks of society. The troubadours never sang for money, but for honor or love, while the jongleur was a paid servant. It is related of one troubadour that he was very much offended because he was called a jongleur. "I give without return," said he, "and will have no other reward for my art than love's reward." *Minstrels, jongleurs*

The minstrels often led wild and irregular lives, wandering like gypsies from place to place without any settled homes, in parties of men, women, and children. In Germany for a long time they were held in contempt and enjoyed no rights, either of church or state. In France and England they received better treatment. In the course of time they settled down in towns and cities and became organized bodies, usually under the protection of some nobleman. It was their custom to choose a leader, who received the title, "King of the Minstrels." In France there were minstrel kings as early as the thirteenth century. In England, a brotherhood of minstrels existed in olden times at Beverly in Yorkshire. The first king of the minstrels was chosen in 1381 through a privilege granted by John of Gaunt, Duke of Lancaster. During the reign of Edward IV, in 1469, a license was granted to the minstrels that they might be incorporated into a body. *Organization of the minstrels*

A clever jongleur united a variety of accomplishments. It was not uncommon for him to be able to play as many as nine musical instruments, to be skillful in the arts of rope dancing and tumbling, in imitating the song of birds, and in playing the fool, — hence the name "jongleur," derived from *joculator*, a jester. The jongleurs commonly accompanied their songs on the harp, or rota, as it was called in mediæval times, the peasant's lyre, a kind of hurdy-gurdy, and the rebec, a three-stringed instrument played with a bow. Besides these there was a great variety of instruments in use; as for instance, the vielle or viola, — a name apparently related to *fides*, a string.[1] Other instruments peculiar to that age were the gigue, sambuca, salteire, armonie, muse, chiphonie, and frestele; they have long since become obsolete, and we scarcely know more of them than the mere names. In the orchestra of instruments — if the name can be applied to such rude beginnings — were included various kinds of drums, horns, trumpets and trombones. The jongleur generally played his own accompaniments in unison with the melody; but the better-trained ones attempted a separate part, something in the style of the organum or discant.

The instruments used by jongleurs

Love, the subject of the poetry and music

The principal subject of Provençal poetry and music was devotion to woman, — the celebration of her virtue and beauty. The poet selected some lady, whether married or single it mattered not, as the object of his inspiration, to sing to her of the bliss and pains of love without any thought of a nearer acquaintance. Some of these lyrics were the chanson, or canso, a chivalrous love song, the seranas, or serenade, and the albas, or aubades, — songs sung at dawn or in the evening to celebrate the bliss of lovers; the tenso was a poetic combat in which love affairs formed the subject of dispute; the planh, a lament on the death of a beloved friend or hero, or on the disappointments of love; the sirventes, a song or poem of service, which was devoted to the praise of some patron,

---

[1] *Fidula* was the general name for stringed instruments, and if we follow the word through all its changes from *fidula* to *vidula*, *videl* (or fiddle), *viele*, *vioel*, we reach *viola*, and finally its diminutive *violin*.

or the rehearsal of some private or public affair. There were also various songs, ballads, and dance rounds, in which the performers formed a circle, one singing the solo, the others joining in the refrain.

The oldest known of these lyric melodies are by the Châtelain de Coucy, of the twelfth century; Thibaut, king of Navarre (1201–1254); Gaucelm Faidit; and Adam de la Hale. If these pieces are correctly deciphered we cannot but be surprised to hear how modern they sound. We feel that they are not the result of a labored theory, but the natural effusions of a poetic spirit. The troubadours were naturalists in music. Their pieces are marked by a melodious flow and sense of rhythm, with peculiar and quaint turns and cadences. They also show a decided affinity for the clear, tonic character which distinguishes modern music in comparison with the mystical uncertainty of key in mediæval church music. Perhaps the most nïave and pleasing melodies among the number are by the tróuvère, Adam de la Hale, who was not only one of the earliest musicians to write in parts or counterpoint, but appears also as the founder of the French drama.

Corresponding to the troubadours of Spain and the south of France were the trouvères of the north of France and England, who made their appearance somewhat later in history. Italy suffered a kind of invasion of troubadours and minstrels, and was for a time under the influence of Provençal poetry and song. Even Dante and Petrarch studied it and copied some of its forms. It is a question whether any specimens of Italian popular songs of this period have come down to the present day.

Of all other European countries Germany was most influenced by the troubadours. The minnesingers and mastersingers were similar classes of lyrists, knightly poets, and musicians. But the Germans did not slavishly copy their neighbors; the original Teutonic element was manifest from the outset. The differences between the Romanic and

Minnesingers and mastersingers in Germany

Germanic types are fully illustrated in the national songs of the respective races. The German minnelied (love song) was more earnest and tender, though less brilliant and pleasing, than the song of the troubadour. The minnesinger was devoted to all womanhood, while the troubadour sought out a single object for his poetical passion. This devotion on the part of the minnesinger was in a measure prompted by his religious feeling; for the *Mariencultus*, or veneration of the Virgin Mary, was an intense, mystical phase of religious worship in the Middle Ages, and had a deep connection with the poet's respect for woman.

Minnesingers skilled musicians

The minnesingers stood in closer relation to the people than did the troubadours, counting as many of the burgher class among their number as of the order of knighthood. As the minnesingers were usually skilled in playing and singing, they dispensed with the aid of the jongleurs or minstrels. The Wartburg near Eisenach, the seat of the court of Hermann, Landgrave of Thuringia, was the headquarters of minnesingers. Among the most celebrated singers were Wolfram von Eschenbach, Walther von der Vogelweide, Heinrich Schreiber, Heinrich von Zwetzschin, all of knightly rank, Biterolf, and Heinrich von Ofterdingen, burgher of Eisenach.

Many specimens of the minnesongs have been preserved, and we are well able to judge of their characteristics. The recitative style of many impresses us; the meter of the words decides the length of the notes. The cadence is often marked by a freer flow of melody. The grave and serious character of the older songs reminds us of Gregorian music. Some of the later specimens, however, are lively and modern, as the following example shows:

DER KUNINC RODOLP

| | Der | ku - ninc | Ro - dolp | myn - net | Got | und |
| | Der | ku - ninc | Ro - dolp | rich - tet | wol | und |

ist an tru-wen ste-te der ku-ninc Ro-dolp
haz-zet val-sche re-te der ku-ninc Ro-dolp

hat sich ma-nigen scan-den wol vur sa-get
ist eyn helt an tu-gen-den unvurt-za get

Der ku-ninc Ro-dolp e-ret Got unde

al-le wer-de vrou-wen, der ku-ninc Ro-dolp

let sich di ke in ho-en e-ren scou-wen ich

gan ym wol daz ym nach sy-ner mil-te heil ge-

scicht der mey-ster syn-gen gi-gen sa-gen daz

hort her gerne unde git yn dar-umme nicht.

The poetry of the minnesingers reached its highest culmination in the thirteenth century, and rapidly declined in the following century.

The mastersingers were a class of poets and singers, gen- Master-erally not of knightly rank, but of the middle class, including singers schoolmasters, clerks, and mechanics. Guilds, or companies of mastersingers (with rules and regulations), were organized in the rich cities of Germany. Mentz was the center of mastersinging for a time; a high school of singing was established there. In the fifteenth century it was cultivated extensively at Munich, Strassburg, and Augsburg.

Nuremberg was the headquarters of mastersinging in the sixteenth century, and it reached its culmination there under the famous Hans Sachs, the cobbler poet. The poems of the mastersingers were always lyrical. The entire poem was called a *Bar* and was divided into three or more stanzas. The melody was called a tone, or *Weise* (air); it was very monotonous and expressionless, and sounded like church psalmody. The music related so indefinitely to the words that the tone was oftentimes composed previously to the text. Curious names were given to these melodies; for instance, the "Proud Youth's Air," the "High Maiden's Air," the "Short Ape's Air," the "High Fir-Tree Air."

Officers and rules of the mastersingers

The rules of art of the guild were very arbitrary. Every little fault of singing or recitation was fined. There were thirty-two important faults to be avoided according to their rules of singing. The ruling officers were the headmaster, the crownmaster, the recorder or markmaster, and the cashier, who represented the four classes of members, — the masters, the poets, the singers, and the classmates, as they were called. The master won his title by the invention of new poems and melodies; the poet sang his own poems to the melodies of others; the singer was able to sing the well-known melodies by heart, without appearing as a composer; and the classmates possessed a complete knowledge of the rules of tabulature, or system of notation, which they used. At their free meeting, or *Freisingen*, persons not members of the guild could appear as singers. They were obliged to sing without any notes, and four officers marked down their faults. One watched the rhymes, another the measure of the verse, another the melody, and another had the open Bible before him to see that no transgressions were made against the Scriptures. At Nuremberg mastersinging did not die out until the eighteenth century.

Other representatives of secular music were the minstrels, a numerous class in Europe from the eighth century to the eighteenth, to whom we owe many popular airs. In their travels they were the means of awakening a love of music among the people, and though often despised, they did a great service. The minstrels are associated with all that is poetical and romantic in English literature, from Chaucer to Scott; they are supposed to be the genuine descendants of the ancient bards, and in England were always welcome at palace and hall. *Minstrels*

Chappell's "Popular Music of the Olden Time" contains many old English airs, some of which were sung by the minstrels. One of the most famous of these is the quaint and charming "Sumer is icumen in." This melody is the theme of a six-part canon,[1] which is a remarkable example of regular counterpoint. If the date 1250 be correct, it proves that England was then much in advance of the Continent in this difficult art. From the time of Alfred the Great to Charles the First, England was as musical a country as any in Europe. The popular airs exercised a great influence in all the leading countries; this was especially the case in Germany. The old volkslieder are to be considered as quite apart from the minnelieder, both in the words and melodies. *Popular airs*

The words of the old songs were metrical and employed rhyme; by this means the music was naturally divided into phrases, with cadences at the ends of the alternate lines. Thus the melodies were in equal divisions, and the rhythm became clear and marked. The natural flow of the rhymes inspired the untutored singers to originate tunes wherewith to clothe and beautify the words; thus many beautiful songs sprang into existence, though when they were composed, and *The German volkslied*

[1] Grove, Dictionary of Music, III, 766.

by whom, is not known. These songs went from mouth to
mouth until they became universal favorites, and in many
cases are still sung by the people. Such heirlooms are better
than precious stones. They sprang up like wild flowers and
have all the aroma and beauty of the flowers. The German
volkslied is more naïve, tender, and rhythmical than the heavy
and religious minnelied, which in most cases approaches the
choral in its slow and equal notes. Among all the popular
airs of the Middle Ages those of the Germans are distinguished especially for their deep and tender feeling and naïve
simplicity. They are like violets among flowers, and the
" Violet " of Goethe and Mozart might serve as a typical
German lied, and reminds us in its simplicity and tenderness
of the old songs. Two beautiful examples of the old German
volkslied are : first, a love song, author and date unknown,
entitled " Unlust det dich grüssen " ; second, a famous love
song of parting, entitled " Entlaubet ist der Walde," which
belongs probably to the fifteenth century. The masters of the
early German school of church music of the fifteenth and sixteenth centuries, Finck, Mahu, Isaac, and others, used many
of the popular airs as themes for contrapuntal treatment.

Ritual best
suited to
develop-
ment of
counter-
point

The words of the ritual service of the church, on the other
hand, were in Latin and not metrical ; the slow, monotonous
notes of the Gregorian song were in strong contrast to the
rhythmical variety of the people's songs. In the first experiments in music in parts, however, the very simplicity and
slowness of the notes of the Gregorian music made it possible
for musicians to work out the problem of counterpoint, or
music in parts ; and it was not until the principal laws that
govern such music were established through long experience,
that the time was ripe for the employment of the popular airs
by learned masters as themes for their works, and such masters did not appear before the fourteenth century.

CHAPTER V

MUSIC IN THE NETHERLANDS

The labors of Hucbald, Guido, Franco, and, centuries later, of Marchettus and De Muris, in teaching the rules of the organum and discant, and of musical notation and measure, gradually opened the way to practical results of inestimable value, and we now approach a great epoch in musical history. During the Middle Ages until toward the end of the fourteenth century, the progress of music was very slow and unimportant, compared with what occurred after that time. The new age, already inaugurated by Dante, Giotto, Pisano, and other illustrious poets and artists, witnessed the revival of literature and art, the invention of printing, and the rapid enlightenment of European society. Scholasticism was destined to give place to modern discovery and invention. This transformation could not fail to influence music as well as the other fine arts. Yet it cannot be maintained that the new life born into architecture, painting, and sculpture in Italy during the fifteenth century inspired a simultaneous reform in music. For the renaissance of music, or what corresponds to the so-called renaissance of the fine arts — that is, the new spirit and style of art brought forth by the study and imitation of ancient classical models — was not attempted until about the beginning of the seventeenth century, at a time when the groundwork of the art had already been firmly laid.

It is a significant fact that the very first experiments in counterpoint were made by northern musicians. Hucbald, Franco of Cologne, Walter Odington, Adam de la Hale, Hieronymus of Moravia, Machault, De Muris, are the names identified with the earliest attempts in harmonic music. It

First experiments in counterpoint by northern musicians

63

was in the Netherlands, Germany, Northern France, and England that the first masters of this new music flourished. It is by no means a settled question, however, which of these countries deserves the honor of having produced the first specimens of developed counterpoint. Burney claims it for England, Fétis and Kiesewetter for the Netherlands, while some of the present German critics believe they have undisputed evidence, in the discovery of an old songbook of the fifteenth century, the " Lochheimer Liederbuch," that good counterpoint flourished earliest in Germany. Finally, Coussemaker has published a numerous collection of early contrapuntal pieces of French origin, which proves at least that the French have an equal right to claim this honor.

There does not exist, however, the shadow of a doubt which of these countries bore the first ripe fruits in this new field. We have only to point to the illustrious names of the Flemish composers who, for nearly two centuries, held undisputed sway, and whose fame spread over the civilized world. Through them polyphonic music, which previously had given only vague hints of its possible future, became so general that unison singing, except in secular and Gregorian song, was totally neglected for over two hundred years ; and even this exception was not absolute, for the contrapuntists chose secular and Gregorian melodies as the subject of their most intricate counterpoint.

It is customary with musical historians to divide the history of the Netherland school into four epochs as represented by the composers of most distinguished merit, — Dufay, Ockenheim, Josquin, Gombert, Willaert, and Orlando Lasso. The epoch of Dufay and his contemporaries marked the first stage in the development of good counterpoint. In the second epoch, that of Ockenheim and Josquin, artistic skill and finesse, — involved contrapuntal progressions, — reached an extraordinary height, while the fame of the Flemish masters became universal. The third epoch notes the return from extravagances in technical skill and abstruse experiments to more reasonable limits.   The fourth epoch closes with the greatest Flemish master, Orlando Lasso, who is nominally to be classed with his countrymen.   Since his day the Netherlands have never regained their prominence in music.

Guillaume Dufay, the pioneer of Flemish music, was born at Chimay in Hainaut.   The date of his birth is uncertain, and we possess only a meager account of his life.   His reputation as a composer began, it is conjectured, about 1436.   Very few of Dufay's musical compositions are extant; several of his masses are preserved in the archives of the Papal Chapel at Rome.   **Guillaume Dufay**

The most prominent contemporaries of Dufay were his countrymen, Binchois, Faugues, Eloy, Brasart, and the English musician, John Dunstable.   The extant works of these contrapuntists show that considerable progress had been made in the use of chords, in the treatment of the voices, and in musical measure and notation.   Discords were introduced on unaccented divisions of the measure as passing notes; generally as regular suspensions, the fourth before the dominant third, or the seventh before the sixth.   The leading note, or seventh of the scale, was resolved into the octave as a passing note in the following manner:

This curious cadence was the fashion for a long time, but in the sixteenth century it became antiquated.   According to the old custom a cantus firmus was selected as the basis of contrapuntal pieces.   The melody, a secular tune, was usually set in the tenor, to which other higher and lower parts were composed in imitation.   The fugal, imitative style was yet crude, though augmentations and short canons in the octave were introduced.   The counterpoint was commonly in three or four parts.

In judging of the counterpoint of Dufay's time we should compare it with that of earlier centuries. The want of flexibility in the several voices or parts, the monotonous character of the harmonic progressions, and the absence of tasteful invention were the prevailing characteristics of style; but if we compare the works of Dufay and his contemporaries with the rude attempts of Adam de la Hale, Machault, Landino, and others, we perceive at once that remarkable progress had been made in melody and harmony.

Johannes Ockenheim

Dufay's most noted pupil was Johannes Ockenheim, or Okeghem, the real founder of the Flemish school. He was a native of Hainaut and was born in 1430. His active career as a composer and teacher began about the middle of the century. His name was recorded in 1443 as a singer at the Cathedral at Antwerp. Subsequently Ockenheim was chosen as one of the sixteen royal chapel singers of Louis XI of France, and after many years of service was appointed treasurer of the Church of St. Martin's at Tours, as a mark of honor from the king. At a later period of his life he made a visit to his native land, and was received with flattering attention; but he returned finally to Tours, where he spent the remainder of his days, dying in 1513.

Ockenheim was called the "Prince of Music," and enjoyed the highest respect of his contemporaries, both on account of his compositions and his extraordinary talents as a teacher; the most celebrated masters of the fifteenth century were among his pupils. Ockenheim has been esteemed as the progenitor of modern music, as the patriarch of counterpoint and canonic writing. Such praise, of course, is unmerited; yet, though Ockenheim was not the inventor of double counterpoint and the modern canon as has been supposed, his mission was an important one. The influence of his music and teachings was far more extended than that of any other musician of his day, reaching into foreign countries. Ockenheim stood far in advance of his predecessors; his compositions bear the marks of higher understanding and intelligence. The forms of counterpoint became so facile under his pen that they frequently led into abstruseness.

His favorite form of music was the canon. A canon then did not signify, as it does nowadays, a composition in which two or more parts enter one after another and follow each other throughout in strict thematic imitation, but primarily the rules, signs, and devices which were written out only on one staff for the solution of a musical enigma or puzzle canon. Tinctoris explains the canon to be a rule to enable one to search out the hidden meaning of the composer. Subsequently, when composers began to write out the canon in vocal score, the word signified strict imitation, as it does at present, and to this style of composition was also applied the word "fuga," because of the flight and pursuit of the theme through all the voices. The modern fugue, however, was not developed before the latter half of the seventeenth century. *Canon; change in the significance of the word*

In Ockenheim's time there were all sorts of canons, — canons in contrary and retrograde movement, in augmentation and diminution, and enigma canons of great variety and ingenuity. Their inventors sought for every device to puzzle the singer instead of aiding him, with the idea, we suppose, that they were accomplishing a worthy object. The several voices of a canon were frequently sung simultaneously, in different kinds of time; and intricacies arose on this score which would drive a modern singer to despair. Voices, not a note of which was intended to be sung, were introduced and carried silently through a whole mass. The singer was often obliged to find out for himself the hidden clef and key of the canon, as well as the entrance of the recurring voices. A Kyrie of Ockenheim has interrogation marks instead of clefs.

Compositions were sometimes written in more than thirty parts. Kircher, in his celebrated "Musurgia," gave the solution of a particular instance of this kind, which consisted of the bewildering number of five hundred and twelve voices, in one hundred and twenty-eight chorus divisions. But these were not real parts, like the double and treble choruses of the Roman and Venetian schools of the sixteenth century; they simply constituted a round of voices, and hence this species of composition was called the circle canon, or round.

Character of music of Ocken- heim's time

In the music of Ockenheim's time we do not commonly find more than five or six real parts. Although the harmony was still harsh and incorrect in places, considerable improve- ment had been gained in the melodious flow of the voices, and there are evident in this music many traces of individuality and expression. There are modern musicians who fail to per- ceive the intrinsic merit of this intellectual music of these mas- ters. It is considered as dry and abstruse, and utterly devoid of interest. But such an opinion only betrays ignorance and prejudice, for even were it not the fact that much of Ocken- heim's music is pervaded with genuine musical feeling and a sense of beauty, we should still be indebted to him and other Netherland composers for the thorough development of the intellectual part of music, which otherwise would possibly never have come to light; and the art would never have reached beyond the primitive forms of the song and dance. By means of the problems worked out with the understanding, musicians were enabled to acquire that technical skill and experience which are indispensable to the composer as a means of giving ready expression to his emotions and imagi- nation in ideal and permanent forms.

Masses and motets based on secular melodies

The forms of music most in fashion with the Netherland composers were the mass, motet, and secular part song. The composer bestowed particular attention on the mass, which called forth his highest talent and skill in designing musical problems and artifices. Every mass and motet was named after the first line of the cantus firmus, which, as I have already stated, was some familiar choral or secular melody on which the whole composition was founded. Accordingly we meet with some very odd titles in church music; for example, "Adieu mes amours," "Des rouges nez," "Fortuna desperata."

The most famous of all the secular melodies used in this way was the Provençal song, "L'omme armé." This was interwoven into numberless pieces, from the time of Dufay, in the fifteenth century, to that of Carissimi in the seventeenth. The melody was placed in the tenor, and if a mass had no such secular tenor, it was called *sine nomine*. In those days men did not generally heed the true meaning of the sacred text, and as the words of the mass, in their constant repetition, were perfectly familiar to the singers, it became the custom to write the words down only at the opening of the various movements, Kyrie, Gloria in Excelsis, etc., it being left to the good taste and discretion of the singers to apply the words to the notes. The result can easily be imagined. The marks of accentuation and quantity were often not only applied to the wrong syllables, but the text itself was frequently misplaced or omitted, so that it speedily degenerated into a series of meaningless syllables.

L'omme armé; missae sine nomine

The text of the motet and secular part song was better treated. The very name, motet, from *mot* (text), indicates the importance of adhering to the sacred words, which were generally selected from the Scriptures. There were people ready enough to condemn these abuses. It should be remembered, however, that so far as the introduction of secular music and words into church music is concerned, it was not an unmitigated evil. No profanation was intended; and, on the other hand, the naïve beauty of the popular songs exerted a good influence on the contrapuntal art. The common people were, in this manner, made to feel and appreciate in some degree elaborate church music, through its association with the favorite melodies which they had sung from childhood. Had the musicians from the outset originated their own themes, the music would have appeared in strange and unwelcome contrast to the songs of the people. These served as a

The text of the motet

safe guide, and protected the art of counterpoint from losing itself in aimless endeavors; for the counter melodies were composed in close imitation of the chosen theme, and thereby the counterpoint won a certain naturalness and ease, which otherwise would not have been attained. It was not, however, any poverty of invention which led these old masters to choose the Gregorian and secular songs as subjects for their music, but it was rather a feeling for that bond of sympathy which, during the Middle Ages, united all artists with the people. The counterpoint of that time, like the architecture, painting, and poetry, sprang from the people and was designed for the people.

Ockenheim was a very productive composer, judging from the number of masses, motets, and part songs which have been preserved, and which are known to be only a small portion of his works. Petrucci, the inventor of music printing, published several books of his compositions early in the six-

Prominent contempo- raries of Ockenheim

teenth century. Some of Ockenheim's most prominent contemporaries were his countrymen, Busnois, Caron, Regis, and the learned musical theorist Johannes Tinctoris, who was the author of the first musical lexicon. His most prominent foreign contemporaries were Johannes Goodendag of Germany and Guarnerii and Hykaert of Naples. Ockenheim had more than his equal in merit, though not in fame, in his countryman, Jakob Obrecht, or Hobrecht, whose music is considered as superior to that of all other masters prior to Josquin. Obrecht's counterpoint was more tasteful and elaborate and his harmony richer than Ockenheim's. It is related of Obrecht that he possessed so much facility and fire of invention that he could compose a whole mass in one night. Glareanus affirms that Obrecht was the musical instructor of the learned Erasmus.

Josquin de Prés

A new and more fruitful epoch is represented by Josquin de Prés, who was the greatest musical genius of his age. Josquin was born about 1445, probably at Condé, in Hainaut. He was a pupil of Ockenheim. His musical career began at

Rome as a singer in the Papal Choir under Sixtus IV. In 1480 he appeared as a famous musician in the employ of Lorenzo the Magnificent, and subsequently he became the leading singer or master of the royal chapel of Louis XII of France. It is not ascertained how long he remained in the service of that sovereign. Afterwards he was chosen court chapelmaster of Maximilian I, emperor of Germany, but he finally returned home to Condé, where he spent the remainder of his life. He was provost of the Cathedral there until his death in 1521.

Josquin became the musical idol of Europe. All his contemporaries and successors were unanimous in pronouncing him as endowed with extraordinary powers ; and this is corroborated not only by the masterly compositions he has left, but also by the troops of eminent masters whom he educated. His popularity was so great that his music fairly superseded all that had gone before it. This exclusive admiration was so extravagant that in the Papal Choir, on one occasion, a favorite six-voiced motet was thrown aside when the singers learned it was not by Josquin, as they had supposed, but by Adrian Willaert, who had already gained celebrity.

Josquin did not open a new path in music, like his countryman, Willaert, the founder of the Venetian school ; neither was he a so-called reformer, like Palestrina. But the materials which his predecessors had brought together he converted into organic, finished, and expressive forms ; and in this sense he was a genuine reformer. He was the first to master thoroughly the art of elaborate counterpoint, which he carried to its utmost limits, — to a development from whence music might take a new direction. The subtle ingenuity displayed by him in his canons and fugal pieces is wonderful. Under his facile guidance the most involved combinations gained an easy and playful form, and all his works bear the stamp of originality and character. It may be asked why Josquin's music is neglected, why it is not made fully known

Significance of Josquin's work

to modern hearers. It can be readily answered that those works which were solely the product of his intellect and skill do not call forth our sympathy except as students of the history of musical forms, but by far the greater number of his compositions are worthy of admiration to-day, and deserve a place among the best music.

The defects shown in his early compositions
Josquin's defects are noticeable in his early compositions, in the dry canons and empty harmonic progressions which conformed to his school and time. He was tempted to perform feats of skill in his writings, and his weak imitators copied his faults but not his virtues. It was during his day that the words of the mass were most neglected. The singers frequently omitted the words altogether, or replaced them with others wholly foreign. Many eminent musicians did not scruple to compose long vocal pieces without having selected any words to be sung to them. They went so far as to apply the words of "Ave regina" to one voice, "Alma redemptoris" to another, and something still different to each of the remaining voices of the piece. This practice of combining all sorts of incongruous elements was in favor for a long time, both in sacred and in secular music. Such potpourri, made up of scraps of melody and verse patched together like a beggar's garment, were named "Messanze" or "Quodlibets."

Vulgar and very offensive words were sung in church, and, on the other hand, church music was made to accompany dancing and other gayeties. We learn from Baini that the composers of church music in that day thought they had accomplished something meritorious if they had succeeded in awakening a desire to dance among the congregation. In this way many of Josquin's church compositions became the entertainment of jovial companions ; they sang his masses and danced to his church melodies. This is corroborated by Erasmus, who says that people run to church as to the theater to have their ears tickled. I fear their criticism may be applied with some pertinence to people of our own day. We read in Baini's life of Palestrina that it was the custom in Josquin's day to color the notes red, green, black, etc., according to the meaning of particular words. The words darkness, thunder, and death were expressed by black notes ; plants, meadow, flowers, by green notes ; the sun, heavens, wounds, blood, by red notes, and so on. This display of decorative art was not the work of the composer, however, but of the æsthetic and imaginative copyists of the times.

Let us now turn from the faults of Josquin and his con- **His merits** temporaries and do justice to his merits as an artist. It is a **as an artist** singular fact that Josquin, notwithstanding the abuses of his time, was the first composer who gave the words their full expression. His best masses and motets are faithful exponents of the sacred text, and are pervaded with the spirit of religious devotion. He discovered the true æsthetic value of the dissonance as a means of musical expression, — not merely as an harmonic device. Josquin used dissonances as suspended notes quite freely in his music, and in such a way as to give profound expression to the words.

"In spite of the constraint," says Ambros, "which the church ritual and the artistic conditions of the age inexorably imposed on him, in Josquin's music there speaks to us a pure and feeling soul, capable of stirring the very depths of our nature. It may be true that he carried musical artifices and witticisms to an extreme, but, nevertheless, even the most trivial of his works bear the stamp of superior genius, when compared with the endless productions of his contemporaries and imitators."

Luther, who was a good judge of music, gives his testimony in favor of Josquin in these words : "Josquin is master of the notes ; he does with them as he wills. Other masters of song must do as the notes will have it done. His music is gladsome, mild, and lovely, and not forced, nor tied down to the rules, but as free as the song of the finch."

Although Josquin produced numerous works, in fertility of genius he cannot be compared with his great successors Orlando Lasso and Palestrina, nor with many of his own disciples. He was too severe a critic of himself; it is said that he reserved many compositions for years before letting them be heard, and meanwhile did not spare any efforts to alter and improve them.

A rich portion of his works has been preserved to the present day. There are nineteen masses in print, besides a good number in manuscript kept in the archives of the Papal Chapel at Rome. In the sixteenth century Petrucci issued several books of Josquin's masses and motets, psalms, and chansons. Josquin's most distinguished contemporaries were his fellow-students with Ockenheim — De la Rue, Brumel, Agricola, Compère. His foreign contemporaries were the French master, Genet, and the German masters, Mahu and Stoltzer. Dietrich, Meyer, and Créquillon may also be considered as musicians of his time.

His most prominent followers and disciples were Mouton, Adrian Coclicus, the theorist, and Nicolaus Gombert; Clemens non Papa, De Monte, van Berghem, Waelrant, and many others belong to this productive period. His most noted French followers were Jannequin and Arcadelt.

Nicolaus Gombert

Perhaps the ablest representative of the progressive musicians directly succeeding Josquin was his pupil Nicolaus Gombert of Bruges, chapelmaster of Charles V. He was a wonderfully prolific and masterly composer, and was not content to remain a mere imitator of Josquin. Finck, the gifted German song composer, declared that Gombert had created music separated entirely in style from the earlier school. And Baini says there were many composers of that time who slavishly and mechanically imitated the faults of Josquin without being penetrated by the peculiar spirit and fire of his genius. Gombert was the true spiritual successor of Josquin; his music is earnest and noble, and is classed among the best of the Netherland school. The Netherlands, at this period, were in many respects in advance of the rest of Europe. The country was rich and prosperous through its skillful artisans, its manufactures, and its commerce. This material development was attended by a corresponding spiritual one, and marked the highest attainment of mediæval civilization.

Italy in the fifteenth century had emerged from the Middle Ages, but in Germany and particularly in the Netherlands the old customs and manners lasted much longer. During the first half of the sixteenth century the Netherland school reached the full tide of its glory; we read name after name of famous composers, theorists, and singers. Their fame and influence spread far and wide; in Rome the Papal Choir was for a long time composed almost exclusively of Netherland masters and singers, while in France, England, and Germany there arose a number of distinguished native masters, under their example and instruction. *Influence of the Netherlands on other countries*

The most celebrated French masters of that age were Jannequin, Certon, Maillard, Coclicus, Arcadelt, and Claude Goudimel, the teacher of Palestrina.

Clement Jannequin was the most original master of this French school. He was a clever contrapuntist and composer of masses and motets; but his favorite style was displayed in some curious descriptive pieces, which quite outrival modern attempts like the "Battle of Prague" and the oft-repeated "thunder storm" of modern organists. In one of his pieces he describes in tones the tumult of a Paris street. We hear the voices of the petty tradesmen, the familiar cries of "Buy my fish, shoes, pastry," etc., from the hucksters as they offer their tempting wares to the passers-by. *Clement Jannequin; descriptive music*

Such descriptive music was very common in that age. "They did not have any æsthetic scruples," says von Dommer, "as to whether they were overstepping the limits of art like the composers of programme music in our day, but went to work more ingenuously. They set music to the coats of arms of their patrons, wrote canons having for their subject rivers, mountains, towers, etc. ; but battles were the particular object of their fancy. Jannequin painted in this way the battle of Marignano, with the calls of command, the trumpet signals, the roll of musketry, the lively march with drum and fife, the clatter of sabers, the whistling of bullets ; then came the flight of the enemy, cursing and making barbarous outcries which were finally drowned by the triumphant shouts of the victors, crying, " Victory ! victory ! for the noble king of France ! " All this was accomplished by human voices, and must have had an indescribable effect. Such music may appear childish to our minds, but at all events it answered one purpose in that age, — it showed what the art was capable of, and enabled it to appropriate whatever would tend to enrich its effects.

The age of the Netherland music was fruitful in musical literature. Johannes Tinctoris was one of the ablest theorists of the fifteenth century. His " Diffinitorium " is the oldest dictionary of musical terms extant. Other noted writers were Gafor, or Gaferius, and Adam de Fulda.

Printing with movable type In conclusion, it may be well to speak of an important invention made about the beginning of the sixteenth century, which was of untold value to the art of music, — the invention of printing music with movable metal types, originated by Ottaviano dei Petrucci of Fossombrone. This invention served as important a purpose for the spread of music and musical knowledge as was accomplished for general literature by the art of book printing. To print notes from wooden tables, as hitherto had been the practice, was a slow and laborious process. This new invention enabled the printers to set up types and strike off copies with readiness and dispatch.

The numerous masters of the Netherland school with their German and French contemporaries were destined to become universally known and appreciated in their printed works ; had it not been for this good fortune we might never have known of their existence, though I fear they are hardly as well known as they deserve to be, notwithstanding Petrucci and his metal types.

The outline which I have attempted to trace of the history of music during the fifteenth century and the early part of the sixteenth may serve to show what a wonderful and rapid evolution was taking place in musical life and experience ; and we are now prepared to witness a grand culmination of *a cappella* music in the works of its greatest representative composers, Palestrina and Orlando Lasso.

CHAPTER VI

THE ITALIAN MASTERS OF THE SIXTEENTH CENTURY

Italy has long been loved and admired as the birthplace of modern literature and art, as the land of the renaissance of painting, sculpture, and architecture. In music, however, during the fourteenth and fifteenth centuries, another land claims our homage for working out the problem of counterpoint. Yet, although the Netherland composers surpassed all others in the mastery of elaborate church music, Italy was not wholly without good native musicians, who, in their comparatively inferior position, were preparing the ground for great masters like Palestrina and Gabrieli.

Netherland counterpoint rested on the naïve but rude songs of the people, while the earliest Italian music, except the Gregorian, was set to refined poetry, and the airs, therefore, were not borrowed, but entirely original. The Italians by innate capacity or disposition were prone to greater simplicity of expression, a richer flow of melody, and a more faithful rhythmical adherence to the metrical structure of the verses than Flemish composers, whose attention was absorbed in the treatment of the counterpoint.

Forms of secular music in Italy The most common forms of secular music in Italy during the fourteenth and fifteenth centuries were the frottola, the villota, or villanella, and the madrial, or madrigal. The frottole were four-part songs of a gay and trivial description, generally popular street songs; but some of them were more earnest and sentimental, being set to good poetry.

The villote, or villanelle, were peasant's songs originally, as the name implies. They resembled the frottole, but were more extended and artistic. The *villote alla Napoletana* were the most artistic of this class, but were often set to frivolous words. The madrigal was known as early as the fourteenth century, but it did not rise into universal prominence as the representative form of secular music before Willaert's day.

The word "madrigal" is probably derived from *mandra*, a flock of sheep, and originally denoted a shepherd's song. There were other favorite vocal pieces of a more general character, which were composed in agreement with a chosen meter to which the poem was afterwards set. The name given to this kind of composition was modus, or air, and from this source was derived the modern name "air," or "aria," which signifies the manner of singing (as we say a person has a certain air or manner), and does not refer, as many suppose, to the medium of song, — that is, the sound of vibrating air. These forms of secular song were inspired undoubtedly by the beautiful poetry which enriched Italian life at that period, — the age of Dante, Petrarch, and Boccaccio.

Petrucci published (1504–1508) as many as eight books of frottole, some nine hundred numbers in all. These are characteristic though primitive examples of Italian music, and mark the essential difference between it and Flemish music. The latter, like the Gothic architecture of the North, was developed organically from germs or motives, while the former corresponds to the simpler forms, — the grand curves and arches of Roman churches, within whose walls the pure and elevated harmonies of Palestrina have resounded through the centuries. As Rome was the center of civilization in the Middle Ages, so it was likewise the central point of the musical world, even before Italy gained the ascendency through the genius of her native composers.

The Papal Choir was for ages the most important musical **The Papal** organization in the world. Its history, in truth, embraces the **Choir** history of church music. During the Middle Ages it performed an invaluable service for the advancement of music. It gave liberal support to the most gifted singers, theorists, and composers of Europe. The members of the Papal Choir were treated with the honor which their ability deserved. They were clothed with the rank of a sacerdotal college. At St. Mark's in Venice the composers and singers occupied an equally honorable official position.

The Papal Choir was composed of different nationalities. They represented separately special branches of the art : the Spaniards were distinguished as falsetto singers, and sang the soprano parts ; the French were noted as clever teachers as well as composers ; the Flemings, who stood in the fore-ground, were remarkable as theorists and composers ; the Italians ultimately excelled in all these branches, although for a while they were humble learners.

Women not allowed to sing in church

According to ecclesiastical law, women were not allowed to sing in church, probably in obedience to St. Paul, who wrote, " Let your women keep silence in the churches." The soprano and contralto parts were performed by male falsetto singers, — castrati, or boys. Under the brilliant reigns of Pope Julius II and his successor Leo X, — the patrons of Raphael and Michael Angelo, — many eminent Flemish musicians were invited to Italy. Their supremacy at this moment was com-plete, but the time was rapidly approaching when native genius would assert itself and the musical scepter pass into the hands of the Italians. We have already learned that a reaction took place within the Netherland school, as exhibited in the works of Josquin, Gombert, Willaert, and others. These masters were cultivating the ground in Italy for such masters as Palestrina and Gabrieli.

The only Italian master worthy of special mention prior to Palestrina was Costanzo Festa, papal singer in 1517. Among the foreigners in the Papal Choir were the Spanish masters Morales, Escobedo, Scribano, and the learned theorist Fran-cesco Salinas. Morales was thoroughly grounded in Flemish counterpoint ; his works display originality and possess the fire of a true Spaniard.

The most distinguished Franco-Flemish masters at Rome were Arcadelt and Goudimel. Arcadelt was a very productive composer. He was one of the originators of the madrigal style, with Willaert and Verdelot.

Claude Goudimel, the teacher of Palestrina, was born at Vaison, in Flanders, early in the sixteenth century. He founded a school of music in Rome, at which a number of celebrated Italian composers were taught, among whom were Palestrina, Animuccia, Nanini, Bettini, and Alessandro della Viola. Goudimel was distinguished not only as a teacher but as a composer. He was the author of the melodies set to the psalter of Marot and Beza, the French Calvinists. The melody of " Old Hundred " has erroneously been attributed to him. He fell a victim to religious persecution, was murdered as a Huguenot at Lyons on St. Bartholomew's night (1572), and his body thrown into the Rhone. *Claude Goudimel*

Other eminent composers and singers in Rome about the middle of the sixteenth century were Ferrabosco, the French masters Barré and Carpentras, and the Flemish masters Dankerts and van Berghem of Antwerp.

Giovanni Pierluigi was born in 1514. He was called Palestrina after his birthplace, a small, ancient town in the vicinity of Rome. His family name was Sante. Very little is known of his early life. He was sent to Rome to complete his musical education under Goudimel. In 1551 he was appointed master of the boy singers and chapelmaster at the Vatican Basilica, as successor to Roselli. Soon after this he composed several four-part and five-part masses which were dedicated to Pope Julius III. This led to his call to the College of Singers in the Papal Choir, though he was not a priest and was a married man, which was contrary to the rules of membership. *Palestrina*

Paul IV, who ascended the papal throne in 1555, issued an order that the three married men who lived in company with the singers of the Papal Choir to the scandal of God's service and the sacred laws of the church should be expelled from the college. These three singers were Palestrina, Barré, and Ferrabosco. When Palestrina was informed of this sentence he was seized with a violent illness which lasted for more than two months. During the same year, however, he was appointed director of music at the Church of St. John Lateran. He held this position for more than five years, — an important period, for he worked assiduously and composed a number of works which were the first fruits of his genius. It was during this period that he composed the work which bears the title of

The "Im-
properia" "Improperia." It proved to be the foundation of his fame, and after the lapse of more than three hundred years is still sung every Passion Week by the Papal Choir. This simple composition, which consists of a succession of chaste concords combined skillfully and effectively for the voices, is animated with the very spirit of religious devotion. Baini applies to it the words of St. Bernard, " This is the song which I sought as worthy of the temple of the Most High, as sweet yet not trivial, but a noble song which pleases the ear and moves the heart."

Agitation
for a return
to Grego-
rian song In 1561 Palestrina was appointed chapelmaster of the Church of Santa Maria Maggiore. It was during the next few years that the effort was made to banish figural or contrapuntal music from the Roman Catholic Church and return to the exclusive use of unison Gregorian song. The question was fully discussed at the Council of Trent (1562), but without reaching any definite decision. Two years later, Pope Pius IV, who was an ardent lover of music, appointed a commission of eight cardinals and eight singers of the Papal Choir to give attention to this matter. They held several meetings in which it was debated whether the sacred words sung by the choir could be rendered more clearly audible. The singers represented that it was not always practicable to make the words perfectly distinct, owing to the fugal imitations in the counterpoint, and that to abolish counterpoint would be equivalent to the destruction of musical art.

The cardinals cited a " Te Deum " by Festa, the " Improperia," and a quartet from a mass by Palestrina as music in which every syllable of the text could be heard. The singers replied that those pieces were short, whereas a Gloria or Credo could not be composed in a corresponding style. They agreed, however, to banish from the choir all masses and motets composed on secular melodies, and all foreign words introduced into the texts. Finally, they decided to make trial of a composition to be written in a ·simple, elevated style, in which the words when sung should' be rendered perfectly intelligible. Palestrina was invited to write a mass for this purpose. In response to this call he composed three six-part masses. On the completion of the masses the papal singers were invited to sing them before the cardinals. The company gave their undivided attention to these works. Their interest grew more and more intense as the performance went on, and the third mass in G, in particular, received enthusiastic applause. It is asserted that Palestrina thus won a victory which established his world-wide fame, and that henceforth no one thought seriously of abandoning figural music. He was called the " Saviour of Music " ; yet this is not strictly true. His style was considered as the model for centuries, and *stile Palestrina* was the name given to *a cappella* music. The famous mass in G was dedicated to Marcellus II, Palestrina's former patron, and it bears the title, " Missa Papae Marcelli."

[margin note: Palestrina's three masses]

Pope Pius IV is said to have remarked of this work, " These are like the harmonies of the new high song which the Apostle John once heard in the heavenly Jerusalem, and of which another John has given us a conception, in this earthly Jerusalem." The Pope rewarded the author by creating for him the office of composer to the Papal Choir, and other honorable positions were subsequently opened to him. He died in 1594, and was buried in St. Peter's. An inscription on his tombstone styles him the " Prince of Musicians."

Palestrina, like most great masters, was a remarkably productive composer. The list of his works embraces many volumes of masses, motets, lamentations, litanies, hymns, magnificats, sacred and secular madrigals. Baini, in his biography of the master, which is valuable to the student in spite of its unreasonable hero-worship, claims for Palestrina no less than ten different styles, corresponding to the various stages of his career. But this refinement of criticism is worthless. We merely observe in the works of Palestrina, as in those of other musicians, traces of the growth of his individuality, but fail to perceive any such sharply marked transformations of style that they may be counted off on the fingers.

It is generally admitted that Palestrina was partly instrumental in bringing about a reformation in church music, but Baini wrests the facts of history out of their proper bearing when he states that Palestrina worked out a great reform almost single-handed. The music of Josquin, Gombert, Willaert, Festa, De Rore, Andrea Gabrieli, Goudimel, and yet more notably that of Orlando Lasso, shows that the sacred text was no longer abused and neglected by composers. The style of counterpoint was growing more simple and chaste. The so-called *stile familiare* of Josquin, or counterpoint note against note, had become universal and was leading the way to modern music through the adoption of chromatic intervals by masters of the Venetian school.

Significance of Palestrina's work Palestrina achieved no reform, but he prevented a retrogression in music. By a turn of good fortune unparalleled in musical history, he was the means of saving counterpoint from being ignominiously abolished from the Roman Church. If such a foolish step had been taken, Italian church music would never have reached a state of high cultivation, and the world would have lost many beautiful manifestations of genius. In Protestant Germany and England, however, counterpoint would undoubtedly have made further progress, but probably in a less artistic form.

In considering Palestrina from an artistic standpoint, he is the highest representative of old church music. His pure and elevated conceptions found appropriate expression in types of form perfectly suited to the tonal system of the fifteenth and sixteenth centuries. The inflexibility of that system demanded a certain obedience of the composer. A church mode once chosen, — as, for instance, the Phrygian, Dorian, Lydian, etc., — forced the composer almost into its own peculiar mood, and for this reason, mediæval music, as long as it was bound down to the typical church modes, lacked much of the free expression of the music of the present era. The individual traits and idiosyncrasies of the artist could not be so sharply outlined. This objective character of mediæval music, however, had its great attributes ; it was in harmony with the age and its religion. The church gave it birth, and under her motherly care it grew up to power and influence. Notwithstanding the frequent absence of tonality, or the adherence to a chosen key with its relatives, and in spite of the want of connection between foreign triads, and abrupt transitions from one to another, the best *a cappella* music of that age will always be interesting. This is additional proof that all genuine and inspired works of the mind and heart of man are of interest in every age, and do not lose their significance with the changes of fashion

Palestrina will always hold a place among the greatest artists. No matter how far removed men may be from the spirit of the age in which he lived, there is in his music something that calls forth our highest admiration, something that lifts us above ourselves. In the words of Leopold von Ranke :

Estimates of his music

Who can listen to his beautiful works and not feel his soul stirred within him ? It is as if nature became endowed with tone and voice, as though the elements spoke and the sounds of universal life mingled in spontaneous harmony to hallow and adore, now undulating like the sea, now soaring heavenward in exulting bursts of jubilee. The soul is borne aloft to the regions of religious ecstasy, on the wings of universal sympathy.

It is not ardent Catholics alone who appreciate Palestrina's music, though it is certain that a part of his power is due to the grandeur and solemnity of the Roman churches, and to the liturgy, which is itself a great work of art. But his music, like all genuine music, stands above the opinions and creeds of religious sects.

Analysis of the art of Palestrina

It is easy to feel the ideal beauty embodied in the works of Palestrina, just as it is in other forms of perfect art, but it is difficult to express in words the secret of their magic power. The true listener perceives in this wonderful music peculiar characteristics which render it the greatest of all purely polyphonic vocal music. He finds the contours, or outlines, of the single voices of wonderful refinement and beauty ; it is a world of ideal shapes and figures so combined with pure sweetness of tones and harmonies that we are transported to a higher sphere, above all human passions. The technical musician appreciates the masterly treatment of the form of the composition. Where the composer avails himself of the learned artifices which the Netherland masters employed in earlier times, they are not placed in the foreground ; they appear natural and simple, and have a higher meaning. The weaving of the voices does not lead to confusion and lack of clearness. All polyphonic music has its origin in melody, lives and has its being in melody — the harmony is only the result of simultaneous melodies. The harmony is not the object but the result. The prime object is the symmetrical leading of the several individual voices. This is true of Palestrina, as of other masters of the fifteenth and sixteenth centuries.

" Palestrina's music, to express it in a word," says Ambros, " breathes the beatitude of worship, the blessedness of adoration." This true appreciation of the Roman school, however, requires a special training. " The music before 1600," to quote somewhat freely from Ambros, " is in comparison with music after that date a foreign idiom, which must be learned. A half knowledge is worse than no knowledge. Representative works like the 'Pope Marcellus Mass,' the 'Well-Tempered Clavichord,' and the 'Heroic Symphony' are very different from each other, in fact, as far apart as the poles. . . . The music of Palestrina is not music for the concert room, the salon, or the circle of refined amateurs : it is purely music for the church — and the Roman Church, by which it was inspired and for which it was created. . . . Its true place is the Sistine Chapel, where Michael Angelo's sibyls and prophets look down, where the beginning and end of all things — the creation and destruction of the world — are brought in dreadful pictures before our eyes. Above the thunder of the Judgment the tones are spanned as a glowing rainbow. The titanic painter speaks of the justice of the living God, but the musician speaks of divine love and mercy, and of the pure harmony of eternal blessedness."

In Rome Palestrina's most eminent contemporaries were Animuccia, Vittoria, Nanini, and Luca Marenzio, the greatest of madrigal composers. The Roman style, or *stile Palestrina*, was called the elevated style, to distinguish it from the elaborate style of the Netherland school and the later beautiful or florid style of the Neapolitans. It was fully established before the death of Palestrina. The most distinguished followers and descendants of this style in the sixteenth and seventeenth centuries were Anerio, Allegri, Cifra, Valentini, Abbatini, Ugolini, Agostini, Domenico and Virgilio Mazzocchi, Benevoli, Bernabei, Steffani, Corelli, Pasquini, Gasparini, Carissimi, Pitoni, and others. *His contemporaries and successors*

About the beginning of the eighteenth century the dramatic style began to eclipse *a cappella* music, and thenceforth Roman church music has lived only in its past greatness. Of all the contemporaries of Palestrina no one could be called his rival except Orlando Lasso, the greatest master of the Netherland school.

Orlando Lasso was born at Mons in Hainaut in 1520, the year that Charles V was crowned as emperor at Aix-la-Chapelle. *Orlando Lasso*

His original name was Roland de Lattre, but he changed it because his father had been sentenced for the crime of counterfeiting money. When he was a boy of sixteen he accompanied the nobleman Ferdinando de Gonzaga to Milan and Sicily; after remaining for two years at Naples he went to Rome, where, in 1541, he was appointed chapelmaster at the Church of St. John Lateran, a very high post for a youth of twenty-one years. Although his reputation increased rapidly, he abandoned this position at the end of two years on learning of the dangerous illness of his parents, and hurried back to his native land, but on his arrival found that they were dead. Homeless and afflicted, he went to England and France, and afterwards spent several years at Antwerp. His reputation meanwhile was steadily growing, and in 1557 he was invited to the court of Duke Albert V of Bavaria, who appointed him chapelmaster. Through the splendor of Lasso's genius this position became one of the first in Europe. He brought into the duke's service many of the best singers and players of that time. His choir and orchestra consisted of sixty singers and thirty performers, fully able to perform the most difficult compositions to his satisfaction.

His honors and titles   Lasso soon became a man of European celebrity; he was the favorite and friend of monarchs and princes, who rivaled each other in bestowing on him testimonials of honor. The Emperor Maximilian conferred on him titles of nobility, the king of France made him Knight of Malta, Pope Gregory XIII made him Knight of the Golden Spur, and a medal was struck in his honor on which were stamped the very flattering words, *Hic ille est Lassus qui lassum recreat orbem* (This is that weary one who refreshes the weary world). He was called the musical phœnix of his age, the " Prince of Musicians "; and all other masters of the sixteenth century, except Palestrina, were obscured by his fame. His compositions were in such demand that even during his lifetime it was a matter of pride to be the fortunate possessor of the least of his manuscripts.

Lasso remained faithfully at his post at Munich until his death in 1594, — about four months after the death of Palestrina.

Lasso is reputed to have been a polished and handsome man, whose amiable disposition, noble character, and cultivated mind rendered his society highly prized. He lived in daily intercourse with men who were distinguished either by their learning, intelligence, or birth. But amidst all the honors bestowed on him, he remained modest and retiring, — a mark of true greatness.

Lasso was a wonderfully prolific composer. His works number, according to Delmotte, his biographer, some 2337 compositions : they have been collected and preserved in the Royal Library at Munich. His sacred music consisted of masses, motets, psalms, hymns, lamentations, magnificats, litanies, and over four hundred Latin and German canticles ; in all more than fifteen hundred compositions. The remainder of his works are secular madrigals, chansons, villanelle, and other Latin and German vocal pieces. Lasso's compositions

Lasso betrays his Flemish origin in his church music, and therefore is rightly classed with the composers of his native country, — the last and greatest of that school. But he is more than this : he is a true cosmopolitan in music, and on this account has been called the Mozart of the sixteenth century. Like that wonderful genius he was a universal master. He united harmoniously the different national styles in a natural and original style of his own. In his masses he appears as a Flemish master, and shows an inclination toward a complex treatment of the voices. In his motets, however, he dispenses with the tiresome cantus firmus and evinces an unusually refined taste. His *a cappella* style reminds us of Palestrina, and although his harmonies may not always possess the chaste and severe purity of the Roman master, yet in the massive strength and grandeur of his musical conceptions Lasso is fully his equal. He was always ready to adopt the latest innovations in music, and although he was not the The cosmopolitan character of his work

originator of chromatic melody and other novel effects of his
day, he boldly used them in some of his pieces. It is said
that he was the first composer to introduce the major third in
the closing chord of a composition. Hitherto only the octave
or the octave with the fifth were allowed.

Burney and Baini have greatly underrated the genius of
Lasso. The former calls him "a dwarf on stilts," the latter
holds him to be "a soulless and spiritless Netherlander."
But more enlightened and impartial critics, who are not
wedded to pet theories or favorites, speak in other terms.
Proske in his introduction to the "Musica Divina" remarks:

> In his works may be discerned the traits of an epic dramatic force
> and truth which seem imbued with the spirit of a Dante or a Michael
> Angelo. If Palestrina can be compared with Raphael, Lasso may be
> classed with the great Florentine artist and poet. Equally great in
> church and secular music, Lasso absorbed the nationality of all the
> European music of his time, which no longer appeared as special
> Flemish, Italian, German, or French music, but, impressed with his
> own spirit, was formed into a characteristic, united whole.

Lasso's full significance as a representative musician has
not yet been measured, for the greater number of his compositions are still unpublished. He is worthy of better treatment, and a biographer is yet to come who will throw a clear
light on the master's life and works.

CHAPTER VII

VENETIAN MASTERS OF THE SIXTEENTH CENTURY

Venice in the sixteenth century was as peculiarly and richly endowed with men of genius in music as in painting and architecture. The world is never weary of praising the unique beauty of Venetian art, the warm coloring of its paintings, and the splendor of its churches and palaces. Venetian music deserves as much praise for its glow of color and beauty of design, yet is now sadly neglected.

The grand Church of St. Mark was the center of Venetian music, just as the Papal Choir was the center of musical life at Rome. In the ninth century organs were used in Venice, owing to its proximity to the East, whence the first organs came. We do not find any historical proof, however, that the public church authorities of the city took any special interest in church music earlier than the fourteenth century. The name of Zucchetto is recorded as organist of St. Mark's in 1318. Since his time the record of the organists of St. Mark's has been preserved. Francesco Landino, the blind organist, and Bernhard the German, the reputed inventor of the organ pedals, are the only distinguished names of the many who officiated at the organ at St. Mark's before the latter half of the fifteenth century. In 1490 Urban of Venice built a new organ for St. Mark's opposite the old one, and before the end of the century there were employed two organists and two well-drilled choirs, able to sing the difficult music of the Flemish masters. Early in the sixteenth century Adrian Willaert, one of the most gifted Flemish composers, was invited to Venice to take the direction of the music there, and he thus became the real founder of the great Venetian school.

Church of St. Mark, center of Venetian musical life

91

Influence of the Netherlands on Venetian music

At this period Venice stood at the height of her political prosperity. Her relations with the Low Countries were much more intimate than with her Italian neighbors and kinsmen, toward whom she held a proud and isolated position. This free intercourse between prominent commercial powers extended to matters of intelligence and art as well as trade and commerce, and we can trace mutual action and reaction. We have evidence that the influence of Titian, Veronese, and Tintoretto was felt in the Netherlands in the works of Rubens and Vandyke, while in music we know that Josquin and Willaert were the forerunners of the Venetian composers, De Rore and Andrea and Giovanni Gabrieli.

Adrian Willaert

Adrian Willaert was born at Bruges in 1480. His father brought him up for the profession of law and sent him to Paris to study, but his love for music was so strong that he abandoned the study of law and became the pupil in music of Mouton and Josquin. He went to Rome in 1516, having previously gained considerable reputation. Subsequently he spent several years at the court of Louis II of Hungary. In 1527 he was called to Venice as chapelmaster of St. Mark's, a post which he held during the rest of his life. He died in 1563.

Composition for combined choirs

Under Willaert's direction the music of St. Mark's became very celebrated, and the office of chapelmaster at that church reached a high point of eminence; from his time until the eighteenth century the place was occupied only by masters of the first rank. Willaert was a pioneer in the broadest sense, for though his style was founded on that of Josquin and his disciples, he began almost where they left off. He was the first master to compose for two or more choirs in combination, — a style of music which his followers developed to its utmost limits with astonishing results.

I mentioned that antiphonal choir singing was introduced into the Christian Church at a very early period, and was a custom borrowed from the responsive chanting of the ancient

Greek chorus and Jewish temple worship. But this did not acquire any remarkable characteristics before Willaert's day. The Netherland musicians employed all their energies in solving the problem of counterpoint with a limited number of parts. In their most elaborate experiments the counterpoint never exceeded eight real harmonic parts, including even their rounds or circle canons, with the multiplicity of recurring voices which characterized them. It probably never occurred to them to mass chorus against chorus, each one as a well-organized body of counterpoint, capable of working when required in full agreement with the others.

Willaert, with his countrymen, Arcadelt and Verdelot, was the founder or promoter of the madrigal, as a highly refined style of music. Hitherto it had been a kind of wild flower, —a simple pastoral; but now it assumed more importance. The poem generally consisted of twelve or fifteen lines of variable length, so that it really appeared more like a free recitation than a versification. "The style," says Mattheson, "is adapted to the emotions of love, tenderness, and sympathy." The closing lines often expressed some witty or happy thought, like an epigram. *Development of the madrigal*

The music was governed more strictly by the meaning of the words than it was in the mass, and the counterpoint was more simple and expressive. In some madrigals the voices were wrought out with exquisite refinement in a delicate web of counterpoint; others were composed in simple harmony, note against note. This latter style possessed a diatonic character, out of which the chromatic element of modern music could gradually be developed. The first hints of this new acquisition we owe to Willaert.

The so-called sacred madrigal was an offshoot of this new style and does not differ essentially from contemporary motets. At a later period the comic madrigal came into vogue through Vecchi and others, and finally the madrigal was introduced on the dramatic stage in the earliest attempts of the opera, and gave rise to the modern opera chorus. The madrigal was accompanied on all sorts of instruments. For over two centuries it was the favorite style of music, and an immense number of madrigals flooded Europe.

Willaert's most noted pupils were De Rore, Zarlino, Porta, della Viola, and Vicentino.

Cipriano de Rore

Cipriano de Rore was born at Mechlin in 1516. He was Willaert's successor at St. Mark's in 1563, and died at Parma two years later. His originality was manifested in his madrigals, which became so popular that the Italians called him " Il Divino." De Rore did not hesitate to use chromatic intervals, and boldly entered upon the new path which his teacher had merely pointed out. Considerable opposition was made to this innovation at first, but soon other bold masters, like Lasso and Luca Marenzio, adopted chromatic intervals in their writings. The diatonic character of most of the counterpoint had grown monotonous, and the introduction of chromatic melody gave variety and coloring to the music and deepened the expression of the words.

The first experiments, naturally, were rude and harsh, for De Rore did not stop halfway, and produced discordant sounds equaled only by some of the latest modern masters. It was not to be expected that De Rore and his imitators should at once thoroughly comprehend the true laws which govern chromatic melody and harmony; such laws could be determined only after long experience. These masters deserve the honor, at all events, of having prepared the way for the modern system of major and minor keys and the chromatic scale. They did more toward the attainment of a newer and higher type of music than all the speculation of learned theorists and scholars had been able to accomplish from antiquity to the modern age.

Gioseffo Zarlino

De Rore's successor at St. Mark's was Gioseffo Zarlino, the greatest musical theorist of the sixteenth century. It is difficult to form any idea of Zarlino's talent as a composer from the few compositions that are at hand; his fame justly rests on his profound theoretical writings. His great work on the principles of music, entitled "Instituzioni armoniche," holds a very high place in musical literature. Before his day musicians avoided the thirds in the last chords of the final cadence of a composition; all pieces ended either with the simple octave, or the octave with the fifth. Orlando Lasso, as I have stated, was the first to adopt this innovation in practical music, but he did not extend it to the minor third, which was not used at the close of a piece until nearly the eighteenth century. Zarlino justified the use of the major and minor thirds and sixths as concords by his so-called pure diatonic system of tempered intervals, which was an improvement on the pure-fifth system of Pythagoras. This new system recognized large and small whole tones in the series of intervals comprising the diatonic scale.

The foundation of organ playing was laid at Venice. The most celebrated organ players of the sixteenth century were trained in the Venetian school. A complete list of the organists of St. Mark's is contained in von Winterfeld's masterly work, "Giovanni Gabrieli and his Age." We read the names of Parrabosco, Claudio Merulo, and Andrea and Giovanni Gabrieli. The two greatest masters of the Venetian school were Andrea Gabrieli and his nephew Giovanni. *Organ playing*

Andrea was born at Venice in 1510. He was appointed organist of the second organ at St. Mark's, and held this position until his death in 1586. He was a productive composer, and enriched church music by the accompaniment of various instruments. Proske pays a high tribute to his genius in the following words: "He understood better than any of his predecessors how to combine choruses of many harmonic parts in superb masses of tone. But the sensuous splendor of these novel effects, which seemed to be an inheritance of the proud island city, did not rob his music of that earnestness and religious feeling which was peculiar to Venetian institutions *Andrea Gabrieli*

and society at that period." Andrea Gabrieli was a remarkable organist. He was the teacher of Merulo, who was very
famous as an organ composer and player.

Giovanni Gabrieli was born in 1557. In 1585 he was
appointed first organist at St. Mark's in place of Merulo. His
genius was manifested in all branches of musical composition.
His church music is as solemn and elevated as Palestrina's.
Although he employed the church modes, he seemed to mold
their rigid forms into a more modern expression. The genuine church style pervades Giovanni's works, but they are
free from the cold impersonality which is characteristic of
most *a cappella* music : he appeals to the individual heart.
"He prays and we pray with him," says Ambros. "If we
compare the same text with Palestrina, whose style is not
less glorious, nor less elevating to the soul, we feel an immense difference; for Palestrina is the last, purest sound of
the older direction in music, while Gabrieli announces in a
wonderful manner the coming musical emancipation of the
individual." In *a cappella* music he has never been equaled
in the production of rich effects of musical coloring — in
separating and massing together choral harmonies.

His compositions for two, three, and four choruses are
wonderful exhibitions of skill and judgment. Each choir is a
complete organization of four-part harmony. Each is stationed
separately at some point of the cathedral to take independent
action, to respond to the other choirs or to blend with them,
according to the master's fancy. The sound of these aërial
harmonies as they rose and fell in echo, now soaring heavenward in many-voiced concord and in glorious praise, now
floating soft and low in prayer or in sad miserere, must
have moved profoundly the hearts of the worshipers in that
grand old cathedral of St. Mark's. We cannot but feel a
pang of regret that such divine art is not universally known
and appreciated, that this musical Titan has been neglected
and almost forgotten. It may not always be thus ; we may

yet be educated to a more universal and enlightened taste, so that our ears may some day be open to noble and beautiful music of every country and age.

Gabrieli made free use of musical instruments, which did not slavishly accompany the voice parts but had an obligato part of their own. Sometimes they preluded the voices, and in the course of the piece instrumental interludes were introduced. Such compositions were called sacred symphonies. He also employed solo voices in combination with chorus and instruments. The instruments used by him were the cornetti (a wind instrument now obsolete), trombones, and stringed instruments. Von Winterfeld gives a number of fine examples of the master's art. One of the most strikingly beautiful and richly effective pieces in this collection is the "Benedictus et Osanna" for three choirs. The first choir is composed of sopranos, alto, and tenor; the second choir, of mixed voices; the lowest choir, of male voices in a low register. The rich color of such music cannot be described. Gabrieli holds a high place in musical history as an instrumental composer and organ player. His pieces for the orchestra of stringed instruments, cornetti, and trombones must have had a superb effect. His sonatas, canzoni, toccatas, and other organ pieces sound musical to-day, notwithstanding the immense progress that has been made since his time. *Free use of instruments*

The use made of chromatic effects by this master is well described by Ambros. He says: *Chromatic effects*

In his madrigals Gabrieli showed that he knew how to treat chromatic progressions much better than De Rore, who occasionally overshot his mark. In the class of music by Gabrieli which may be termed chromatic, the master has proved himself to be thoroughly familiar with the laws of chromatic harmony, producing effects of which his predecessors and even his contemporaries had hardly a conception. We find modulations, sequences of chords, digressions, half cadences that refer to the tonic of a foreign key, retrogression, etc., — musical effects, which, though closely related to our modern system of keys, were not very far removed from the mediæval church modes. He accomplished this through the agency of the raising and lowering of the key which had become general; that is, the so-called *musica ficta*, or transposed keys.

Giovanni Gabrieli stood at an important turning point in musical history. He witnessed some of the first attempts in monodic dramatic music, — the beginning of the opera and oratorio in the first year of the seventeenth century. If he had lived longer, he might possibly have composed specimens of these new styles, as did his gifted pupil Heinrich Schütz.

Gabrieli
compared
to Bach

Gabrieli may be compared to Sebastian Bach, who also stood at a turning point in music, and marked equally well the culmination of an older epoch and the beginning of a new one. Both these musicians did a great work for instrumental music; both introduced new and bold effects in harmony and remarkable combinations of voices and instruments, of which their predecessors had not availed themselves; and both were more individual, or subjective, in their music than their greatest contemporaries. While Gabrieli can be compared with Bach, Palestrina may be matched with Handel; and from a worldly point of view this analogy also holds good, for the genius of Palestrina and Handel has been universally recognized and admired, while the other two musicians are still unappreciated by the millions.

CHAPTER VIII

MUSIC IN GERMANY

The Reformation of the sixteenth century exerted a power- Effect of the ful influence on the development of music in two ways : first, by means of the Protestant Church ; and secondly, through the reaction which it caused within the Roman Catholic Church.

Effect of the Reforma- tion on music

During the early stages of the Reformation great violence and harm were done to the fine arts. Churches were sacked and burned ; the paintings and statues destroyed. But this fierce spirit of iconoclasm did not extend to music, except among the Presbyterians and Puritans, who banished trained choirs and musical instruments from their places of worship. The great body of the Protestant world, however, retained music as the handmaid of religion. To men engaged in a terrible struggle with Roman tyranny and persecution, music was a precious boon. It expressed more deeply than any other form of art the aspirations and hopes of those who were destined perhaps to suffer at the hands of a cruel enemy.

As Germany was the central point of the Reformation, so it was likewise the starting point of this new and peculiar phase of musical progress. Although that country at an earlier period had able musicians like Isaac, Finck, and Mahu, who were contemporaries of the earlier Netherland school, yet the real national characteristics of German music sprang into life through the Reformation.

Martin Luther himself, the head and front of the great movement, took the deepest interest in music, which he exem- plified in his own grand " Ein' feste Burg ist unser Gott " and other famous melodies and hymns. Some of the noblest

Martin Luther

words in praise of music were uttered by him. He said:
" Next to theology there is no art to be compared with music.
Music makes people more gentle and tender-hearted, more
virtuous and reasonable. Singing is an excellent art and exercise. There dwell the germs of many good virtues in hearts
devoted to music. Those who are not moved by music I hold
to be like sticks and stones."

If we compare the early Protestant church music of Germany with the Roman and Venetian music of the sixteenth
century, we are struck with one marked difference. The
German church music was of a more popular character; it
sprang directly from the people. It was more simple, lyrical,
and expressive, but less artistic and elaborate than Italian
church music, which was the outgrowth of skill and genius.
The powerful encouragement which the church had given for
ages to the cultivation of sacred music produced great results
while German music was yet in its childhood. Rome was still
the center of the world in art and knowledge as well as in
wealth and refinement. Germany was but a poor country in
comparison; its people were rough and uncultivated. Nevertheless the foundation of the future greatness of German
music was laid during the Reformation, and in the course of
the following two centuries Protestant Germany produced
two of the greatest masters of sacred music who ever lived,
— Bach and Handel.

Sources of
music of
the Lu-
theran
Church

I refer all those who desire to gain a complete knowledge
of this branch of musical history to the great work of Carl
von Winterfeld, entitled " Der evangelische Kirchengesang."
There are three sources whence the Lutheran Church has
derived its music: first, from the early Latin hymns and
melodies of the Romish Church; second, from the popular
sacred music in Germany prior to the Reformation; third,
from the secular music of the Middle Ages. Many of the most
beautiful Latin hymns were eagerly translated or imitated in
German, furnishing rich material for the new church. The

melodies in many cases were also appropriated, and a few specimens have lived to the present day and are still in general use in the Lutheran Church. The three oldest Latin songs are the following beautiful chorals : " Veni redemptor gentium " (Come, Saviour of the Heathen), from the fourth century, and attributed to St. Ambrose ; " A solis ortus cardine," from the fifth century ; " Veni creator spiritus " (Come Creator, Holy Ghost), from the eighth century, and erroneously attributed to Charlemagne.

In regard to the German sacred songs prior to the Reformation, it is a well-authenticated fact that long before that age it was the custom to sing a part of the religious service in German instead of Latin. Even as far back as the ninth century there existed German popular sacred songs, and in succeeding centuries, especially in the thirteenth and fourteenth, the age of the *Mariencultus*, they were very common, and finally were used in the church. On the other hand, Latin words were not wholly dispensed with in the Lutheran Church before the seventeenth century. Some of the best specimens of this old, popular sacred music are the chorals, " Christ ist erstanden " (from the twelfth century), " Also heilig ist der Tag " (from the fifteenth century), " Nun bitten wir den heiligen Geist," " Gelobet seist du, Jesu Christ," etc., and the old German Christmas song, " Ein Kindelein so löbe- lich," known as " Der Tag, der ist so freudenreich." German words sung in the church

The German popular secular songs of the Middle Ages, which we met with in the minnelieder and meisterlieder of the thirteenth, fourteenth, and fifteenth centuries, together with the rich collection of melodies contained in the " Lochheimer Song Book " enable us fully to appreciate the noble character of much of this old music. It is easy to account for the very generous supply of fine chorals that owe their origin to this source. Perhaps the most beautiful and touching melodies, the very jewels among the many chorals now in use, were set originally to secular words.

Old German songs peculiarly adapted to religious worship

We might suppose, judging by the music of the present day, that the custom of introducing secular melodies into the church would have led to a profanation of religion. In the Netherlands this was the case, because profane and sometimes very offensive words were introduced, as well as other abuses which I have already enumerated. But the old songs of Germany were generally earnest and elevated in their tone; many of them, indeed, were profoundly sad and religious. When the trying times of the Reformation came the people could not help singing; nothing could restrain them from expressing their religious ardor in song. And what could be more natural than to sing the familiar melodies which they had known from childhood, and which were endeared to them by earliest associations? In this way the words were changed; instead of some secular object the higher worship of God became the burden of the song. From that day forward the people took a more active part in the services of public worship. Simple melodies were required for congregational singing, and none could serve them so well as their own favorite songs, for the elaborate counterpoint of Catholic church music was far too difficult for them. These are sufficient reasons to account for the great number of German chorals which owe their rise to the people and not to distinguished masters of the art. At first considerable opposition was shown by many to the adaptation of sacred words to secular melodies on the ground that that which is once dedicated to the world and the devil is not fit for the church. But von Dommer remarks that Satan, according to Luther's own words, is no lover of music, and his Majesty seems to have been very indifferent to the fate of these secular songs, never having troubled himself to look after his stolen property, but leaving it in the hands of the Protestants.

Modern secular music not adapted to worship

The custom of appropriating secular melodies continued for a long time, almost till the present century; but the more modern examples offend our taste, because the secular style in music has diverged so far from the church style. The exquisite beauty of some of the melodies of mediæval origin has deservedly rendered them great favorites, and celebrated masters like Schulz, Graun, Bach, and, in the present century, Mendelssohn, Schneider, and others, have introduced them into their finest cantatas, passion music, and oratorios.

It will suffice to give the names of a few such melodies well known to the admirers of German chorals. The lovely choral, "Nun ruhen alle Wälder" (the Forests are now Reposing), was a secular melody composed by Heinrich Isaac about the beginning of the fifteenth century. Another deeply expressive melody, "O Haupt voll Blut und Wunden" (O Sacred Head now Wounded), was originally a love song by Hans Leo von Hasler, and has been used by Sebastian Bach in his passion music. The melody to " Ich dank' dir, lieber Herre " (I thank thee, dearest Lord) was adapted from the secular song, " Entlaubet ist der Walde," which I mentioned as the oldest specimen extant of good three-part harmony. Early in the sixteenth century various collections of secular songs were printed by Oeglin, Schöffer, Forster, and others, and in the latter part of the century they were arranged to sacred words for congregational use by Knaust, Vespasius, and others. *Famous German chorals*

But since these publications first appeared the choral melodies have greatly changed their form. At the present day the notes are of nearly equal length, but before the middle of the seventeenth century their rhythm was more varied than since that time : notes of various lengths were freely used ; triple measure, syncopations, and sudden changes of tempo were common. These effects sprang naturally from the peculiar meter of the secular poetry and music of that age and not from the elaborate contrapuntal art. *Change in form of choral melodies*

Since the time when the choral melodies assumed their modern simple form, efforts have been made to return to a more florid and varied rhythm, but without success, for the simple and equal notes are more solemn and much more easily sung in unison by a large congregation. This is the only practical solution of the question, for no congregational singing can be grand and inspiring unless it be of a simple character.

Contemporaneous with this simple style of church music for congregational singing was enriched artistic choir sing-ing, the contrapuntal treatment of choral melodies in many parts being very common in the sixteenth and seventeenth centuries. The usual form of such compositions was brief and closely wrought. The choral was frequently placed in the tenor, as cantus firmus, and the other voices were set to it in free, imitative counterpoint. The mediæval church modes lay, of course, at the foundation of their harmonic and melodic structure. Luther describes this kind of music with unqualified admiration.

> We recognize with astonishment the great and perfect wisdom of God as exhibited in his wonderful works of music ; but we perceive it only in part, for it is most surprising that while one voice is singing a simple air or tenor, other voices leap and play about it as with shouts of joy, adorning this same air or tenor with manifold grace and beauty, and led like a heavenly choir, they fondly encircle and greet one another. Even those who have but a slight understanding of this art are deeply touched by it, and think that there is nothing more remarkable in the world than such a song adorned with many voices. And he who has no love nor desire for it, and is not moved by such a delightful master-piece, must be a coarse clod for whom such music is too good ; he is only fit to listen to the howlings of animals.

The twofold character of Lutheran church music is shown in the choral books of the sixteenth century : one kind con-tains the simple melodies and text, and was intended for the use of the congregation ; another was printed in separate voice parts for the choir, and contains the full contrapuntal treatment of the chorals. These harmonies were not com-posed simultaneously with the melodies to which they were set, but were the later work of educated musicians ; the melodies were generally the productions of singers or unknown authors. Many of these choral melodies have been attributed erroneously to the harmonists, while in fact they were composed long before their day.

This contrapuntal choral style soon attained a high degree of cultivation; and at the same time the chorals were gradually sifted out, leaving a rich residue of melody in the many examples now in use, which sound ever new and beautiful. They are the embodiments of religious enthusiasm and devotion, and will always move the hearts of men. We have reaped the fruits of the Reformation, not only in our modern religious and social freedom, but also in some of the highest forms of musical art. The double significance of this new movement in music which the Reformation inaugurated is that the popular element — the source and life of musical inspiration at that time — was combined with the development of the more artistic forms of expression, as displayed in the cantatas and passion music of noted masters, who freely introduced favorite choral melodies into their most elaborate works as illustrative of some significant passage of the text, while the remainder of the composition followed the original epic, lyric, or dramatic style, with corresponding recitatives, solos, and choruses, which the composer arranged according to his fancy or conception. This style of music reached its culmination in the eighteenth century in the cantatas and passion music of Sebastian Bach, which are the highest expression of Protestant church music.

The prominent names which we first meet in connection with Protestant church music in Germany, besides Luther, are those of the musicians, Johann Walther and Ludwig Senfl. Their labors did not extend beyond the middle of the sixteenth century, and this may be called the first period of Protestant church music. Johann Walther was master of philosophy and court musician at Torgau, and was afterwards called by Luther to Wittenberg with the singer Conrad Rupf to arrange the German mass. Walther's was the first choral book published, and appeared at Wittenberg in 1524, under the supervision of

Johann Walther and Ludwig Senfl

Luther, who wrote the preface to the work. Several editions of this choral book were printed in the course of the following years. In the last edition of the work in 1551 the melody, which hitherto had been placed chiefly in the tenor, appeared frequently in the upper voice as in modern music.

Walther was not distinguished as a master of music, and beyond his choral book did not leave any impression on his age. The ablest musical personage of that period was Ludwig Senfl, who, like Walther, is reputed to have been associated with Luther in advancing church music. He was born and educated in Switzerland, and was a pupil of Heinrich Isaac. He became a member of the chapel of Emperor Maximilian, and in 1530 was chosen as director of church music at the Bavarian court at Munich, — the position which was occupied subsequently by Orlando Lasso.

Senfl was a great favorite of Luther, who praised his compositions above all others. The panegyric which I quoted may have been suggested by Senfl's harmonies. Senfl not only composed motets and other church music, but also set music to ancient odes, particularly those of Horace, according to the custom of his day. A collection of these odes was published in 1534 at Nuremberg. He did not compose original chorals, but displayed a higher degree of skill and taste than others of his time in his contrapuntal treatment of them, and was the forerunner of masters like Eccard and Michael Praetorius. A pure religious spirit animates his works, and the chaste style of his themes and counterpoint, though not so flowing as with later masters, renders his music interesting.

Among the names of other German masters of the first half of the sixteenth century are Heinrich Finck, Rhau, Resinarius, Martin Agricola, Ducis, Mahu, Dietrich, and Stoltzer, most of whom were educated in the Flemish school.

Second period of German church music

The second period in the development of German Protestant church music began about the middle of the sixteenth century, when it became the custom to set the melody in the highest part of the harmony, as in modern music. Placed in the tenor, the melody could never assert its rights, for, while the other voices played about it in canon or imitative counterpoint, it was so oppressed that it was often lost to the ear.

I have already spoken of a similar movement as taking place in Flanders and Italy. The *stile familiare* of Josquin and his followers, the simple frottole and villanelle of Italy, were the first attempts in homophonous music, and were soon imitated in Germany in the later choral books. The French Calvinists, under the direction of Clement Marot, published as early as 1542 a French translation of thirty of the Psalms, which were sung to the popular secular melodies then current in France. Calvin himself increased this number during the following year.

In 1552 Theodore Beza, a banished French nobleman living at Geneva, completed a French translation of all the Psalms, which was published in 1565 with corresponding melodies and full harmony by Claude Goudimel, and was adopted for use by the authority of the Calvinist Church. These melodies were of popular origin. Goudimel's harmony was very simple, usually note against note, with the melody in the tenor, which, as the other voices rarely cross it, can generally be distinguished from the other parts.

During the latter part of the century the prominent masters were Matthieu Le Maistre, a Netherlander, who for a long time was royal chapelmaster at Dresden; Antonius Scandellus; Jacob Händl, or Gallus as he was called; Seth Calvisius; Joachim a Burgk; Nicolaus Hermann, who composed the famous chorals "Erschienen ist der herrliche Tag" and "Lobt Gott, ihr Christen, allzugleich," the latter appearing in mutilated form in books of American psalmody. Among other composers of chorals and church music of a more elaborate description were Johann Steuerlein, Melchior Vulpius, Hieronymus and Jacob Praetorius, David Scheidemann,

Prominent masters of the last half of the sixteenth century

Bartholomäus Gese, and Lucas Lossius. Several of these representatives of early German music were distinguished in other fields than music. A number were cantors, — an **Cantors** office of high distinction in those days. The cantors were masters of singing appointed to take full charge of the music of the church, and even before the Reformation they held an honorable position. During the first two centuries of the Lutheran Church the cantors were in many cases the most noted musical characters of their time. The oldest and most prominent of these cantorships now in existence is that of the St. Thomas School at Leipzig, which is noted above all others for a brilliant array of names of musicians like Johann Kuhnau, Sebastian Bach, Doles, J. A. Hiller, Schicht, Weinlig, and Moritz Hauptmann. But with this, and a few other exceptions, the office of cantor has lost its ancient reputation.

Hans Leo von Hasler The ablest representatives of German church music in the sixteenth century were Hasler, Eccard, and Praetorius. Hans Leo von Hasler was born at Nuremberg in 1564 and died in 1612. He was educated in music by Andrea Gabrieli at Venice. He was one of the first organists of his time and a clever contrapuntist and composer. Although he was a disciple of the Venetian school, his compositions have a genuine German simplicity and strength. The wonderfully beautiful and pathetic choral, " Herzlich thut mich verlangen," was composed by Hasler.

Johann Eccard The most justly celebrated German composer of the sixteenth century was Johann Eccard, who was born at Mühlhausen in 1553. It is conjectured that he was a pupil of Joachim a Burgk and Orlando Lasso. On the completion of his training under those masters, it is affirmed that he visited Venice to advance his musical studies, this being the time of Zarlino, Merulo, and Andrea Gabrieli. He returned to Germany in 1578, and subsequently held several musical positions there. In 1608 he was called to the court of Frederick at Berlin, where he died three years later, in 1611.

Eccard's music was simple compared with that of his con- temporaries of the Venetian and Roman schools. He was content to use his gifts in a more narrow range ; nevertheless his festival songs deserve a place among the best church music, for they are the perfect embodiment of religious devotion, and show a complete mastery of the peculiar form which he adopted. His festival songs are midway between the motet and the choral, approaching rather nearer the latter kind of music. The melody appears always in the soprano, and is not sufficiently individualized to be separated from the harmony. The harmony is clear and full; it is written generally in five parts, which move freely and are well adapted to the voices of the singers. These festival songs were set by royal command to the sacred airs most common in Prussia at that time, and were used on festival days of the church during the year. A selection of the best of these pieces was edited and published in 1858 by Teschner in Berlin.

Eccard was likewise the composer of sacred odes and secular songs, which are noble in comparison with similar music of his day, but his attention was devoted chiefly to church music. Two of his pupils became celebrated musicians, Johann Stobäus and Heinrich Albert, the founder of the German Lied.

Michael Praetorius stood on the boundary line between the sixteenth and seventeenth centuries and witnessed the great change which was then taking place in music without contributing much toward it. He was a great collector and publisher of church and secular music. His most important work was his " Syntagma musicum," which is an invaluable source of information regarding old musical instruments.

CHAPTER IX

MUSIC IN ENGLAND

Cultivation of counter-point Music was cultivated in England from the time of Alfred the Great. English minstrelsy was universal during the Middle Ages. John of Fornsete was one of the first English musicians (1226). It is held that the art of counterpoint was farther advanced in England in the thirteenth century than on the Continent. One of the most ancient specimens of good counterpoint, as I previously mentioned, is the six-part canon, " Sumer is icumen in," the author of which is unknown. If the date (1250) be correct, it proves that counterpoint was practised in England in a more advanced form than elsewhere. Chappell has brought to light four more specimens of English counterpoint of the thirteenth century, — a find which seems conclusive. John Dunstable was one of the best contrapuntists of the fifteenth century. Toward the end of this century we find the following names of composers of contrapuntal church music : Hamboys, Saintwix, and Abyngdon. Turges, Cornyshe, Fayrfax, Newark, Tuder, Sheryngham, Banester, Brown, Davy, Sir John Phelyppes, Dygon, and others flourished in the time of the early Netherland masters, and evidently imitated their style.

It was not until the reign of Henry VIII that any composers arose who merit special attention. Of those who flourished before the middle of the sixteenth century may be mentioned Redford, Thorne, Edwards, Johnson, Taverner, Parsons, Sheppard, Etheridge, Testwood, Smearton, Abel, Marbeck, and even Henry VIII himself, who cultivated music with enthusiasm in his younger days. The music of these masters compares very favorably with the best contemporaneous works of the Netherlands and Italy. A part of their numerous works was destroyed by the Puritans, but an immense collection still remains. One of the finest examples of this early English school is Redford's anthem, " Rejoice in the Lord." The counterpoint of these masters reminds us strongly of the Flemish style. Their secular music is decidedly their best. A fine example is Edwards' madrigal, " In going to my naked bedde."

The first master who marked the epoch of the highest Christopher
excellence in English music was Christopher Tye of West- Tye
minster, who was made Doctor of Music at Cambridge in 1545 and was organist of the royal chapel in Queen Elizabeth's reign. Burney says of him that he was as great a musician as Europe then could boast of, and prints in the second volume of his history a selection from one of his masses. This piece certainly proves that he was decidedly superior as a composer to his English predecessors ; one is struck with the purity of the harmony and the effective massing together of the voices, — a massing which strongly resembles the style of the best Italian masters. Dr. Tye was a man of great learning. His anthems are said to be his best compositions. His chief work was to set the Acts of the Apostles to music, but he did not get any further than the fourteenth chapter. This music is highly praised. Among his contemporaries were Causton, Oclande, Knight, Heath, White, Shepherd, and Johnson whom I have already mentioned.

Robert White, whose death occurred early in Elizabeth's reign, was a true master of church music in the style of Palestrina. Burney prints in his third volume a fine anthem by White, which fully testifies to his excellence as a composer.

During the age of Queen Elizabeth England was decidedly a musical country. Music was cultivated by all classes of society from the throne downwards. It was considered to be a necessary branch of education ; singing and playing were universal accomplishments. Queen Elizabeth herself was a remarkably skillful player on the lute, and gave encouragement to the cultivation of music. Her reign abounded in talented composers like Tallis, Byrd, Dowland, Morley, Wilbye, and others, who deserve to be compared with the foremost Italian masters of that epoch. Marbeck accomplished a good work for English church music by setting the whole cathedral service to music. This was first published in 1550 under the title, "The Book of Common Prayer, noted."

Thomas Tallis

Thomas Tallis and his pupil William Byrd are held to be the most eminent masters of their time. Tallis was born early in the reign of Henry VIII and died in 1585. It is believed that he was organist of the royal chapel under Henry VIII, Edward VI, Queen Mary, and Queen Elizabeth. Burney pronounces him to be one of the greatest musicians not only of England but of Europe during the sixteenth century. This praise is certainly not undeserved; though, in comparison with Palestrina and Orlando Lasso, he manifests less skill in his counterpoint and in the treatment of the church modes than the latter composer, and falls far short of the elevated grandeur and purity of the Roman master. But compared with his predecessors and contemporaries among his own countrymen Tallis exhibits a greater mastery of form; his noble style, rich harmony, and bold use of accidentals give a peculiar strength and individuality to his compositions. His cadences are particularly energetic and significant.

Although it is easy to perceive that Italian music had begun to exercise a powerful influence on English musicians, the imitation of foreign models of musical art did not rob English madrigals and anthems of the sixteenth century of a certain native simplicity and healthy strength which prevent them from ever becoming antiquated.

William Byrd

William Byrd, a disciple of Tallis, was born in 1538 and died in 1623. He was the son of the musician Thomas Byrd, one of the gentlemen of Edward VI's chapel. His musical career began as oldest choir boy at St. Paul's. In 1563 he

was appointed organist of Lincoln Cathedral. Six years later
he was chosen Gentleman of the Chapel Royal in the place
of Robert Parsons, and at the same time Organist to the
Queen in company with his teacher, Tallis. Ambros says of
Byrd, " He was the master who completed what his predecessors had aspired to, and was an artist in as full a sense as
Palestrina." But the German critic does not go quite so far
as Burney, who maintains that Byrd's " Graduals " are
" equally grave and solemn with those of Palestrina to the
same words, and seem in no respect inferior to the choral
works of that great master."

There is a tonic clearness in the harmony of Tallis and Modern
Byrd which distinguishes it from the mystical, mediæval style quality of
of music of contemporary foreign masters. It has a positive his work
modern quality, a peculiar simplicity and strength. Byrd was
a very industrious and productive composer. A large number
of his compositions were published during his lifetime, consisting of psalms, sonnets, graduals, sacred songs, and madrigals.
He composed three masses, one of which, the five-voiced mass,
is published by the Musical Antiquarian Society of London.
Byrd was a master of the organ and virginal, — another name
for the spinet, probably given to it in honor of Queen
Elizabeth, who was a clever player on that instrument. In
a splendid manuscript which bears the name of " Queen Elizabeth's Virginal Book," and is preserved in the Fitzwilliam
Museum at Cambridge, there are nearly seventy of Byrd's
instrumental pieces. These pieces consist of dances, fugal
movements, fantasies, and variations on popular melodies. They
remind us of similar compositions by Giovanni Gabrieli, whom
Byrd surpasses in this branch of music. The homophonic element and modern tonality of key are very prominent in these
pieces. This is evident in the variations on the old English
tune, " The Carman's Whistle," which is not only figured in
the usual contrapuntal manner but is also harmonized quite
in the modern fashion.

John Dowland

John Dowland, a celebrated lute player and composer of madrigals, was born in 1562, and was a great favorite in his day. Shakespeare praises him in his "Passionate Pilgrim" with the lines, "Dowland to thee is dear, whose heavenly touch upon the lute doth ravish human sense." The degree of Bachelor of Music was conferred on Dowland at Oxford in 1588; on his return from a journey through Germany, France, and Italy, he was elected a member of the royal chapel. One of his most remarkable works is entitled "Lachrymæ, or Seven Teares, figured in seaven passionate Pavans." It was composed in five-part harmony, for lutes, violins, and violas, and consists of pavans, galliards, and allemandes, — dances that have long since become obsolete. Among his madrigals is the charming "Awake, sweet love."

John Bull

One of the most famous men of his time was John Bull, born in 1563. He was a remarkable virtuoso on the organ and virginal, and was also a learned contrapuntist and fruitful composer. The title of Doctor of Music was conferred on him at both Cambridge and Oxford in 1592, and soon afterwards he was appointed professor of music at Gresham College. He resigned this position after holding it ten years, according to Burney, "having been more praised at home than rewarded." He afterwards went abroad (1611) and entered the service of the Grand Duke of the Netherlands.

Dr. Bull was the composer of more than two hundred works, of which the greater part were pieces for the organ and virginal. His unremitting diligence both as an instrumental composer and performer soon won for him a continental reputation. Some of his pieces are difficult even for advanced players of the present day. Specimens of his music from "Queen Elizabeth's Virginal Book" are printed in Burney's "History of Music." The first specimen consists of variations on the hexachord — a series of ascending and descending notes of the scale — played by the right hand, while the left hand executes difficult passages of double thirds and sixths as well as a perplexing combination of unequal rhythms, three against two and nine against six quarter notes in rapid motion. Another specimen is called "Dr. Bull's Jewel," which is far from being a musical gem.

An absurd story is related of Dr. Bull. During his travels in France he met with a director of music who laid before him an original composition in forty-part harmony, which the author considered as the *ne plus ultra* of music, but he was so completely astonished when Dr. Bull on the spot added forty parts more to his composition that he exclaimed, "You are either Bull or the Devil."

Thomas Morley (born about the middle of the sixteenth century, died 1604) was one of Byrd's scholars; he was made Bachelor of Music at Oxford in 1588, and became one of the gentlemen of Queen Elizabeth's chapel. He was a noted composer and writer on music, and was the author of an excellent treatise on the theory of music, entitled "A Plaine and Easie Introduction to Practicall Musicke." His madrigals, canzonets, and ballets rank among the best of the time. A charming madrigal is "April in my mistress's face." Other prominent madrigalists and composers of this time were Thomas Weelkes, John Ward, John Bennet, John Mundy, Michael Este, John Milton, father of the poet, Wilbye, Hilton, Ford, Cobbold, Bateson, and Kirbye. Wilbye's "Sweet honey-sucking bees" is a charming madrigal. It is universally admitted that the madrigals of Queen Elizabeth's reign are unsurpassed. They stand as the best types of English music, notwithstanding that this form of composition was copied from the Italians. The English excelled all others as madrigal composers. There is something essentially English both in the words and music of these composers, whose madrigals sound as fresh and beautiful now as when first composed; and it is no wonder that great pains have been taken to preserve, publish, and perform this noble old music, the pride of all true Englishmen.

Thomas Morley

Orlando
Gibbons

Orlando Gibbons, the youngest of three brothers, all of whom attained fame as musicians, is the last of this group of English composers to be mentioned. He was born in 1583, and died of apoplexy in 1625 at Canterbury, whither he had gone with the court to conduct the festival music composed by him for the marriage of Charles I. Although he was distinguished as a writer of madrigals and instrumental music, he gained even greater reputation by his church music, which won for him the title of "The English Palestrina." His pieces for the virginal are among the best, and led to his association with Byrd and Bull in the publication of "Parthenia," the first collection of music for the virginal ever printed. His galliard is an interesting composition.

PART II

ORIGIN OF DRAMATIC MUSIC

Opera and Oratorio

CHAPTER X

ESTABLISHMENT OF THE OPERA

It was a primitive custom with the cultivated nations of antiquity to give dramatic representation to the most solemn ceremonies of religious worship. In the ancient heathen temples the responsive choral songs, the offering to the gods, the sacred dances, and other devotional and symbolical rites of religion assumed a scenic form. The Greek drama was at first wholly religious, but at a later period it became also the model of classic art, by representing national and social ideas and actions. Like Greek life itself, its ideal was to blend in perfect harmony all its single elements; in this manner poetry, music, dancing, scenic display, and action were combined so as to constitute a grand, harmonious whole.

In the first ages of Christianity great opposition was shown to theatrical performances; but, in spite of all the efforts made to extinguish the theater, there sprang up within the church itself a dramatic element which soon became a prominent feature of the services of religious worship on all great occasions especially at Christmas, during Passion Week, and at Easter. The Passion, Crucifixion, and Resurrection of Christ were the subject of the most impressive of these representations, and for this purpose the text of the Evangelist was recited literally, and not acted until at a later period.

Dramatic element in early Christian worship

One priest recited the story, a second the sayings of Jesus, another the words of other characters, and a choir of voices represented the disciples and the people. The text was interspersed here and there with ritual verses sung in Latin, to give variety and expression to the recital, as do the chorals in the cantatas of the German composers of church music of the eighteenth century. Thus gradually there developed a kind of religious drama. Such dramas were known before the tenth century, and ultimately became very popular throughout Europe. They served a good end in the Middle Ages, for the subjects of many of these plays exercised a powerful influence over the people, whose ideas and aspirations were often elevated by the solemn spectacles.

Miracle plays

These miracle plays were given at first in churches and monasteries, exclusively by ecclesiastics. Subsequently they were exhibited by laymen in the public squares and streets, and at length priests were forbidden to take any part in them. The plays grew more and more extended in form until their performance lasted several days and was attended by thousands of people. Great corporate societies were founded at Paris, Rome, and other places. Jongleurs and other vagrant minstrels and actors contributed their clever buffoonery to the performances, which in consequence were rendered thoroughly secular and vulgar. No subject was too holy to escape the coarse and burlesque wit of the participants, and these festivals degenerated into mere occasions of high carnival.

The stage

"The stage," we are told, "consisted commonly of three platforms, raised one above another. On the uppermost sat the Pater Caelestis, surrounded by his angels; on the second appeared the saints and glorified men; while living men occupied the lowest. On one side of the stage appeared a dark, pitchy, flaming cavern, from which issued hideous howlings, as of souls tormented by demons; its occupants were the greatest jesters and buffoons of the company, and constantly ascended upon the stage to act the comic parts."

The immense popularity of miracle plays in England is well attested by the full records that exist of the great performances that were held in various parts of the country, particularly at York, Chester, Coventry, and Woodkirk. At Chester they were represented by the incorporated trades, and the play lasted several days. The representation covered the whole period from before the creation of the world to the day of judgment. Among the subjects are the fall of Lucifer, performed by the tanners; the creation, by the drapers; the deluge, by the dyers; Abraham, Melchizedek, and Lot, by the barbers and wax chandlers; the slaughter of the innocents, by the goldsmiths; the descent into hell, by the cooks, etc.

The miracle plays entirely disappeared in the eighteenth century, with one exception, which is the only important remnant of the popular sacred play now in existence. It is the solemn and impressive Passion Play, given once every ten years by the villagers at Oberammergau in Bavarian Tyrol.

Notwithstanding the opposition of the church to the popular plays, the ancient custom was continued through the Middle Ages of giving a solemn musical and dramatic representation of the Passion of Christ during the religious services of Passion Week as a part of the Liturgy. The practice of representing the Evangelist, Christ, and the other characters of the drama by persons can be traced back as far as the twelfth century. Not a word of the text was spoken, but the single parts were intoned by priests, while a chorus sung the words of the people. The oldest specimens of passion music which have been preserved are in Latin text, and are by the composers, Obrecht (1500), Galliculus (1538), and Resinarius (1544). The words of Christ and the other characters were not sung by single voices, but by a four-part chorus. This exclusive chorus treatment of the text is also followed, in later examples, by Cipriano de Rore, Orlando Lasso, and others. It testifies to the absolute sway which full counterpoint exercised at that time. Toward the end of

Passion music

the sixteenth century, when the first efforts were made to introduce solo singing and the modern recitative into dramatic music, the passion music began to show signs of artistic improvement. In two examples by Vittoria, the Spanish contemporary of Palestrina at Rome, the text of the Evangelist is intoned by single voices, while the chorus of the people, called "turbae," are short pieces composed in four-part harmony. One of these passions, that according to St. John, is performed in the original manner, it is said, at Rome on every Good Friday. Very curious examples are those of Scandellus, Stephani, a Burgk, and other German composers of the latter part of the sixteenth century; the words of the Evangelist are intoned by a single voice, but the words of Jesus are generally sung by four voices, and those of other persons by two and three voices, with turbae sung by a full chorus. It was not before the eighteenth century that the passion was developed into a noble, artistic form of music, though Heinrich Schütz and other composers of the seventeenth century gave the older type new life and expression, as we shall learn later.

Secular musical drama

During the age of the troubadours, in the thirteenth century, a kind of secular drama was in vogue. It was a simple, unpretending play, something like the modern vaudeville,—a mixture of dialogue and songs, very bright and pleasing. Adam de la Hale was the author of several of these little plays, one of which, entitled "Robin and Marion," I have already mentioned. It is a love affair between Robin and Marion.

"Robin and Marion"

When Marion has sung her simple song young Auburt, who has just returned from the field of tournament, enters with a falcon perched on his wrist. He addresses soft words to Marion; she retorts by declaring that she loves Robin, and begs Auburt to leave her in peace; whereupon the young man pretends he is deeply in love, and leaves her with the assertion that he is going to drown himself; but, instead of replying seriously, she turns his speech to ridicule. Robin then enters and chats about the approaching wedding. As he turns to go away to engage a minstrel and invite his friends to the festival, young Auburt appears again and picks a quarrel with Robin, under the pretext that he has hurt his falcon. They come to blows ; Robin gets a good beating, and is left lying on the ground, while Auburt forcibly carries off Marion. Gautier, the minstrel, who witnesses the abduction, now comes forward and calls out to Robin, and endeavors to restore him to his senses. We do not quite see how the affair will end, but Auburt, tired of Marion's opposition, returns of his own free will and delivers the bride up to Robin. At this happy result they all dance and make merry ; the minstrel sings a ballad, and thus the play ends.

During the fifteenth and sixteenth centuries we observe an **Masques** increasing love for scenic representations, which grew more artistic and cultivated in a corresponding degree with society itself. At Italian courts it was the custom to perform all kinds of mythological and allegorical spectacles and masques, in which music generally bore a part, though a subordinate one. We read in Fink's " History of the Opera " the description of a singular masque which was performed at the wedding feast of Duke Sforza with Isabella of Aragon, at Milan in 1388.

In the center of a magnificent hall, which had a grand gallery around it occupied by instrumental players, the table was laid for the royal feast. As soon as the royal party had arrived and taken their places the feast began. The scene opened with Jason and the Argonauts. They strode about with a menacing air, bringing the celebrated Golden Fleece, which they laid on the table after they had danced a ballet to express their admiration for the beautiful bride. Mercury now appeared and related how he and Apollo, at that time shepherd of King Admetus in Thessaly, had stolen the finest, fattest calf of the whole herd to bring as a present to the newly married pair. When they had placed it on the table Diana entered the Hall, dressed as a huntress and accompanied by her nymphs who, to the sound of hunting horns, brought Actæon changed into a stag, on a golden litter, adorned with green branches. The affair continued in this way to the end of the feast.

"A dramatic attempt," says Kiesewetter, "having for its argument the bill of fare." The whole object of this masque was to bring in the dishes. A century later we witness a decided progress in the dramatic quality of such scenic display, when Francesco Beverini produced a sacred play called "The Conversion of St. Paul," which was performed before Pope Innocent VIII at Rome.

In the sixteenth century the Italian princes encouraged the drama, and sought to excel each other at their respective courts with the splendor and variety of their entertainments. The first masque performed in England was at Greenwich in 1512, "after the manner of Italy," as we read. They soon became very common as court entertainments, and were given in splendid style; the several parts were generally represented by the first personages in the kingdom; if at court, the king and queen and princes of the blood often performed in them. Burney says, "The English seem at all times to have received more delight from dramas in which the dialogue is spoken and the songs incidental, than from such as are sung throughout. . . . Of the fourteen comedies of Shakespeare, there are but two or three in which he has not introduced singing; even in most of his tragedies he has manifested the same predilection for music." Milton's "Comus" and "Arcades" are beautiful specimens of the masque; Ben Jonson may be considered as the chief writer of this kind of drama, and Henry Lawes was famous as the composer of the music to many of them, including "Comus."

The music of the Italian masque now began to be considered of greater importance. The dialogue, however, was spoken throughout. The music consisted of choruses in the madrigal style. They were generally sung between the acts, merely to give change and variety to the performance, or else they were introduced into the dramatic scenes called intermezzi or intermedii, which were played between the acts, and were generally independent of the rest of the drama.

Some of the most noted dramas of the sixteenth century were set to music by Alphonso della Viola, a talented musician of Willaert's school and director of music at the court of

Ferrara. His pieces were performed on several grand occasions at Ferrara, Bologna, and Venice. Similar dramas are reputed to have been composed by Zarlino and the noted organist Luzzasco of Venice. In all these compositions we receive no intimation of the future recitative and air, the dialogue being invariably spoken.

I have already stated that in the time of the Flemish composers unison or solo singing no longer existed, except as rude, popular music. This peculiar one-sidedness continued until toward the end of the sixteenth century, when we meet with the first regular efforts to allow the single voice to be heard. Before that time counterpoint ruled supreme in secular as well as sacred music, and melody in the proper sense was literally forgotten by the learned musicians ; consequently melody had to be rediscovered again, so to speak, about the year 1600. The simple and natural songs of the people dwelt in obscurity, and, for the most part, the educated musicians neglected to develop them into extended artistic forms or failed to invent original melodies of equal beauty and native simplicity. At the most they made no further use of popular melodies than as a cantus firmus around which they might weave a network of elaborate counterpoint. The result was, that in the masses and motets of the most celebrated masters melody in the free modern sense was wanting : the individual found no voice for his personal emotions in church music. The absolute power contrapuntal music then exercised is fully displayed in the vocal music of the drama previous to this revolution in style. Not only did the choruses consist invariably of full-voiced madrigals, but even the principal characters of the play did not sing their parts individually, being represented by a chorus behind the scenes singing the madrigals in full harmony. Vecchi published comedies composed for chorus, dialogue, and monologue, all as five-part madrigals. Orlando Lasso wrote a comic duet for two choruses, the subject of which was Pantaleone and his servant. The servant,

Solo singing a lost art

who is at the wine cask in the cellar, is called by his master, and, being rather tipsy, in his fear lets the spigot drop. The master then goes into the cellar, and while groping about, they berate each other in five-part chorus till the spigot is found.

Attempts to introduce the solo voice

The first feeble attempt to free the single voice from the web of counterpoint was made at the performance of an intermezzo at the wedding festivities of the Duke de' Medici in 1539. The happy idea occurred to some one to sing the highest part of a four-part madrigal by Francesco Corteccia as a solo, while the other parts were played on strings and wind instruments. This rude beginning found imitation, and in a similar piece by Corteccia, performed in 1565, the music of Venus, originally written for an eight-part chorus, was sung by a single voice on the stage, while the remaining voice parts were executed by instruments behind the scenes. Let me not give the impression, however, that this step led immediately to the desired emancipation; for though now the solo voice could be heard, yet it was nothing more than a mere thread or fraction of the contrapuntal whole, and when sung separately was distinguished by no beauty of its own, but was quite dependent on the harmony furnished by the other voices. Nevertheless, musicians began to vary the stiffness of the solo part by the introduction of runs and other ornaments. This practice became so common that it soon led to a bravura style of singing, proving that the art of vocalization had already begun to be highly cultivated in Italy before the year 1600. This peculiar attempt to introduce solo singing on the dramatic stage was a makeshift, and yet it served to show that the feeling was growing stronger and stronger for solo music, that the lyric element was essential to musical art, and that the absolute reign of polyphonic, unaccompanied choral singing was over. This revolution of style and struggle against counterpoint was a new birth, — the musical renaissance, which came two centuries after the renaissance of the other arts.

The introduction and establishment of the opera and oratorio, the invention of the recitative and air with orchestral
accompaniment, and other innovations and improvements
in music about the beginning of the seventeenth century
represent an important turning point, — a new stage of progress which has been paralleled only during two other periods
of musical history, namely, the rise and development of
counterpoint in mediæval church music and the development of instrumental music in the eighteenth and nineteenth
centuries. These are the three great historical stages in
modern music.

Mediæval church music did not fulfill the entire mission of
the art. Although its object was the highest, and it employed
the most elevated thoughts and emotions in the adoration of
God, it did not embrace in its scope all the nature of man,
leaving out an important element of artistic representation, —
his earthly acts and passions. It was reserved, therefore, for
secular music to supply this want, without derogating anything from itself, though the name would naturally suggest
the worldly in opposition to the spiritual. We call it secular
music because it is independent of ecclesiastical interests,
and owes its origin and cultivation to the natural impulse of
the people. 'Music expresses, outside of the church, the
highest embodiments of religion and morality, at least as far
as their principles exert a deep influence on the sentiments
and actions of men, and then it stands on as high a plane of
adoration as within the church. But without the church, it
can also give full expression to purely human sympathies and
acts. The Reformation was undoubtedly the means of giving
a new impulse to the cultivation of secular music, just as it
was the source of a new style of sacred music of popular
origin. In that age of new ideas light could not fail to pene-
trate the minds of lovers of music as well as of literature and
art in general. Italy was rich in art and learning; an increasing interest was taken in antiquity, especially in Greek

literature, philosophy, and art. This led to the ardent desire on the part of cultivated men to restore Greek tragedy. Enthusiasts painted in glowing colors the splendors of Greek music ; they unanimously believed that modern counterpoint could not compare with ancient music, either in regard to the simple beauty of the song, or the rhythmical clearness and rhetorical expression of the words ; but no monuments of Greek music existed, and they had to trust to their own imaginations as to its nature.

The monody

This idea of restoring the ancient drama and music was first advanced at the meetings of a society of scholars and artists, held at the residence of a Florentine nobleman, Giovanni Bardi, count of Vernio, a man well versed in literature, besides being a composer and a poet. The first attempt to put the idea into execution was made by a member of this society, Vincenzo Galilei (father of the celebrated astronomer), a clever player on the lute and a composer. He obtained a copy of three ancient hymns with their melodies, which he published in 1581, but without understanding the musical notation. He also attempted to compose for a single voice in imitation of ancient music, notwithstanding his ignorance of it, and set some of the lines of Dante and the Lamentations of Jeremiah to music. These crude experiments were called monodies ; they were the first regular pieces for a single voice not developed from counterpoint.

Another member of this society was Giulio Caccini, a Roman attached to the Florentine court, who composed monodies of a more pleasing character than Galilei. He adopted a kind of arioso style, suggestive rather of the future aria than of recitative. Caccini was more distinguished as a singer and master of singing than as a contrapuntist. To him belongs the honor of being the first to present this new kind of music to the world; his monodies were published in 1601.

Church concertos. Ludovico Viadana

Almost simultaneously with the monodies of Galilei and Caccini sprang up a similar class of sacred music, called church concertos (*concerti da chiesa*), which were melodies for one or more solo voices set to an organ bass. They were originated by Ludovico Viadana, who after leaving Rome was made director of music at the cathedral at Fano in 1600, and afterwards went to Mantua. The first of these sacred concertos he composed as early as 1595, but they were not published till the year 1602. In these pieces the instrumental accompaniment acquired a new significance ; formerly it could not be distinguished from the web of counterpoint, but with Viadana it held about the same relation to the solo voice as it does at the present day, at least, so far as it enriched and supported the melody with its simple harmony.

Viadana's concertos were accompanied on the organ. He inaugurated a new and valuable effect of employing an independent obligato bass, called basso continuo. By this continuous bass the solo voices were not only sustained, but enabled to move more freely and independently, inasmuch as any thin places in the harmony that might arise from the movement of the voices could easily be filled by means of this bass, and chords introduced at the right moment. Viadana was not the originator of the *basso generale*, or thorough bass, as reputed. This invention, which enabled the organist to supply the full harmony from figures and other signs applied to the bass, was in use at a previous time.

In the year 1590 Emilio de' Cavalieri, also a member of the Bardi society at Florence, attempted a revival of the ancient musical drama in two pastoral plays, called " Il satiro " and " La disperazione di Fileno " ; and the following year with another, entitled " Il giuoco della cieca." Although these were the first dramas ever set to music throughout, they did not meet with favor from the society ; and these separate efforts of Galilei, Caccini, Viadana, and Cavalieri had not brought about the expected revival of Greek music. The arioso style did not suit the dramatic form, since they supposed the dialogue of the ancients to have been not exactly speech

Emilio de' Cavalieri

nor song, but something midway between declamation and melody, or what we call recitative.

Jacopo Peri   The honor of inventing the modern recitative is due to Caccini and Jacopo Peri. Peri was a Florentine by birth, and was a clever singer and master of the clavichord. He devoted himself with zeal and enthusiasm to this "new art" of music, and became a member of the society, which after the departure of Bardi to Rome, met at the house of a certain Corsi. It was in this connection that Peri composed the drama entitled "Dafne," by the poet Rinuccini, and the piece was performed at Corsi's house in the year 1594 or 1595. It met with general applause, for their aspirations had in a measure been fulfilled. Thus arose the recitative, or *stile rappresentativo*, which was developed in the following century into its modern form. In 1600 Rinuccini and Peri brought forward a new play called "Euridice," which was given at the marriage of Henry IV of France with Maria de' Medici.

"L'anima e il corpo"   During the same year there appeared at Rome a kind of moral, allegorical drama called "L'anima e il corpo," composed by Cavalieri, which was played on a stage in the oratory of the Convent Maria in Vallicella, with scenery, decorations, and dances. The characters are Time, Pleasure, the Body, the World, Human Life, etc., from which an idea may easily be formed of the nature of the subject. The orchestra was placed behind the scenes, in order not to drown the voices of the solo singers, and the actors were recommended to carry instruments in their hands, so as to give the appearance of accompanying their own recitations. The dances were performed to the music of the chorus. "The performance," says the author, "may be finished with or without a dance. If without, the last chorus may be doubled in all its parts, vocal and instrumental; but if a dance is preferred, a verse is to be sung, accompanied sedately and reverentially by the dance. Then shall succeed other grave steps and figures of the solemn kind." Considering the place of representation, these directions sound very odd. This was the origin of the name " oratorio," but comparing this piece with the later specimens of music bearing that name we can trace no resemblance.

These feeble beginnings of the musical drama, not called opera till the middle of the century, soon spread to other parts of Italy. As early as 1601 the " Euridice " of Rinuccini and Peri was brought out at Bologna, and in 1604, Peri's " Dafne " was performed at Parma.

In all these operas the recitative was exceedingly stiff and inexpressive ; the chorus held a very subordinate part, and was insignificant in ideas and treatment, and the solos were crude in melody. Yet these works possessed the general outlines of the future musical drama, — the recitative for the dialogue, the solo arioso style for the more emotional places in the text, and the chorus to give voice and expression to the sentiments of the people. The use made of the instrumental accompaniment well illustrates the primitive character of the first opera. The orchestra was composed of a singular combination of instruments. Some of our modern instruments had already been invented, but the players had not yet learned their full capabilities ; yet these dramatic experiments soon led to a much wider field of musical expression, and in the course of the seventeenth century instrumental music began to claim universal attention. Besides various stringed instruments played with a bow, like the viola, viola da gamba (our modern violoncello), viola da braccio, and others, there were various mediæval wind and stringed instruments, such as the lute, clavichord, chitarrone, harp, cornetto, storto, lirone, rebec, etc. The drama opened generally with a madrigal accompanied by the orchestra, which merely played the voice parts, or else it was introduced by a flourish of trumpets twice repeated. During the course of the play the instruments performed several short pieces, — interludes, introductions, and dances.

The orchestra

Compari-
son of opera
with Greek
tragedy

It is evident that the first opera had hardly more than a mere external likeness to its ancient Grecian model. To reproduce the spirit of Greek tragedy implied similar conditions of life, the same belief in the gods of their mythology; and though Christians might study the artistic representations of gods and heroes as they appeared on the ancient stage, they could not return to phases of thought and feeling characteristic of a more juvenile age of the world. It is true that the first opera composers copied at the outset the general form of the Greek tragedy, — the recited dialogue, the chorus, the personages, as well as the general action and story of the play; but even this likeness gradually disappeared as the music grew more independent — as the recitative and air were developed. The ancients had a kind of musical recitation which was subordinate to the rhythm and rhetoric of the words, or else merely accompanied movements of the body in dancing. This absolute bondage to the words did not admit of the melody as we understand it. Even in the Christian era it was long before the tones were freed from this slavish dependence on the meter of the words; and when this had been attained in part in the Gregorian age, the slow, monotonous intoning of the psalms in the Catholic Church, which was practised for centuries, hardly answered to the name of recitative or melody.

A new
form of
recitative

Peri and his contemporaries thought they were restoring the ancient recitative,. but in reality they were unfolding a new element in music; for the instrumental accompaniment on which the new recitative was built up, rude as it was at first, stands in marked contrast to the *a cappella* church music, which gave no scope for instrumental accompaniment or solo melody. A simple ground bass was held with few changes, while the voice accommodated itself to the harmonic intervals agreeing with this bass. The specimens at hand of Peri, Caccini, and others seem intolerably monotonous to our ears, but subsequently a rapid improvement took place, both in

regard to the melodious treatment of the voice part and to
the changes of harmony which accompanied it. At points
where the arioso style was introduced, the accompaniment
became more animated, and when the voices paused short
ritornelles were played, in order to relieve the voice and give
variety to the effect. This new music must have been listened
to with delight by ears not yet surfeited with higher beauties.
As regards the chorus, it held a place and meaning in Greek
tragedy which was almost entirely lost in the modern drama;
for then it expressed by the mouths of the people the voice
of Fate, judging of the sentiments and actions of the characters of the play. The founders of the modern musical dramas
selected the subjects of their plays from ancient mythology
and history, but they took no deep interest in the religious,
national, and social ideas and deeds which lay at the foundation of Greek life and art. The refined dilettanti of Florence
in the sixteenth and seventeenth centuries could well appreciate the classic beauty of ancient art, but the gods and heroes
they sought to bring to life on the stage were the mere pup-
pets and shadows of their former selves. Love, and that not
of the highest type, was the predominating subject of the
drama, while all mythology, all history, real or reputed, were
made to serve the most frivolous and dreary commonplaces
of modern gallantry. "Gods and heroes were made to sigh
like amorous shepherds. Simple Thracian shepherds gave
utterance only to the most fashionable, lackadaisical speeches,
in the style of genteel Florentine society."

The
chorus

CHAPTER XI

PROGRESS AND SPREAD OF THE OPERA

Opposition
to the opera   The progress of the opera in the early stages of its career
was slow and insignificant in regard to the character of
both the music and the play. The efforts of dilettanti and
musicians of limited attainments, like Cavalieri, Caccini, Peri,
and their associates, could not be rewarded with immediate
results, yet they are deserving of acknowledgment as the first
indispensable steps in a new field of musical endeavor. At
the outset the learned contrapuntists were naturally opposed,
or at least indifferent, to a branch of art so wholly unlike the
venerable church music to which they devoted their talents.
The drama, with the exception of the sacred plays, had for
ages been given up to buffoonery and vulgar amusement.
The decorations and glitter of the stage, the pomp and show
of the spectacle, absorbed the attention; so much so that the
text was almost entirely disregarded, and the slow and heavy
recitative which the Florentine dilettanti had introduced
remained for a long time a kind of experiment.

First
public per-
formances   The opera was at first reserved for the exclusive pleasure
of the rich and great at princely marriages and entertainments. The earliest public exhibition of the opera was given
at Venice in 1637, on which occasion the "Andromeda,"
composed by Francesco Manelli, was performed. Under Monteverde, Cavalli, and Cesti the opera at Venice soon became
famous. Other opera houses were opened in the course of a
few years, and representations were given almost daily, while
at Rome, Bologna, and other Italian cities, opera houses
were not so common. Before the end of the century no less
than three hundred and fifty-seven operas, the work of forty

composers, were performed at Venice. It was not, however, until the musical drama had attained general publicity and popularity that the name "opera" was applied to it; hitherto it was called "dramma per musica," or simply "tragedia."

The first important steps in the musical advancement of the opera were taken by Claudio Monteverde (born at Cremona in 1568). He was a pupil in music of Ingegneri, and was a fine viola player. His career began at Mantua, as director of music at the court. His first opera, "Orfeo," was produced there in 1607; in the following year appeared his "Arianna," and the opera with ballet, entitled "Il ballo delle Ingrate." The most important years of his life were spent at Venice, from 1613 till his death in 1643. As director of music at Venice he composed several operas, the "Proserpina rapita," "L'incoronazione di Poppea," "L'Adone," "Il ritorno d'Ulisse," and "Le nozze di Enea con Lavinia." His "Arianna" was performed again in 1640 with particular success. Some of these works are known only by name. Monteverde's reputation was gained chiefly as a composer of operas and madrigals, though he wrote some sacred music. He holds a notable place in musical history as a bold innovator in his treatment of harmony, and the honor is claimed for him of having been the first composer to use discords freely without preparation. He did what no other musicians before his day had ventured to do, namely, to employ unprepared minor sevenths and diminished triads, even in the extreme parts of a composition, as well as suspensions of the seventh with the second and fourth and other dissonant combinations. Indeed, there is scarcely any combination of dissonant intervals which he did not boldly adopt in order to give expression to the words.

Like the innovators of the present day Monteverde met with determined opposition from many of his contemporaries, one of the most prominent of whom was Giovanni Maria Artusi, of Bologna, the learned writer on counterpoint, who

Claudio Monteverde

Opposition to Monteverde

published a severe criticism of Monteverde's music of the future. Monteverde did not suffer in worldly estimation, however, from opposition; on the contrary, his name subsequently acquired an importance which it has not entirely deserved, though many of his steps were in the right direction. Monteverde was anticipated in his use of discords, in a very large degree, by Cipriano de Rore and other Venetian masters. The most substantial service which Monteverde rendered music was to heighten the effect of the dramatic action and lyric passion of the play by means of a more liberal use of the orchestral accompaniment and by the introduction of the true arioso style of singing. Before his day the instruments served a very subordinate rôle, merely doubling the vocal parts of the madrigals which then formed the entire chorus of the opera, while the only accompaniment for the recitative was the lute, harpsichord, or chitarrone. But Monteverde adopted for this purpose a number of bowed stringed instruments and wind instruments, as, for example, regals and organi di legno, which were small portable organs with flute stops. They were selected to accompany the recitatives singly or in combination, according to the personation and the requirements of the words. Thus, in his opera "Orfeo," the genius of Music, who speaks the prologue, is accompanied by two *clavicembali*, or harpsichords; Orpheus by ten *viole da braccio*, or tenor viols; a chorus of nymphs and shepherds by an *arpa doppia*, or harp with double strings; Hope by two *violini piccoli alla Francese*, or violins; Proserpina by three *viole da gamba*, the forerunner of the modern violoncello; and Pluto by four trombones.

His services to music

Analysis of the opera "Orfeo"

The overture was called a toccata; it was a short piece of harmony in five parts, for a trumpet and other instruments, and was directed to be played three times before the raising of the curtain. Then the prologue is delivered in recitative, its purport being to explain the argument of the piece and bespeak the attention of the audience. The opera begins with a monologue in recitative by a shepherd, followed by a chorus in five parts, accompanied by all the instruments. Other choruses are directed to be accompanied in different ways, — by viola, flutes, and guitars. There are no airs for a single voice, but recitatives, choruses, trios, and duets make up the piece, which concludes with a dance to a lively strain called a moresca, probably a Moorish air. In the course of the opera short instrumental movements called symphonies and ritornelles were played ; this was an idea borrowed from Venetian church music. Monteverde originated the peculiar effect of the tremolo of the stringed instruments. In order to express vividly the agitation and passion of a battle scene, he made the violinists repeat their notes in rapid succession by an upward and downward movement of the bow. This novelty was at first derided by the musicians, but, nevertheless, has continued to be used ever since as a perfectly legitimate, indispensable, and characteristic effect of modern orchestral music.

At Venice, Monteverde's successors in dramatic music were Cavalli and Cesti. Francesco Caletti-Bruni, called Cavalli, was born at Crema in 1600. In 1617 he was singer under Monteverde at St. Mark's. He was appointed organist of the second organ in 1638, and chapelmaster in 1668. His career as an opera composer began in 1639, and in the course of the following thirty years he produced at least thirty-nine operas, some of which became great favorites. His "Giasone" and "Ercole amante" achieved marked success all over Italy.

Marco Antonio Cesti, a Florentine monk, was born in 1625. He was appointed chapelmaster by Emperor Leopold I, and died at Venice in 1670. His operas became universally popular, his first one, "Orontea," holding its place on the stage for nearly forty years. From a specimen of this opera, printed by Burney, we discern a decided improvement on the recitative and arioso style, in comparison with Monteverde and earlier opera composers. Cesti composed numerous cantatas in the style of his teacher, Carissimi.

Carissimi

Giacomo Carissimi, chapelmaster at the church of St. Apollinare at Rome, was the most remarkable musician of his day. He was born probably about the year 1604, in the vicinity of Rome, and died in 1674. It is not known that he composed for the stage, but he is honored as the originator of the chamber cantata. This music is dramatic, but is performed without any scenic display or action. There are no dramatic personages, but musical characters who sing in recitative and air. In form the cantata resembled the modern oratorio, with the exception of the subject, which was always secular. It is possible that the idea of this kind of music was suggested to Carissimi as a substitute for the opera, which was less encouraged at Rome than in other Italian cities. The church gave its powerful support exclusively to the cultivation of sacred music. By means of the cantata the composer could adopt all the new effects of music without resorting to the stage and shocking the severe taste of those educated to the

Development of the air and recitative

solemn harmonies of Palestrina. Under Carissimi's genius the air and recitative now gained, as if by magic, the principal characteristics of style that distinguish them at the present day, although the musical periods have since become far more extended and refined. Carissimi also rendered valuable service to the development of the oratorio, not only indirectly by means of the cantata but by his works bearing the name of oratorio. His oratorios display remarkable chorus effects, and the recitatives and airs are acceptable to our modern taste. His orchestral accompaniments do not mark any particular progress; they are quite simple parts, played by violins, contrabass, and the organ. Carissimi composed a number of masses and other church music. He was also remarkable as a master of singing and vocalization, and was the direct forerunner of the famous Pistocchi and Bernacchi, who brought the so-called chamber singing to its full development. Carissimi's works were models to his disciples and successors, and the chamber cantata soon became the favorite style of music, and influenced the entire art of composition, as the madrigal did a century before. The pleasing, attractive style of the cantata stood in strong contrast with the older church music, and *a cappella* singing soon gave place to a more varied and florid style. Solo singing and free instrumental accompaniment, lyric and dramatic expression, worked their way into church music, and in the course of the following eighteenth century, the so-called beautiful style supplanted the elevated style of church music. These terms "beautiful" and "elevated," however, are not used to imply that the beautiful was unknown in the older music, nor that elevated and sublime effects were no longer common after the time of Palestrina and Orlando Lasso.

A celebrated contemporary of Carissimi was Alessandro Stradella, whose works, as far as they are known, are among the best of that period. Burney prints some five extracts from his sacred compositions, and a romantic account of his life. The power of his music is illustrated by his incredible escape from assassination at the hands of hired ruffians employed by his implacable enemy, a Venetian nobleman. It was at the performance of one of his oratorios in the church of St. John Lateran that the assassins determined to dispatch Stradella, "but the excellence of the music joined to the rapture that was expressed by the whole congregation made such an impression and softened the stony hearts of these ruffians to such a degree as to incline them to relent, and to think it would be a pity to take away the life of a man whose genius and abilities were the delight of all Italy. An instance of the miraculous powers of modern music," says Burney, "superior, perhaps, to any that could be well authenticated of the ancient." The famous piece called "Stradella's Prayer" has found a permanent place in music, but it is hardly probable that Stradella was the composer of it, for the work gives internal evidence of a later origin. Stradella's compositions are numerous; among them are eleven dramas and six oratorios.

Alessandro
Stradella

The dramatic incidents of his life furnished the subject of the famous opera, "Stradella," by Flotow.

Allegri

Among the most distinguished Italian composers of church music in the seventeenth century were Allegri, Benevoli, and Bernabei. Gregorio Allegri, of the Correggio family, a pupil of the elder Nanini, was appointed papal singer in 1629, and died at Rome in 1652. The only music of his that has lived to the present day is his celebrated "Miserere," which is still performed every Passion Week at the Papal Chapel. This is the composition which travelers have described so often, and which has been held in awe and wonder as something supernatural. Although it was forbidden to take a copy of it from the choir on penalty of excommunication, Mozart and Mendelssohn succeeded in writing down the piece by ear. The extraordinary fame of this composition is due in large part to the solemn ceremonies of worship of which it bears a part, and the way in which it is sung. It is, however, one of the best examples of the Roman style of the seventeenth century.

Orazio Benevoli was appointed director of music at St. Peter's in 1646 and died in 1672. He composed, in the *a cappella* style of Palestrina, for two or more choruses combined. His music is pronounced by such judges as Burney, Reichardt, and Fasch to be wonderfully fine counterpoint. His pupil, Giuseppe Ercole Bernabei, director of music at Rome and afterwards at Munich, was also distinguished as a composer of church music.

Alessandro Scarlatti

In Italy, toward the end of the seventeenth century, the opera, oratorio, cantata, and melodious style of church music had fully superseded the old music, and there now appeared a master who was destined to accomplish a great work in the further development of these new forms. This illustrious musician was Alessandro Scarlatti, the founder of the so-called Neapolitan school. He was born at Trapani, in Sicily, in 1659 and died in 1725. It is supposed that he was a pupil of Carissimi in Rome. Later he appeared at Naples as a celebrated singer and player on the harp and harpsichord. In 1680 he composed an opera, " L'onestà nell' amore," for Christine, queen of Sweden, which was performed at her palace in Rome. This fact indicates that he had already gained some reputation as a composer. His opera " Pompeo " was performed at the royal palace at Naples in 1684, and he was styled a "maestro di cappella" to the queen of Naples. Ten years later, in 1694, Scarlatti was appointed chapelmaster to the viceroy of Naples, and the rapid succession of works which he produced year after year gave wings to his fame; yet it is remarkable that so little is known of the events of the life of a great musician. This has hardly a parallel in musical history, except perhaps in the case of Sebastian Bach. The production of Scarlatti's " Laodicea e Berenice " in 1701 added greatly to his reputation. In 1705 Scarlatti was appointed assistant chapelmaster at Rome, and soon after he received the order of the Golden Spur. In 1709 he returned to Naples where he died.

Scarlatti was a wonderfully prolific composer in all branches of music; he manifested as much learning in counterpoint as originality and pleasing skill in dramatic music. He is said to have composed no less than one hundred and fifteen operas, of which only forty-one are extant. His secular cantatas exceeded four hundred in number. Two hundred masses, of which few have been preserved, numerous madrigals and serenades, seven oratorios and a passion music, besides a number of instrumental pieces for the organ or harpsichord, furnish proof of his versatility and industry. The glory of the Italian opera begins with Scarlatti. As a teacher at the Naples Conservatory of Music, he was sought by pupils from all countries, and is said to have taught all Italy and Germany. Among his pupils were the celebrated Hasse, and Quanz, the flute teacher of Frederick the Great. Scarlatti was also one of the best singers, clavichord and harp players of his time. Quanz declared, " He knew how to play skillfully on the

His versatility and industry

clavicymbal, though he did not have the execution of his son." Domenico Scarlatti, his son, became one of the greatest masters of the clavichord. He was excelled on that instrument only by Sebastian Bach.

Influence of
Scarlatti on
the opera
The elder Scarlatti exercised a great influence on the dramatic art of singing, just as Carissimi did on the chamber style, and he was also distinguished as an orchestral master. Under his direction the orchestra at Naples became famous. He enlarged and refined the instrumental accompaniment, especially in respect to the treatment of the stringed instruments. He adopted an innovation of Lully, the French opera composer, namely, the instrumental overture to the opera, but his overtures differed from the French in having a grave movement placed between two allegro movements instead of a quick movement between two slow ones. Scarlatti continued to build on the foundation laid by Monteverde and Carissimi in developing the modern recitative and air. His genius molded them into more graceful and flexible forms of beauty, and he fairly inaugurated the era of melody. Scarlatti has been erroneously regarded as the inventor of the *da capo* aria. This form was known before his day; we find examples of it in the operas of Cesti and Cavalli. But he did originate the obligato-accompanied recitative. He likewise employed the orchestral accompaniment in a more independent manner than formerly; we often find melodious phrases in the instrumental part. It is a great pity that this genuine master, whom Handel and other composers studied and imitated, should not be better known; but, alas! the world does not possess more than the merest fragment of his works. They were scattered and lost, — a common occurrence at that period. It is easy to account in most cases for this negligence in preserving operas, for the music and text were of secondary interest to the mere spectacle of the play.

CHAPTER XII

ITALIAN COMPOSERS OF THE EIGHTEENTH CENTURY

The genius of Alessandro Scarlatti gave such a powerful impulse to the advancement of the opera and cantata that his disciples and successors had only to follow the course which he indicated, in order to reach a high point of attainment from which Italian music could command the whole world. During this epoch the number and excellence of Italian composers and singers were more remarkable than ever before or since, and for nearly a century they held Europe in musical bondage. The direct pupils of Scarlatti at Naples were Durante, Leo, Porpora, and Greco; and they were succeeded by a second generation of masters, — Jommelli, Piccini, Paisiello, and others; at Rome by Steffani ; at Venice by Marcello and Lotti ; and at Bologna by Bononcini, and others. Supremacy of Italian music

Francesco Durante, the pupil and subsequent rival of Scarlatti, was born in 1684. He received early musical instruction from Scarlatti and Greco at the conservatories dei Poveri and St. Onofrio, institutions of music which Durante directed in after years. He also studied at Rome under Pasquini, the great organist, and gained there a mastery of the church style of composition. He afterwards returned to Naples, where he remained during the rest of his life, except for a short journey made to Germany. He died at a ripe old age in 1755. Durante was not distinguished as a dramatic composer ; his talent was exercised chiefly in church and chamber music, and he was more skillful as a contrapuntist than as a melodist. He advanced the art of orchestration in some degree, inasmuch as he produced a better instrumental ensemble than his predecessors. To the stringed quartet of the orchestra he Francesco Durante

141

added flutes, bassoons, horns, and trumpets. Durante's church music shows the tendency of the period in which he lived; it is less elevated and religious than the music of the older Italian masters. It bears the traces of the new secular style, which was becoming the favorite style even in church music. His "Lamentations" are still performed at Rome during Passion Week; his "Magnificat in D" has been revived of late years, yet it is not a remarkable composition. Durante was an industrious composer; he produced a great number of masses, psalms, hymns, madrigals, duets, and sonatas for the harpsichord. He lived to be a great favorite of his countrymen, while Scarlatti, in his old age, was greeted with cold respect. Durante was much more remarkable as a teacher than as a composer; he trained a number of the most noted masters of the eighteenth century, — Vinci, Jommelli, Terradellas, Traetta, Piccinni, Sacchini, Paisiello, and others.

Leonardo Leo

As a composer Durante was eclipsed by his younger contemporary Leonardo Leo, who was for a time the delight of all Italy. Leo was born in Naples in 1694, and pursued his musical studies under Pitoni in Rome and Scarlatti in Naples. He possessed great versatility of talent, and was equally successful in church, chamber, and opera music. His light and pleasing style soon rendered him very popular, and his operas were represented all over Italy. As a melodist he was excelled by no one of his day. His most celebrated piece of sacred music is the "Miserere" in eight parts.

Antonio Caldara, born in 1678, a pupil of Scarlatti, was a noted composer of church music. Francesco Feo was a prominent contemporary of Durante and Leo. He founded a vocal school at Naples, and was distinguished as a composer of dramatic and sacred music. Gaetano Greco, a pupil of Scarlatti, earned a high reputation as a contrapuntist and teacher; he counted a number of noted masters among his pupils.

Niccolò Porpora

Niccolò Porpora is the best known of these older masters of Scarlatti's school. He was born at Naples in 1686, and was placed at an early age under the instruction of Scarlatti. His career as a dramatic composer began at Venice, where he found a formidable rival in Hasse. His present fame rests principally on his remarkable talents as a teacher of singing, yet for a time he met with considerable success as an opera composer. He was invited to England to take charge of the opera, which had been set on foot in opposition to Handel, but was unable to withstand the genius of the German master. Porpora spent a number of years at Vienna. It is related of him that while he was poor, and struggling for recognition, the emperor, Charles VI, was not pleased with his music, which, he said, was too full of shakes and other vocal ornaments. Through the friendship of Hasse the imperial dilettante was prevailed upon to listen to an oratorio of Porpora's composition. Porpora, having received a hint from his friend, did not introduce a single shake in the course of the oratorio. The emperor was much surprised, and kept continually repeating, "Why, this is quite a different thing; there is not a single shake!" At last, however, the concluding fugue began, and the emperor observed that its theme set out with four trilled notes. These, of course, were taken up in succession in the answers by the different parts, and worked upon according to the rules of that species of composition. When the emperor, who was privileged never to laugh, heard in the full height of the fugue this deluge of shakes, which seemed like the music of a set of crazy paralytics, he could no longer preserve his gravity, but laughed outright, perhaps for the first time in his life. This pleasantry was the beginning of Porpora's good fortune. In George Sand's famous novel, "Consuelo," both Porpora and Haydn figure as characters.

Leonardo Vinci, a fellow-pupil of Porpora, was born at Naples in 1690. He is said to have run away from the Conservatorio dei Poveri in consequence of a quarrel with Porpora, who seems to have been his rival in after life. His career as a dramatic composer began early. His "Siroe" was

Leonardo Vinci

brought out at Venice in 1726, and was successful over the "Siface" of his rival Porpora. His "Didone abbandonata" was produced at Rome in the following year, and added greatly to his reputation. His music speedily became all the rage ; at London his "Elpidia" was repeated fifteen times in one season. Yet with all this admiration and success his compositions have long since been forgotten. For a time he was lauded to the skies by musicians as well as dilettanti, but Scheibe, a German musical critic of the last century, complains of Vinci and other Italian composers, saying, "An Italian lets his heroes sing, *alla, alla*, over and over again, and one learns at the end of a quarter of an hour that he wishes to say, *alla vendetta !*"

Pergolesi

The example and teachings of Durante, Greco, and the other earlier Neapolitans reached their full value in the works of the younger generation of composers. One of the most renowned masters of this second period was Giovanni Battista Pergolesi, born in 1710. At an early age he became a pupil in the Conservatorio dei Poveri, where he produced the first specimens of his genius. His first opera was brought out at Naples, but, in consequence of its doubtful success, he turned his attention to the comic style, which had come into vogue through Niccolò Logroscino, the founder of the *opera buffa.*

" La serva padrona"

Pergolesi wrote an intermezzo called "La serva padrona," which soon became celebrated throughout Europe. At Paris it almost caused a revolution in the national taste ; Rousseau asserted that henceforth one must go to Naples to learn how to compose. This famous piece has only two characters, the third person introduced being merely a mute. They are an old bachelor and his pretty servant maid. She provokes her master to such a degree by her willfulness that he declares he will go immediately and take a wife to be rid of her impertinences. "Very well," says the maid, "take me !" The old gentleman, who at first flies out at this impertinent proposition, comes round in the course of the piece to the damsel's own view of the case, and gives her his hand in the presence of the only witness, the pretended lover of the maid, — the lay figure of the play.

Pergolesi, on the strength of his brilliant reputation, composed in 1735 a serious opera for Rome, to the "Olimpiade" of Metastasio, but it failed to interest the public, while they lavished their fickle applause on the "Nerone" of his fellow-student Duni. Deeply mortified at his failure, he returned at once to Naples and wrote no more for the stage. Henceforth he devoted his pen exclusively to the composition of church music; but his health became impaired, and he fell a victim to consumption, brought on, it is held, by his deep melancholy. He died at the premature age of twenty-seven years. No sooner was it known that he was dead than the world glorified him by the performance of his works in every theater and church. His "Olimpiade" was revived at Rome with the utmost splendor. Pergolesi's last work was his celebrated "Stabat Mater" for two female voices and accompaniment of stringed instruments. This work has held a place in the musical world beyond its worth. Pergolesi's music lacks vigor and grandeur; it is soft and pleasing to the ear, and possesses a certain sensuous charm. When the "Stabat Mater" is sung by five singers it is highly enjoyable on account of its religious expression and the pure sweetness of the strains. His music exerted a strong influence on his contemporaries and successors, as his best works presented in concentrated form what was subsequently embodied in hundreds of works. His operas and intermezzi number fourteen; his church compositions, fifteen; his cantatas, five. He wrote thirty trios for violins and violoncello. *[Attempt to write serious opera]*

One of the greatest masters of the Neapolitan school was Nicola Jommelli, born in 1714. In his boyhood he studied under Durante and others at Naples. His first operas were brought out there with applause, and led to his call to Rome, *[Jommelli]* where he won a great triumph. The Romans found his melodies so noble and charming that they called him the greatest musical genius of the age, and were so enthusiastic for him that on one occasion they carried the maestro on their shoulders to his place in the orchestra. Jommelli's melodies courted the ear with their beauty ; and the vocal parts of his operas were treated with such masterly skill that the admiration of the singers as well as the public was unbounded. He improved the orchestral accompaniment, and paid more attention to the effects of *forte* and *piano, crescendo* and *diminuendo.* Subsequently he found a rival in the young Portuguese composer Terradellas, who was richly endowed with genius. During the Carnival at Rome, each rival produced a new opera. Terradellas won the victory, while Jommelli's opera was hissed. In commemoration of the event the friends of the successful maestro had a medal struck off, on which was impressed a representation of Jommelli being drawn through the streets as the slave of Terradellas. On the next morning Terradellas was found dead in the Tiber, yet no suspicion was ever cast upon Jommelli in connection with this murder. On the contrary, he was honored with the position of vice chapelmaster at St. Peter's, but did not remain much longer at Rome. He

Chapel-master at Stuttgart

went to Stuttgart, having been appointed royal chapelmaster and composer to Charles of Würtemberg. He remained in this service a number of years, — from 1754 to 1765. His stay in Germany was productive of the best results to his music. He composed eighteen operas, which were received with high favor and appreciation. His harmony improved greatly, and he wrote more carefully than before he went to Germany. This was brought about through the influence of the more dignified and serious taste of the Germans. The orchestra at Stuttgart won the foremost place in Europe under his unequaled direction. On his return to Italy, his " Demofoonte " and " Ifigenia in Aulide," two of his latest and best operas, failed to interest the Italian public ; they did not appreciate the beauties of his music. He was so much affected by this that his health was undermined. He was struck with palsy, from which he never recovered, and died in 1774. An explanation of his failure to please the Italian public is found in the following extract from Burney:

> Jommelli had acquired considerable knowledge in other arts than music. His poetry was full of taste. Though in his musical works he had the esteem of consummate musicians, they sometimes lost him that of the multitude. He found the theater at Naples, and indeed almost all the theaters of Italy, in the greatest corruption; where, in and out of the orchestra, all is noise and confusion. A learned music like that of Jommelli, full of harmony and contrivance, which requires careful execution and the utmost stillness and attention on the part of the audience, could not satisfy the frivolous taste of the Italians, who used to say that Gluck, Jommelli, Hasse, and Bach were too rough and German, and pleased them less than the songs of the gondolieri, and airs with a few accompaniments and many graces and florid passages.

Jommelli was held in high estimation by the musicians of the eighteenth century. Mozart said of him, "The man has his specialty in which he excels; only he should not have attempted to compose church music in the old style, but should have been content within his peculiar sphere."

Nicola Piccinni, born in 1728, was a pupil of Leo and Durante. He in turn was the favorite of the fickle Italian public. His genius was displayed at the best advantage in the *opera buffa*, in which branch he surpassed all others of his time. His "Cecchina," brought out first at Rome in 1761, met with extraordinary success. It was a standing piece at all the theaters; it was performed in all parts of Europe, and was the foundation of the composer's fame. He gave a new meaning to the *opera buffa*, for although Logroscino originated this form, the credit of having fully developed it belongs to Piccinni. The invention of the *opera finale*, or that species of concerted music terminating each act of an opera, in which a portion of the business of the piece is carried on, was made by Logroscino, but Piccinni infused more life into the dramatic

Piccinni

action of the finale by grouping together various parts, and by frequent changes of movement and measure in the music. He also employed the air and duet in a free form; he often left out the *da capo*, so that the first slow part did not recur after the second quicker part of the air had been sung. Piccinni was called to Paris by the anti-Gluck party as their champion.

Sacchini

Antonio Maria Gaspare Sacchini was born at Naples in 1734. Like his fellow-countryman Piccinni, he became the idol of the Italian opera party at Paris. He had gained a reputation previously, and was already famous as an opera composer at Stuttgart and Munich, and in Holland and England. In *opera seria* (serious opera) he was more successful than Piccinni. His works are distinguished by their fine taste and melodic beauty, and he produces great effects by simple means. His instrumental accompaniments were superior to those of others of his school; being a fine violin player, his parts for stringed instruments are especially well written. He wrote some fifty operas, serious and comic, oratorios, masses and other church music, besides a number of trios and quartets for stringed instruments, and pieces for the harpsichord.

Paisiello

Giovanni Paisiello, born in 1741, was one of the most celebrated composers of the eighteenth century. He was educated at Naples at the Conservatory of St. Onofrio. His first operas were brought out at Bologna, and subsequently he composed about ninety serious and comic operas for different Italian theaters. He was director of music at St. Petersburg for a number of years, and during this period was active as a composer. His name and works became universally known, and his operas are almost the only ones of the Neapolitan school of the eighteenth century which are performed nowadays.

Other Neapolitan masters of lesser fame than these whom I have mentioned were Sarri, Davide Perez, Francesco di Majo, Paradies, Cimarosa, Zingarelli, Cafaro, and others.

The progress made in the Italian opera during the first half of the eighteenth century was not so important in its dramatic as its musical character. First, the air was ennobled and beautified by regulating and enlarging the rhetorical divisions of the whole. Previously the cadences had occurred too often in the course of the piece, and were out of all proportion. The air was henceforth composed in three general parts or divisions, — a first and second part with the *da capo*, besides which there were ritornelles, or instrumental preludes and interludes, which interrupted the continuity of the vocal part, and prepared the hearers for the new entrance of the voice. Secondly, the orchestral accompaniment acquired greater motion and variety in the rhythm, and the art of instrumentation began to show some signs of its modern characteristics. In the ritornelles and interludes of the airs and recitatives composers had begun to introduce motives and passages for the wind instruments, but this innovation met with opposition at first. The chorus was the most neglected part of the opera ; if it was not omitted altogether from the work, it held a very insignificant place. The air, as I have previously stated, absorbed the interest of the performers and the public ; the personages of the drama had degenerated into mere singing machines. Mere execution and *tours de force* were expected of a singer rather than passion and dramatic fire. Among other absurdities common at that period were pieces called " pasticcio," a kind of musical patchwork, made up of all sorts of favorite airs from different composers. One of these incongruous pieces, called " Griselda," was composed of airs by Porpora, Vinci, Bioni, Caldara, Gasparini, Orlandini, Boniventi, Sarri, Porta, Handel, and others. The irregularity of construction, inconsistency of character, and want of poetical beauty which distinguished even the most noted musical drama before the coming of Metastasio and Zeno stood in the way of the rapid advancement of the opera. Mythological personages still walked the

Development of the opera

Musical absurdities

boards of the stage, but they were recognizable only by name. All true development of character, all individual traits were entirely wanting. "Gods and devils," says Arteaga, "were banished from the stage as soon as poets discovered the art of making men speak with dignity." This evil state of things was happily satirized by Marcello, the celebrated Venetian composer, in a work called "The Theater of Fashion." He professes to give useful advice to poets, composers, singers, managers, and all connected with the opera, both in its production and its representation. The author begins by telling the poet that there is no occasion for his reading, or having read, the classical authors, for the very good reason that the ancients never read any of the works of the moderns. He will not ask any questions about the ability of the performers, but will rather inquire whether the theater is provided with a good bear, a good lion, a good nightingale, good thunder, lightning, and earthquakes. The incidents of the piece should consist of dungeons, daggers, poison, boar hunts, madness, etc., because the people are always greatly moved by unexpected things. A good modern poet ought to know nothing about music, because the ancients, according to Strabo, Pliny, and others, thought this knowledge necessary. The modern composer is told that there is no occasion for his being master of the principles of composition. He need not know anything of poetry nor give himself any trouble about the meaning of the words or even the quantities of the syllables. He will serve the manager on very low terms, considering the thousands of crowns that the singers cost him ; he will therefore content himself with an inferior salary to the lowest of these, provided he is not wronged by the bear, the attendants, or the scene-shifters being put above him. The singer is informed that there is no occasion for having practised the solfeggio, because he would thus be in danger of acquiring a firm voice, just intonation, and the power of singing the tune. Nor is it very necessary that he

Marcello's "Theater of Fashion"

should be able to read or write, know how to pronounce the words, or understand their meaning, provided he can run passages, make trills, etc. He will always complain of his part, saying that it is not adapted to him, that the airs are not in style, and so on.

The prima donna receives ample instructions in her duties both on and off the stage. She is taught how to make engagements, to screw the manager up to exorbitant terms, etc. A modern manager ought not to have a knowledge of music, acting, poetry, painting, or anything belonging to a theater. The author goes on in this vein at ample length; if these satirical counsels were more deserved in his day, we might find them somewhat applicable at the present time.

Metastasio marked a new era in the history of the opera. He is the only poet who has ever won a great name by devoting himself almost exclusively to writing for the musical drama. There is no doubt that he was a born poet for music; his verse and rhythm are wonderfully smooth and elegant. "No one before Metastasio," says Arteaga, "ever felt and understood more deeply the philosophy of love. No other possesses in so high a degree the eloquence of the heart, or knows better how to awaken the fancies, engage the interest, and put them to the proof; to mark distinctly the several circumstances that occur in an action, and to combine them; to detect the motives which are most immediately effective, and most consistent with the character of a person. . . . But on the other hand, simply to preserve the custom of introducing love everywhere, useless scenes are inserted here and there, which, far from conducing as they ought to the principal object, and preparing for the catastrophe, serve only to destroy the unity, break the chain of connection, and injure the energy of the most animated situations." Metastasio's opera texts are complained of as being too much alike; his characters are not marked by strong individual traits. Nevertheless, he exerted a great influence on the opera of the eighteenth

Influence of Metastasio

Defects of his opera texts

century. His texts were composed over and over again by all
the prominent masters of Europe ; through his genius they
were led to higher efforts than they otherwise would have
attempted, and such illustrious musicians as Pergolesi, Vinci,
Jommelli, Hasse, and even Handel, may be called the pupils
of Metastasio, for they were warmed by his fire, and perfected their dramatic talents by means of his works.

The brilliant achievements of Italian genius in music in the
eighteenth century did not find their source in Naples alone ;
but other cities like Venice, Rome, and Bologna were rich
in musical composers and singers. At Venice the opera
first flourished as a public entertainment under Monteverde,
Cavalli, Cesti, and others. Later Venetian masters were
Giovanni Legrenzi, fruitful in all branches of musical composition and highly distinguished as an excellent teacher,
Lotti, Caldara, Marcello, Galuppi, and many others less
remarkable.

Lotti

Antonio Lotti, born in 1667, a pupil of Legrenzi, was appointed organist and, in 1736, director of music at St. Mark's.
He composed seventeen operas. Although he was successful
in dramatic music, he was greater in his church and chamber
music. He displayed great power of expression and remarkable skill in counterpoint ; he united the profundity of the
older masters with the pleasing grace of the later. In the
madrigal he is called another Luca Marenzio ; in his church
music, a worthy descendant of Palestrina. He was a thorough
master of vocal style and an excellent teacher.

Caldara

Antonio Caldara, another pupil of Legrenzi, was born at
Venice in 1678. His career as a composer began at Mantua ;
at the end of a four years' sojourn in that city he went to
Vienna, where he held a position at the Imperial Court as
associate director of music. Fux, the noted Viennese composer, exerted a powerful influence on Caldara as a harmonist.
In 1738 Caldara returned to Venice, where he remained the
rest of his life, dying in 1763. Caldara's charming melodious

style rendered him a universal favorite, yet his operas did not enjoy a lasting reputation, for they displayed neither learning nor passion. His sacred music is of a more earnest character; his sixteen-part " Crucifixus " has been published recently, and is held in high esteem.

Benedetto Marcello, whose famous satire I have already quoted, is a noted character in Italian music. He was of noble birth, and held several important offices under his government. He was born in 1686 and died in 1739. In music he was the pupil of Gasparini and Lotti, but he never became more than a cultivated dilettante. His principal work as a composer was the setting of fifty of the Psalms to music. They are written in simple style, generally for one or two solo voices. Marcello attempted to unite ancient simplicity with modern clearness in the expression of individual emotion. His church music is dull enough compared either with the great style of Palestrina or Gabrieli, or with that of later masters like Bach and Handel, but it deserves some recognition as one of the earliest and most determined attempts to give church music a more subjective, individual expression. On no other grounds can we explain the fact that this dry music of the fifty Psalms has been reprinted again and again, and can be found in bulky volumes in all our principal libraries.

Marcello

Of all the Venetian masters Baldassare Galuppi (1706–1785) is the best representative of the dramatic style. He was a pupil of Lotti. In 1762 he was appointed director of music at St. Mark's. Afterwards he went to St. Petersburg, where his " Didone abbandonata " created a great furore, and to London, where he was engaged as a composer for the rival opera to Handel's. His comic operas are his best, and had a perceptible influence on English dramatic music.

Galuppi

Among the Roman masters of the eighteenth century the most prominent were Pitoni, Gasparini, Baj, and Steffani. They were distinguished chiefly in church music. The most remarkable of these composers was Agostino Steffani, who

Steffani

was born in 1655. He was a pupil of Johann Kerl and of Bernabei at Munich, but his first operas were brought out at the court of Hanover. Subsequently he was honored by the Pope with the office of foreign minister, and made an abbé and bishop. Steffani's excellence was displayed best in his chamber and sacred music, his so-called chamber duets being justly celebrated. They unite elegant and flowing melody with contrapuntal skill and learning, and were highly esteemed by the most refined musicians and dilettanti of his age. Handel was influenced by this master, as his twenty-two chamber duets give proof. Steffani's great "Stabat Mater," in six vocal parts with accompaniment, is a work of high merit. It shows in every measure the thorough contrapuntist and vocal master, and is full of religious feeling.

Florence, the cradle of the opera, produced fewer great masters than other Italian capitals in the eighteenth century. One of the best dramatic composers, however, was the Florentine, Francesco Conti, who was also a distinguished player on the theorba. At Palermo was born the Baron Emanuele d'Astorga in 1681, who became a noted composer.

Colonna and Clari

In the eighteenth century Bologna enjoyed the reputation of such great masters as Colonna, Clari, and Bononcini. Giovanni Paolo Colonna was the founder of a school which attained celebrity. He was born in 1640, and is said to have studied at Rome under Carissimi. His numerous compositions are mainly in the church style. Colonna was chiefly celebrated on account of his learning and talents as a teacher, and pupils came to him from all directions. His pupil Giovanni Carlo Maria Clari was born in 1669. Clari's first opera was brought out with much success at Bologna, yet he was more at home as a writer of church and chamber music than as a dramatic composer. His "De profundis" has been performed in modern times.

Bononcini

Giovanni Bononcini was born in 1672 at Modena. He received his first musical instruction from his father, Giovanni

Maria Bononcini. He first appeared as a violoncello player and composer at Vienna and Berlin, and his reputation soon spread abroad. In 1720 he was invited to England, and arrived at London almost simultaneously with Handel. Bononcini's operas became very popular, and the intense party feeling which was aroused on his and Handel's account forms a chapter in musical history. The party spirit ran so high that it became political; it is said that Handel's cause was espoused by the Tories and Bononcini's by the Whigs. For a time Bononcini won the victory. John Byrom ridicules this dispute in the well-known lines:

> Some say, compar'd to Bononcini,
> That Mynheer Handel 's but a ninny;
> Others aver that he to Handel
> Is scarcely fit to hold a candle.
> Strange all this difference should be
> 'Twixt Tweedledum and Tweedledee.

But posterity has awarded immortal fame to the one and a mere remembrance to the other. Bononcini's most popular operas were "Griselda," "Astarto," "Crispo," and "Astyanax." Not one of them has lived to the present day, which is also true, however, of Handel's forty operas.

Italian opera in the eighteenth century found no richer field of conquest than Germany, at Dresden, Munich, Stuttgart, Berlin, and other courts. Vienna, in particular, grew to be veritably an Italian colony. This influence of Italian music on the native musicians of Germany was shown in the works of masters like Fux, Graun, Kerl, and Hasse. *Italian opera in Germany*

Johann Joseph Fux was royal chapelmaster at Vienna for the first forty years of the eighteenth century. He composed a number of operas in the Italian style, which were richer in harmony than the most of that school, but he wrote more church music than secular music. As a learned contrapuntist his teachings have lasted to the present day. His "Gradus ad Parnassum" has served as a standard for many eminent musicians.

Karl Heinrich Graun was born in 1701. In his youth he was an ardent admirer of the Italian opera, and became a singer on the stage. In the year 1740 he was chosen the royal director of music by Frederick the Great, an office which he held for the remainder of his life. He composed thirty-six operas and a large collection of church music. His well-known oratorio, "The Death of Jesus" (Der Tod Jesu), is still sung at Berlin and other places, although it no longer holds the place it once did in Germany.

The most celebrated German master of the eighteenth century, who dedicated himself heart and soul to the Italian style, was Johann Adolph Hasse, born at Hamburg in 1699. He first appeared as a singer in Keiser's opera at Hamburg, and afterwards at the court of Brunswick, where his first opera, "Antigonus," was brought out when he was only eighteen years old. In 1724 he went to Naples to study under Porpora, but fortunately came under the notice of Scarlatti, who was so attracted by Hasse's brilliant performance on the harpsichord that he accepted him as his pupil, and treated him with the affection of a parent. It was not long before his talents found an opportunity to be made known to the Neapolitan public. His "Sesostrato" was performed there in 1726, and it so completely established his reputation that he was henceforth in universal demand, both as director and composer. The Italians named him "il caro Sassone." In the following year he went to Venice, where he was appointed chapelmaster, and there he met the celebrated singer, Faustina, whom he afterwards married. In 1730 he was invited to Dresden, as composer and chapelmaster to the court. The king placed at his command full power and ample resources to put the opera on the most complete footing, and gave him a salary of twelve thousand dollars per year for himself and his wife, Faustina. In this honored position he remained for many years, and the Dresden opera became very famous. He was invited to take the direction of the opera in London in opposition to Handel. On the reception of this invitation his question was, "Is Handel dead?" When they answered "No," he would not stir a foot, declaring that where Handel was there was no room for any one else in the same profession.

Hasse and Graun were lauded to the skies by their contemporaries, while Bach was obscure and unappreciated except as an organist and teacher, and Handel had too many enemies to overcome. "Hasse and Graun," says Scheibe in his "Kritischer Musicus," "are the excellent masters who in their time have succeeded in covering themselves and their country with glory, for it may be said that with them a new period has begun. . . . I have listened at various places to church music by Handel, Hasse, and Graun, and invariably have found that the last-named composer has always produced the greatest and most general impression." But in the opera Scheibe finds that Hasse is preëminent. Time soon confuted the critic. Hasse was a superior singer, and understood how to write for the voice as few others did. "He had better taste," says von Dommer, "than most Italians of his time, and possessed a greater dramatic power. Through him the Italian opera of the school of Scarlatti, when considered within its own limits, reached its highest point of excellence. For Hasse had become an Italian to all intents and purposes, while Handel had not studied any less attentively but still remained a German in spirit. The Italian opera as a whole came to no completion under Handel, although it acquired a higher dramatic musical expression, with resources hitherto unknown, and contained the germs of a new form of development which ultimately came to light in the grand oratorios of that master."

The national German opera at Hamburg, which will come under our notice in a succeeding chapter, did not attain the result to which its supporters aspired; for the Italian opera in Germany, with Hasse at its head, stood in the way of its enduring success. It was not until the advent of Gluck and Mozart that Germany could point with pride to its national opera.

Contemporary praise of Hasse and Graun

CHAPTER XIII

ITALIAN MASTERS OF SINGING

Superiority
of the Ital-
ian school
of singing
The Italian school of singing is universally acknowledged
and admired as the only great vocal system. This unrivaled
supremacy may be accounted for naturally, as the result of a
musical language, a beautiful climate, and a musical temperament which prompts the Italians to sing as spontaneously as
the birds. Yet this natural love of singing would have signified but little if it had not been guided into the right chan-
nel by fortuitous events. We trace the source of this school
of artistic singing back to the sixteenth century, the age of
a cappella music. It was not, however, before the advent of solo
singing, in the seventeenth century, as manifested in the recitative and aria, that the peculiar characteristics of Italian
vocalization came to light. With the advancement of the
opera arose remarkable masters of singing like Pistocchi,
Bernacchi, and Porpora, and great singers like Senesino,
Faustina, and Farinelli.

The development of vocal composition and the art of vocalization went on hand in hand. In a preceding chapter I stated
that many of the most celebrated Flemish masters were
singers in the Papal Choir at Rome, and that with few exceptions the members of that body were the foremost singers as
well as the foremost composers of their time. Subsequently,
the founders of the opera and cantata — Caccini, Carissimi,
Scarlatti, and others — were singers and teachers of singing
as well as composers.

Soprano
and con-
tralto parts
In the church music of the Middle Ages the soprano and
contralto parts were not supplied by women, who were
debarred from this service by ecclesiastical law. In the age

of the Flemish school these parts were taken by falsetto singers, the best of whom came from Spain. This combination of voices accounts for the low range of the soprano and contralto parts in much of the *a cappella* music previous to Palestrina. In his day boy singers became common and soon replaced the falsetto singers, who were not so competent to sing high notes. They in turn were superseded in a degree by male soprano and contralto singers (castrati), none of whom, however, entered the Papal Choir before 1625. This class of singers became numerous, and the greatest virtuosi of the eighteenth century are counted among their number. It is related of Baldassare Ferri of Perugia (1610–1680), a soprano singer, that with his wonderfully trained voice he could execute a chain of trills running through two octaves of the chromatic scale, ascending and descending, all in one breath, and with absolute purity of intonation. This difficult feat appears entirely credible when we read of the severe studies pursued by students of singing at that time. Bontempi, the Italian musical historian, gives an account of the daily exercises to which the scholars of the Papal Choir were subjected under Mazzocchi in 1636, and which, if faithfully followed out, ought certainly either to have made or unmade singers. He says :

Training of the Papal Choir

The pupils had to give one hour daily to the practice of difficult vocal passages, in order to acquire easy execution ; another hour to the study of the trill ; a third to pure intonation,—all in the presence of the master, and standing before a mirror that they might observe the position of the mouth and avoid all grimaces while singing. . . . Two hours more were devoted to the study of expression and taste. In the afternoon half an hour was devoted to studying the theory of sound ; another half hour to counterpoint; an hour to hearing the rules of composition; another to the study of literature, and the rest of the day to playing the clavichord, or to the composition of some psalm, motet, or other style of piece, according to the pupil's own inclination. These were the ordinary exercises of the day. Besides, occasionally they sang at church, or went thither to hear the work of some celebrated master. On their pleasure walks they often went to the Porta Angelica of Monte Maria, to sing there, and listen to the echo of their voices, that they might in this way judge of their singing and detect their faults. And when they returned to their school, they spent the rest of the evening in the improvement of certain points, and in giving to their masters an account of what they had seen and done.

Caccini's "Nuove musiche"

The first regular treatise on the art of singing was published by Caccini in the year 1601, at Florence, in the preface of his " Nuove musiche." He treats of the art of perfect intonation, — how to swell and diminish the tone tastefully and expressively. He gives directions how to execute the trill — which in his day consisted of the rapid reiteration of the same tone, like the modern tremolo — as well as the *gruppo*, or modern shake. He also declares that extended roulades and florid passages are by no means important to a good style of singing, but are oftentimes intended merely to please the ear; and that they should be introduced only in the least passionate places, and in the final cadences of the piece; always on the long syllables and never on the short ones. This advice did not much please his contemporaries, and certainly was not strictly followed by his successors.

Caccini's fame and system spread over Italy. He is accepted as the founder of the so-called dramatic style of singing in distinction from the chamber style, which was introduced by Carissimi. The dramatic style of singing was further advanced in the school of Scarlatti, Leo, and Porpora, and the later Neapolitans. Chamber singing was cultivated at Bologna under Pistocchi, Bernacchi, and others. The greatest singers of the eighteenth century — Senesino, Carestini, Cuzzoni, and others — combined these two styles and carried the art of singing to the highest perfection. The host of singers, performers, and composers in Italy during this epoch was unprecedented.

Pistocchi

The vocal school of Francesco Antonio Pistocchi, founded at Bologna in 1700, taught the method which has remained as the foundation of all good singing even to the present day.

All the arts of practical singing were systematized. Particular attention was paid to the quality of tone, and correctness and beauty of style were demanded as essential conditions of the art of musical delivery. Pistocchi possessed the secret of training the voices of his pupils according to the peculiar nature and capabilities of each one. He was a thoroughly educated musician, and an excellent soprano singer. His most celebrated pupils were Bernacchi, Antonio Pasi, Minelli, Fabri, Carlani, and Faenza.

Antonio Bernacchi followed in the path laid out by his master, and was even more fortunate in the number of remarkable singers whom he trained. He had at the outset only a feeble voice, but he developed it so wonderfully under the direction of his teacher that he became one of the best singers of his day, and was pronounced to be the king of singers by Handel and Graun. He was connected with Handel's opera in London for a long time. Among his many direct pupils were Mancini, Amadori, Guarducci, and Anton Raaff, the German tenor for whom Mozart wrote his "Idomeneo." The influence of Bernacchi's teaching extended beyond his direct pupils, for the greatest singers, Senesino, Carestini, and Farinelli, adopted his style to a great extent. *Bernacchi*

About the middle of the eighteenth century Italian singing attained its greatest excellence. "The sway which a flexible throat exercised over the public was fabulous; the happy possessor of such a voice returned home from his triumphal travels with his golden spoils. Caffarelli was so rich that he actually bought a dukedom, but continued to the last to get well paid for his singing." Doni scolds about these singers, saying, "They get money eagerly in order to revel and gormandize to their hearts' content; they hold themselves in such high honor that everybody else is of no importance. Real scholars are laughed at by them, while they imagine that they possess all the musical knowledge worth having. I have never seen such a perverse and peevish kind of humanity *The composer the slave of the virtuoso* as this." The public forgot everything in its eager desire to hear these wonderful voices. Tenors and basses disappeared entirely from the opera. The only music of the opera which aroused any real interest were the solos which gave the singer full opportunity to display his voice and execution. In the long *da capo* arias it was the custom of the singers to introduce new passages and adornments as often as the principal motives were repeated. The composer had become the slave of the virtuoso, and even the manly, nay heroic, struggles of Handel, carried on for years against the cabal of Italian singers, were for a time unavailing.

Senesino

Among this number was Francesco Bernardi, commonly called Senesino, born at Siena in 1680. He was engaged by Handel in 1720, and sang in London at the "Haymarket" until the musical quarrels broke out, when he became a member of the hostile company set up in opposition to Handel. Senesino is said to have had "a powerful,,clear, equal, and sweet contralto voice, with a perfect intonation and an excellent shake. His manner of singing was masterly, and his elocution unrivaled."

Carestini, also called Cusanino, succeeded Senesino in Handel's opera in 1733. It was said by judges in his day that those who had not heard Carestini were ignorant of the perfect style of singing. He had a remarkable voice, which changed from a strong clear soprano to a beautiful sonorous contralto with a range from D to G, and he controlled it with wonderful ease and flexibility. His highly impressive dramatic representations were enhanced by his majestic figure.

Caffarelli

Caffarelli, one of the most celebrated singers of the Neapolitan school, was born in 1703. He received instruction from Porpora, who is said to have taught him in the following extraordinary manner : for a period of five years he gave him nothing to practise but scales and exercises, all of which he wrote down for his pupil on a single sheet of paper. In the sixth year he proceeded to give him instructions in articulation, pronunciation, and declamation. Caffarelli submitted to this treatment without a murmur, though even at the end of six years he imagined he had got a very little way beyond the mere rudiments of the art. But to his great astonishment his master one day addressed him : " Young man, you may now leave me. You have nothing more to learn from me. You are the greatest singer in the world." This story has often been repeated, but probably contains only a grain of truth, for had Porpora subjected Caffarelli to such a strict and pedantic drill as this, neither master nor pupil could ever have gained his present fame. Caffarelli was looked upon as Farinelli's rival, and some critics considered him the greater singer of the two ; but he never enjoyed such universal popularity as Farinelli.

Vittoria Tesi, of the school of Bernacchi, was a contralto singer of remarkable powers. The extraordinary compass of her voice enabled her to sing with perfect ease the bass airs in the opera, and at Dresden she was often called upon to take this part, as there was a great scarcity at that time of bass and tenor voices. She had a grand and majestic style, and great powers of declamation.

Vittoria Tesi

Faustina Bordoni, born at Venice in 1700, was the greatest woman singer of the eighteenth century. She was trained in singing by Gasparini, and made her first public appearance in the opera at Venice in 1716, but afterward became the wife of Hasse, and for many years was the chief ornament of the opera at Dresden. Faustina was remarkable for her personal charms as well as for her acting and singing. She had a mezzo-soprano voice that was less clear than penetrating ; her manner of singing was expressive and brilliant ; her execution, finished. She had a fluent tongue for pronouncing words rapidly and distinctly, and a flexible throat for passages, with so beautiful and quick a trill that she could put it in motion easily at any moment. In rapid skips she could rival any instrument, and possessed peculiar skill in executing swift

Faustina Bordoni

reiterations of the same note, or tremolo. She sang adagios with great passion and expression, had a very happy memory, and her powers of mimicry and action were wonderful. She succeeded equally well in serious, amorous, and tender parts. Her only successful rival among her own sex was Cuzzoni, who, however, was inferior as an actress.

Francesca Cuzzoni

Francesca Cuzzoni, a native of Parma, began her career at Venice, where she appeared in the opera with her rival, Faustina. She went to England in 1723, and was held in high favor there for a number of years, until her return to her native land. While Cuzzoni and Faustina were in London together the spirit of rivalry and jealousy took possession of them, and each found partisans among the ladies of fashion. It is told by Horace Walpole that his mother, Lady Walpole, had them at her house to sing in a concert at which an assemblage of the best people of the kingdom was present. Finding it impossible to prevail on the one to sing while the other was present, she took Faustina to a remote part of the house, under the pretext of showing her some curious china, during which time the company obtained a song from Cuzzoni, who supposed her rival had quitted the field. A similar device was practised in order to get Cuzzoni out of the room while Faustina performed. The party feeling in regard to these rivals soon became extravagant and furious, and the fashionable world was convulsed by their feuds. The mutual jealousy of the two singers was intensified to such a degree by this foolish partisanship that on one occasion, when they happened to meet in public, they actually came to blows before the spectators. It is no wonder that, under such circumstances, the directors of the opera found their interests in jeopardy, and so they resolved to put an end to the nuisance by taking advantage of an oath which Cuzzoni had sworn to one of her noble partisans, Lady Pembroke, that she would never take a lower salary than her rival, Faustina. The time for a new contract was at hand, and, as the directors offered her a guinea less than they offered Faustina, Cuzzoni, bound by her oath, was obliged to refuse the engagement, and soon left the country. After a life of various vicissitudes she died, poor and neglected, at Bologna in 1770.

The greatest singer of all the remarkable virtuosi of the eighteenth century was Carlo Broschi, commonly called Farinelli. He was born at Andria in Naples in 1705, and was a pupil of Porpora, who bestowed the utmost care on his education. At the early age of seventeen he accompanied his teacher to Rome to make his début in opera, and on this occasion he performed the celebrated vocal feat which gave him great notoriety. In an air with obligato trumpet accompaniment, Farinelli held out a note with the trumpeter so long that the player was obliged to give up the contest, while Farinelli, with apparent ease and with a smile on his face as if he had only been sporting with his rival, not only continued to hold, swell, and shake the same note, but at last, in the same breath, introduced a series of rapid and difficult runs and passages, when his voice was finally lost in the storm of applause. Farinelli possessed a wonderful voice of an extraordinary compass, which in later years grew deeper without losing the power of reaching the highest notes. Farinelli stayed in England a few years, and was engaged by the party of noblemen who were carrying on the opera in opposition to Handel. On leaving that country he went to Madrid, in response to an invitation from the queen of Spain. The king, Philip V, was suffering under great dejection of mind. He was an ardent lover of music, and it was thought that this art might be made to serve as an alleviation, if not a cure, of his infirmity. With this in view the greatest singer of the age was called in as his physician. The experiment succeeded far beyond all expectations. The king was so much pleased with Farinelli that he granted all his wishes, and the singer used his influence to have him take medical advice, which previously he had refused; it was not long before the king was restored to health.

Farinelli

Invitation to Madrid

Farinelli was taken into the service of the court at a high salary, and was not permitted to sing any more in public. During the first ten years of his residence at court he sang every night to the king the same four airs, which, if considered in the light of medicine, must have been extremely hard to take in such repeated doses, and would in ordinary cases be more likely to kill than to cure the musical patient. Farinelli grew into such favor that the king conferred high honors on him, and he was regarded as his prime minister. But in holding this elevated position, he behaved himself with so much modesty and prudence that he gained the esteem and confidence of the

His prudence and modesty

Spanish nobility. It is related of him that one day, as he was going to the king's closet, he overheard an old officer of the guard curse him, and say to another, "Honors can be heaped on such scoundrels as this, while a poor soldier like myself, after thirty years' service, remains unnoticed." Farinelli, without seeming to hear this reproach, took occasion to remind the king that he had neglected an old servant, and procured a regiment for the man who had spoken of him so harshly. In passing out after leaving the king he gave the officer his commission, telling him that he had heard him complain of having served thirty years without promotion. "But," he added, "you did wrong to accuse the king of neglecting to reward your zeal."

After a service at the Spanish court of four and twenty years, on the death of Ferdinand VI, Philip's successor, Farinelli was obliged to leave Spain, for the new king hated music and did not appreciate the character or talents of the man. He retired to Bologna on a pension, where he passed the remainder of his life. The extraordinary events of his career have formed the subject of several plays and operas.

Farinelli was one of the greatest singers that ever lived, not only in regard to wonderful range, power, and flexibility of his voice, — which enabled him to sing the most difficult passages with perfect ease and clearness, so that the composers of that day were literally unable to invent difficulties for him, — but more particularly in his rare power of moving the feelings of his hearers. It is undoubtedly a fact that some of the music of the present century demands of the singer greater depth of feeling and more execution than the most difficult roulades and passages which were composed for Farinelli; yet in his perfect intonation, noble style, and power of artistic expression, Farinelli has never found a superior. Such were the singers of the eighteenth century.

CHAPTER XIV

OPERA IN FRANCE

First performances of opera in Paris

In France, as in other countries, mysteries and masques were common for a long time previous to the establishment of the opera. Italian dramatic music was first introduced into France by Rinuccini, who went to that country in the suite of Maria de' Medici, on the occasion of her marriage with Henry IV. But the first regular opera performed in Paris was by an Italian company, brought to France in 1645 by Cardinal Mazarin. A few years later the " Euridice " of Peri was performed, and it was not long after this that the French began to do something themselves in this branch of music, independently of Italy, and to realize the dream of a national opera. The earliest attempt was made by Pierre Perrin and Robert Cambert, who wrote and composed the first French comedy with music, as it was termed. This was brought out in 1659. Ten years later Perrin was authorized by the king to establish an opera at Paris and other places in the kingdom. This was the beginning of French opera, although the real founder and promoter was Lully, to whom this honor is deservedly given.

Independent development of opera in France

Thus at the very outset France did not resign herself to the charms of Italian opera, but for over a century pursued her own independent path in the development of a national style of musical drama. It is not difficult to find the reason for her exceptional career. France had no great traditional school of church music in the sixteenth century to educate and refine the taste, as was the case in Italy, and even in Germany and England. In the sixteenth century, France had no names to match with Palestrina, Orlando Lasso, Schütz, and William

Byrd. The new style, which sprang up in the seventeenth century, was as much the offspring of previous culture as it was the expression of a new ideal. Consequently, the most musical countries readily adopted Italian music; but in France this was not the case with regard to the style, although it borrowed the idea of a drama with music from its neighbors. It was this very deficiency and sterility in the musical life and organization of the French that turned to their advantage, for in the absence of great works of musical art, their musical drama could approach nearer to its ancient prototype, the Greek tragedy with music. We have seen that the Italians, in spite of their first attempt to produce a recitative which should closely imitate the ancient type as well as learning and imagination could devise, were ultimately baffled and forced to abandon the project by their instinctive love of sweet tones, which could not long endure the dry monotony of mere dramatic recitation in which the tones are entirely subordinate to the words. Thus the arioso style and the aria arose, and soon became so florid and sensuous that the original idea of a pure dramatic music, with recitative all but absolute, was abandoned forever by the Italians. The French taste for the classic tragedies of Greece, and the imitative drama of Racine and Corneille, fully account for the subordinate position early occupied by French music, as the handmaid of poetry. Lully, Rameau, and their successors fully appreciated the rhythmical value of the words. In the Italian opera, on the contrary, the words were often disregarded and perverted; the syllables were drawn out inordinately and the words repeated beyond the limits of strict taste, in order to serve the voice of the singer and the sensuous flow of the melody. The French composers sought merely to intensify the dramatic expression by means of the tones, and though the recitative possessed this declamatory force and truth of expression, it was at the cost of beautiful melody.

Jean Baptiste Lully was a Florentine by birth (1633). At the age of twelve he was taken to France as a page to

Imitation of Greek tragedy

Jean Baptiste Lully

Mademoiselle d'Orléans, the niece of Louis XIV. The lady, however, not liking his appearance, sent him into the kitchen as an under-scullion. His talent for music had received some cultivation previously, and he managed to spare time from his menial occupation to practise on the violin. Some one, overhearing his performance on this instrument, drew the attention of the princess to his talent, whereupon she provided regular musical instruction for him. The proficiency which he early acquired as a violinist led to his appointment as a member of the king's band of twenty-four "Violins du Roy," as it was called. He was speedily promoted to the place of leader of this band, and was employed to compose music for the royal festivals. The king, subsequently, chose him intendant of the royal music, and granted him the privilege of controlling the opera, which had already been established. Lully invited the poet Quinault to write texts for him, and an engagement was made that Quinault should write an opera every year. They held true to this engagement for many years, and nearly all Lully's music was composed to Quinault's words. The opera became the favorite pastime of the court, and Lully grew in position and wealth. The king granted him letters of nobility and made him one of his royal secretaries, an office of high honor and held only by distinguished men. Lully's character was made up of strange contradictions.

Lully's character

He was avaricious and insinuating, but perfectly honest in his dealings with men. In his management of the opera he was strict but just, and kept the singers and performers in orderly behavior. His bluntness of speech often offended the courtiers, but the king always took it in good part. At the production of one of his operas the performance was not ready to begin at the proper time. The king sent word that he was weary of waiting, and desired the piece should begin without further delay. The messenger told Lully that his majesty was out of all patience, and in a violent passion, but the composer, absorbed in his preparations, said coolly, "His majesty can wait." The king laughed at the answer and quietly waited until Lully was ready.

Lully understood the French taste and how to minister to it. His talents as a musician were decidedly inferior to his clear understanding of stage effects ; he improved the dresses of the players, and showed refined taste in decorating the stage. He remodeled the general form of the drama, and had a keen insight into the true action of the play. It is certain that his operas would not have maintained their place on the French stage for a century had it not been for all the appliances which he cleverly adapted to make his pieces attractive. His sagacity, too, was displayed when he selected such a poet as Quinault as the writer of his opera texts. Lully paid him twice as high a salary as the king would, and tyrannized over him to his heart's content, as an equivalent. He was an unmerciful critic of Quinault's work, and when the poet had furnished him with a new libretto Lully did not hesitate to draw his pen through many a line. Quinault is known to have altered some scenes as many as twenty times before the musician was satisfied ; but Lully was judicious in his criticism, and knew better than the poet what would prove advantageous to the play, and this severe pruning really added to its worth in the end. On the other hand, had Lully in turn found as good a critic of his music, he would have been benefited ; Quinault's poetry is still read, while Lully's music is almost forgotten. The merits of his operas lie more in the rhetorical expression of the words than in his melodies. There is very little beauty of melody in the solo parts, and the ensemble effects of the chorus or concerted voices are very simple. The chorus, however, occupied a definite place in the drama, which was not the case in the Italian opera. He was an enemy of colorature, or the holding out of a syllable while a series of tones are sung to it. The Italian composers of the eighteenth century carried this practice to excess, but modern music cannot wholly dispense with colorature without loss. Lully would

Attention to stage effects

not permit the slightest infringement of the law of verbal meter. The tiresome monotony of the recitative was hardly ever relieved, except by the introduction of the arioso style now and then in the course of the scene. His instrumental accompaniments were simple, but sometimes effective. Lully is reputed to have given a definite form to the orchestral overture, which he composed in three short, well-contrasted movements.

Lully's first opera, "Les fêtes de l'amour," was produced in 1672. Among the eighteen works which followed, the most noted were his "Alceste," "Bellérophon," "Phaëton," "Atys," "Isis," and "Armide." He also invented a number of grand ballets and other pieces. His "Armide" was at first coldly received; the music was not liked. Lully, who was passionately fond of his own music, had it performed for his personal gratification, he himself forming the whole audience. When this odd circumstance was reported to the king, he thought that the opera could not be bad if Lully himself had so good an opinion of it. Having, therefore, ordered it to be performed before him, he was charmed with it, and then both the court and the public changed their opinion of its merits. Lully died in 1687, leaving an enormous fortune for his time, — over half a million livres. He was a rough man both in looks and manner, but was honest and manly. His operas held their place on the French stage for a century. He had two sons who were musicians. Among his followers was Colasse, the author of several operas, but his most noted successor was Rameau, who created a new era in French opera.

Jean Philippe Rameau

Jean Philippe Rameau was born at Dijon in 1683. He was the son of an organist, and evinced in his early years remarkable intelligence and rare talent for organ playing and counterpoint. As a boy of fourteen years he was able, it is said, to improvise fugues with several subjects. His good and bad traits of character came to light early in life. He ran away from home and joined a traveling theatrical company as musical director. At Paris his talents as an organist made his name speedily known. His industry was great, his ambition insatiable. He became a pupil of the celebrated organist Marchand, and afterwards went to Naples to continue his musical studies. On his return to France he composed the opera " Hippolyte et Aricie." The appearance of this work created a sensation in Paris. The worshipers of Lully found innovations in it which they considered as attacking the very foundations of the French national opera ; but their fierce opposition ceased when it was found that he was not seeking to revolutionize but simply to develop the principles which his predecessors had laid down. His declamation and musical rhythm were more sharply pointed and defined than Lully's ; in fact, Rameau was greatly superior to him as a musician. He was gifted with more talent and invention than the older French masters. The choruses of his operas were of a much higher order ; they did not consist of a lifeless succession of simple chords, but the vocal parts moved freely in good counterpoint, which was often imitative and fugal, showing the skill of the organist rather than that of the dramatic composer. Rameau was influenced considerably by his Italian studies ; his arioso style resembled that of contemporary masters like Scarlatti and Bononcini. His orchestral accompaniments were characterized by a certain freedom of movement, by the introduction of motives here and there, and by a better combination of instruments than was known to his predecessors. Rameau wrote thirty-six works for the stage. His compositions for the clavichord are charming, and in this branch of music he stands as one of the foremost of his time. His treatise on harmony is the first published work on the subject, and it laid the foundations for a true science of harmony. The titles of a number of his works are proof of his research and invention in the field of musical theory.

His merits as a composer

The absolute supremacy of the national opera of Lully and Rameau was greatly shaken by the introduction of the *opera*

Opera buffa

buffa by an Italian company in 1752. They exhibited "La serva padrona" of Pergolesi. This piece, which I have already described, had a wonderful success; it drew crowds to the theater night after night. The public was divided into two great parties for and against this new appearance in the musical world. Ink was shed freely by the literati. Rousseau himself entered the arena, and declared himself enthusiastically in favor of this music, and proved his words by composing his comic opera, "Le devin du village." It is no wonder that the public accepted the comic opera from the outset. It was more attractive to the French, whose lively gayety quickly responded to the light and pleasing character of the music and the play. They were quite ready to break the heavy fetters imposed on them by the stiff and pompous tragedy. The Italian company, or "bouffons," as they were designated, were very prosperous for a while, but as they sang in a foreign tongue, they were not appreciated by the mass of the people. Finally, they were neglected and took their departure from the country; but they had sown the seed which one day bore good fruit. After the Italians had gone, "La serva padrona" was translated into French and performed to full houses.

The operetta. Duni and Grétry

Duni, the Italian contemporary and rival of Pergolesi, came to Paris in 1757, and introduced a new kind of musical drama, in which there was a good deal of spoken dialogue in the less emotional parts of the play; this was the origin of the so-called operetta, which was subsequently developed by French and German composers into a noble form, as shown in the great works of Mozart, Beethoven, and Cherubini. The immediate French composers of the comic style were Philidor and Monsigny; and a generation later, Grétry, Dalayrac, and Gossec. Grétry brought the comic opera to its full maturity, and gave it the form and character which have rendered it the truest expression of the French taste in dramatic music. He was also remarkably fertile in ideas and a very prolific composer, having produced no less than fifty operas in the space of thirty-eight years, sometimes as many as three in a single year. His principal operas are "Le Huron," "Zemire," "Anacréon," and "Richard Cœur de Lion." This last-named work became famous; it was translated into German, Italian, English, Russian, and Swedish, and performed in various capitals. It is still frequently performed at Paris and, together with the other operas named, deserves a permanent place in the repertory of every great theater. Grétry had a rare talent for natural expression and musical characterization; his melodies are simple and pleasing, and his orchestration graceful and varied.

CHAPTER XV

OPERA IN ENGLAND

Opera in
England
under Ital-
ian influ-
ence

In England the opera was under Italian influence almost from the outset ; it enjoyed only a brief native existence under Purcell and Locke, and since that period, even to this day, has been in the hands of foreigners, notwithstanding the various attempts that have been made to raise up a national school. If as liberal and intelligent support had been given to English musicians after Elizabeth's reign as was the case during that wise monarch's lifetime, a great national school of music would have arisen to match and far excel the work already begun by Tallis, Byrd, Dowland, and other masters of the sixteenth century, and England would never have become so dependent on Germany and Italy for her musical life as she has been during the last two centuries. Puritanism could not tolerate art in any form, and consequently, during its revolutionary sway, the only noble school of music of which England could boast in her history was cut off. I refer, of course, to the church and secular music of Tallis, Byrd, Morley, Wilbye, and others. We can form an idea of the fanatical abhorrence of the Puritans for artistic music from the words of Prynne, who published a book directed against all kinds of plays or entertainments, dancing, dicing, health drinking, and the like. He is the bitter enemy of all music except psalm singing, and denounces all plays as "sinfull, heathenish, lewd, ungodly spectacles, condemned in all ages as intolerable mischiefs to churches, to republics, to the manners, minds, and soules of men. . . . Play-haunters are little better than incarnate devils."

I have already mentioned the plays with music in the Middle Ages and during the time of Queen Elizabeth, as well as

the music by Henry Lawes, the talented and popular composer of the music to Milton's "Comus." During the rule of
the Puritans theatrical performances of all kinds were pro-
hibited. The only exception was made in 1656 in favor of
Sir William Davenant, who opened an exhibition which he
called "an entertainment in declamation and music, after the
manner of the ancients," — which served as a kind of blind
to the fanatical Puritans. The music for this entertainment
was composed by Henry Lawes and other noted musicians of
that time. This was followed by "The Siege of Rhodes," in
stile recitativo, and consequently was the first real opera sung
in England. Davenant produced next a piece with scenes
and decorations, called "The Cruelty of the Spaniards in
Peru." These rude attempts do not merit the name of opera;
meanwhile Italy had produced a Monteverde and a Carissimi,
and the opera had gained a permanent hold on society.

It was not before 1670 that the restrictions on stage plays
were withdrawn. Charles II encouraged theaters, music, and
the other arts. It was during his reign that Locke, Purcell,
and Carey flourished; but it was beyond their power to repair
the loss which English music had suffered during this long
neglect. The Italian opera was now all-powerful. Had England enjoyed inward peace and tranquillity during the half
century succeeding the introduction of the secular style, a
class of native musicians would have arisen to instill new life
into English music. As the direct successors of the celebrated
madrigal writers of the sixteenth century, those masters would
have been able to compete with the best foreign contemporaries of the art; but Purcell, though he was a man of
undoubted genius, could not accomplish this desired result
single-handed. The Italians invaded England in full force, and
at last, Handel, the master of them all, arrived to hold the
natives in subjection as a musical conqueror.

Matthew Locke was born at Exeter, and brought up as a Matthew
chorister in the cathedral of that city. He was employed to Locke

compose the music for the public entrance of Charles II at the Restoration, and was soon after appointed composer in ordinary to the king. His best known works are his opera " Psyche," and the music to Shakespeare's " Macbeth." This latter work is still performed, and holds a permanent connection with the great tragedy to which it was composed.

During Charles II's reign the fashionable taste in music was influenced considerably in favor of French music by the Duchess of Mazarin, who made England her residence in 1675. Cambert, one of the first French opera composers, was called to England by the king, and appointed his royal director of music. The duchess held at her house musical dramatic entertainments which were very magnificent and fashionable.

Henry Purcell

Henry Purcell, one of the greatest musical geniuses England has yet produced, was born in the year 1658. He was the son of the well-known musician, Henry Purcell, gentleman of the Chapel Royal in Charles II's reign, and was a pupil of Dr. Blow. His genius showed itself at a very early age ; while he was a mere boy he composed anthems which are sung to this day. At the age of twenty-two he was appointed organist of Westminster Abbey, and two years later he was appointed to be one of the three organists of the royal chapel. His talent for dramatic music was displayed equally early in life, and his first essay was made in this style when he was but nineteen years old, in the form of an operetta called " Dido and Æneas." This youthful work showed decided evidences of genius, though it lacked the ripeness of his later efforts. The success of the piece soon opened the way to new undertakings. He was engaged by several managers of the theaters to write music for the stage. In this way he composed overtures, pieces to be performed between the acts, and incidental songs. Dryden, the poet, became a warm friend of Purcell and wrote the text of " King Arthur " for him, and with Davenant altered Shakespeare's " Tempest " for the purpose of affording room for scenic decoration and music. "King Arthur" appeared in 1691, and was brought out with great splendor and success. This opera is considered one of Purcell's best, and has been adapted to the modern stage under the name of "Arthur and Emmeline." Other operas by Purcell are the "Indian Queen" (which contains the celebrated recitative and air, "Ye twice ten hundred deities"), "Tyrannic Love," "The Prophetess," "Bonduca," and "Don Quixote."

Purcell's church music holds an honored place in the cathedral service of Great Britain. His facile genius was not confined to one branch, but he excelled alike in dramatic, church, and chamber music. His sonatas for two violins and a bass are worthy to be compared with the best of his time. In his preface to the first set of twelve sonatas he admits his obligations to the Italian composers. The trios of Corelli were published in the same year with Purcell's, so that they could not have served as a model to the English master, although his sonatas belong to the same school.

In the field of dramatic music Purcell is to be compared only with the very greatest masters in force and truth of dramatic expression. Although he studied foreign masters diligently, he had a decided style of his own. His imperfections are slight, and are to be ascribed to the state of music in England in his time. Purcell well-nigh created English secular solo music, for although there were many popular airs current long before his day, he was almost the first master to write cantabile and dramatic airs, in the new higher style which Italy had originated. All critics admit that the supreme merit of Purcell's music is its genuine English character; that it is more truly national than any music before his time. "Though his dramatic style and recitative," says Burney, "were formed, in a great measure, on French models, there is a latent power and force in his expression of English words, whatever be the subject, that will make an unprejudiced native of this island feel more than all the elegance, grace, and refinement of modern

His dramatic excellence

music, less happily applied, can do. And this pleasure is communicated to us, not by the symmetry or rhythm of modern melody, but by his having fortified, lengthened, and tuned the true accents of our mother tongue; those notes of passion which an inhabitant of this island would breathe in such situations as the words describe."

Purcell is the direct forerunner of Handel in the musical health and strength that animate his works, and in unity of form and effect, in the lofty spirit of his choruses, as well as in his many-sidedness. From the one master to the other is a natural step. Purcell, like Mozart, died young. After a short illness, he died in 1695, at the age of thirty-seven, and was buried in Westminster Abbey. Purcell did not live to see grouped around him great musicians of his own country and school; he laid the foundation of a grand national school, but no English successors arose to complete the work so ably begun.

French opera enjoyed only a brief career in England; it disappeared wholly after the year 1690, and the Italians began to invade England toward the end of the seventeenth century. The actual introduction of the Italian opera, however, was preceded by adaptations of Italian pieces to the English stage. An Italianized Englishman, Thomas Clayton, brought out several of these pieces. The era of Italian opera in England did not fairly begin until the arrival of Handel in 1710.

Henry
Carey

Henry Carey (1695–1743), the only English musician of that time worthy of being called, in some degree, the successor of Purcell, was the author of the words and music of charming songs and ballad operas. His melodies have a genuine popular and national ring. One of his songs, the quaint and lovely "Sally in our Alley," is as great a favorite to-day as it was two centuries ago, and is one of the finest specimens of an English song extant. His life on earth was a sad one, full of want and despair; but now he is rich in the love of all who have learned to know him in his imperishable melodies. Chrysander justly styles him the "King of English Minstrels."

CHAPTER XVI

GERMAN OPERA AT HAMBURG

Italian opera was introduced into Germany early in the seventeenth century by Heinrich Schütz, but it was not generally cultivated in that country before the era of the Neapolitan masters of the eighteenth century, although at Hamburg there sprang into premature existence a native style of musical drama under Keiser, Mattheson, Handel, Telemann, and others. A more favorable place could not have been chosen for this experiment, as it may be termed, for Hamburg was even in those days a rich and flourishing city whose citizens were well able to provide the means indispensable to such an undertaking. It was mainly through the zeal of Gerhard Schott, an alderman and jurist of Hamburg, that the opera was set on foot and supported, and as long as he lived it did not lack encouragement. This period embraces over sixty years, and witnesses the highest musical attainment of the Hamburg stage. The first ambitious attempt in dramatic music was made in 1678, when the opera house on the Goose Market was opened with a musical play called "Adam and Eve," by Theile. This sacred allegorical play was succeeded by a number of similar pieces by the same composer, who was a good musician. The spectacle of the play seems to have been the chief attraction of all these pieces, which are quite as remarkable for their rude, incongruous character as any that have received our notice in the early history of the opera in other countries. During this first period of the Hamburg opera the successful masters besides Theile were Franck, Strungk, the celebrated violinist, Förtsch, Conradi, and Kusser. This last-mentioned composer was appointed chapelmaster in 1693.

Theile's musical dramas

Kusser

Kusser produced a number of original operas, but it was chiefly by means of his remarkable talent as a disciplinarian, and by the introduction of a better style of music and singing, that he accomplished a decided improvement in the German opera. Steffani, whose duets are so remarkable, was his model as a dramatic composer, and Kusser brought out this master's operas on the Hamburg stage. He found it very difficult at first to provide singers for his opera rôles, and was so hard pushed that he had to make use of all kinds of people. " Hidden behind the masks of the Olympian gods and heroes," says von Dommer, "were cobblers and tailors, wild students, and all sorts of vagabonds, who had little or no voice. Market women, leaders in the fish and vegetable line, figured as ancient goddesses and queens." But Kusser's unexampled talent and energy overcame all obstacles. Mattheson declared that Kusser never had an equal as chapelmaster. During his brief stay at Hamburg he elevated the musical character of the place in a remarkable degree, and smoothed the path for Keiser, the presiding genius of this epoch.

Reinhard
Keiser

Reinhard Keiser was born near Leipzig in 1673, and was educated at the St. Thomas School and at the university in that city. He was appointed chapelmaster of the Hamburg opera in 1694. Keiser was a man of undoubted genius ; his productivity as a composer was immense, and seems almost incredible. He composed about one hundred and twenty operas, many of which contained no less than forty or fifty airs, besides choruses, recitatives, etc. In all his serious operas there was no spoken dialogue ; all was sung throughout. His operas were performed all over Germany, and were sung even in Paris. His activity was not confined to the stage ; he also composed church music, passion music, and cantatas.

Keiser had a rare and inexhaustible gift of melody ; his recitatives are masterly ; but the form of his music lacks that breadth and massive strength which distinguish his successor, Handel. "All that Keiser wrote," says Mattheson, "was

uncommonly easy to sing, and was so easily caught by the
ear that one had rather admire his music than praise it." But
he failed to take that deep and earnest interest in music which
is absolutely requisite in order to accomplish lasting results.
His course of life was not exemplary; he was more fond of
wine and jovial company than of his art. Keiser, therefore,
did not exert an enduring influence for good on the Hamburg
opera, although for a short time his brilliant genius led it
onward. He appeared to the public as a bright light, but
though the opera under his able direction reached for the
moment a higher point of excellence, his disorderly course
soon brought it down again from its elevation. He did not
refrain from lending his art to the most trivial and nonsensi-
cal farces to afford amusement to the rough and common
people. Mattheson compares him with the more earnest composer, Rosenmüller, whose sonatas were "like fresh blue salmon
of the Elbe," while Keiser's light music was "like the smoked
golden herrings of the North Sea, which tickle the palate, but
awaken a thirst for drink."

Instead of the sacred spectacles and plays which at the
outset formed the subject of the drama on the Hamburg
stage, the gods and heroes of ancient mythology and the most
vulgar farces now divided the attention of the eager public.
The stage spectacle grew more and more sensational; fireworks, devils, serpents and dragons, battle scenes, and all
kinds of noises and sights became indispensable to the opera.
Not content with mere humanity on the stage, the lower
animals were called upon to contribute to the effect. Horses,
camels, asses, and apes were introduced, and the roars and
cries of wild beasts produced very expressive music. Again,
in some operas no less than four different languages were
sung indiscriminately, — French, Italian, High German, and
Low German. Yet in spite of all these abuses and absurdities the Hamburg operas remained worthy of the services of
a Handel and a Mattheson.

The opera
deteriorates

Johann Mattheson (1680–1764) was born at Hamburg, where he began his musical career as a singer at the opera, and made his last appearance in that capacity in Handel's "Nero," in 1705. He was a man of wonderful versatility of talent. A finished performer on the harpsichord, a good actor and singer, and a very prolific composer, but did not possess originality nor depth of conception. As a literary man he still holds an eminent place in musical history. He used his facile pen first on an opera or passion, then on musical essays, or the translation of a pamphlet on the " Properties and Virtues of Noble Tobacco." His music, which was once so lauded, no longer lives, but his writings are still of value to the student of musical literature. Although his pen was not always guided by a wise understanding and a right heart, he left much that is interesting. His writings give valuable information of his time, and are full of wit and humor. The most famous of his books are : " Der vollkommene Kapellmeister " (Complete Chapelmaster), " Das neueröffnete Orchester " (Newly opened Orchestra), and " Die Ehrenpforte " (Triumphal Arch), which contains the biographies of contemporary musicians. These works have a permanent place in every musical library.

Soon after Handel's arrival at Hamburg, at the age of nineteen, he came into contact with Mattheson. The latter's public position and seniority of age justified him in taking Handel somewhat under his patronage. Handel behaved himself in a very modest manner, and quietly took his place in the orchestra below the second violins. An opportunity was soon afforded him to display his ability as a harpsichordist and accompanist, and he was sometimes invited to fill this post at the opera. On one occasion Handel accompanied at the harpsichord while Mattheson was singing, in his own opera of "Cleopatra," the part of Antony. On the death of Antony, which happened early in the piece, Mattheson divested himself of his royal trappings and came into the orchestra to take his usual place at the harpsichord, but Handel would not resign his seat. On leaving the theater Mattheson gave Handel a smart box on the ear, and when they had come to the open square they drew their swords and a desperate encounter ensued; but fortunately, it is said, Mattheson's sword broke on a large button on his adversary's coat, or, as others say, against the score of Mattheson's opera, which Handel had thrust into his bosom. This foolish quarrel went no farther and they soon became reconciled. Mattheson philosophizes on the affair thus: "If you break your sword on your friend, you do not injure him so much as if you spoke ill of him."

Handel's first opera, "Almira," was produced at Hamburg in 1705, and was so well received that it had a run of thirty nights, when it was withdrawn to make place for his "Nero." These two youthful works were the only ones which Handel brought out under his own direction, though he also composed for the Hamburg stage the operas of "Daphne" and "Florindo," which were performed there after his departure. The impression which they made was undoubtedly considerable, for even at that early period of his life he must have stood in favorable contrast to his associates in musical originality and skill. It is undoubtedly true that he could not appear to them as a matured master; for he had yet to gain that experience which years and contact with the world alone can give, before his grand, manly character could be impressed in strong and unmistakable outlines on his works. But he was already acknowledged to be their superior as an organist and contrapuntist. Handel left Hamburg in 1706, and during the same year went to Italy. His manly independence is well shown in this connection; he was invited to accompany an Italian prince whom he had met at Hamburg, but rather than be one of the prince's retinue, he declined the invitation, and preferred to pay his expenses out of his hard-earned savings; he traveled thence alone.

After the death of the chief director Schott, the opera at Hamburg rapidly degenerated, though strenuous efforts were made **Telemann at Hamburg** to sustain the musical fortunes of the place. To this end the celebrated composer, Georg Philipp Telemann, was invited to take the position of chapelmaster. This musician was born at Magdeburg in 1681. Before his call to Hamburg he had acquired a wide reputation as a chapelmaster and composer. His oratorios and sacred cantatas were considered to be masterpieces, but, like his contemporaries Hasse and Graun, his fame hardly outlived his days. He was a wonderfully productive composer, and the quantity of his music can best be appreciated by turning to the list of his works, which comprises about forty operas, six hundred overtures, a number of oratorios, forty-four passions, twelve complete annual sets of church cantatas, and other sacred music, besides instrumental music of all kinds. We cannot say much for the quality of these works. Telemann sought for originality at the cost of beauty and naturalness ; he sacrificed melody for declamation ; his hasty manner of composing gave rise to grave deficiencies. It was not long after Telemann had resigned his place that the Hamburg opera lost its distinctive character.

Italian opera at Hamburg In 1740 it was succeeded by the first Italian troupe in that city, under Mignotti. But although the Italian opera had meanwhile gained absolute possession of all the principal theaters of Europe, the sixty years of German opera at Hamburg were not spent in vain ; for this premature attempt gave conclusive proof that the time was rapidly advancing when the creative musical impulse of the German people would assert itself. The representative works of Bach and Handel, Gluck and Mozart, were destined to replace all that had been accomplished hitherto in Germany.

It is a remarkable fact that there is hardly a single form of music, except popular songs and dances and the masses and motets of the old church masters, which the rest of the world has not borrowed from Italy. The choral, passion music, madrigal, recitative and air, opera and oratorio, sacred concerto and secular cantata, the various forms of instrumental music, such as the sonata, symphony, modern fugue, toccata, etc., all owe their names and origin to Italy. But while we gratefully acknowledge this fact, our deeper homage should be paid principally to Germany, where these various forms of music were enlarged and ennobled, and in most instances raised to the highest point yet attained in history.

For centuries Germany rendered the tribute of respect and admiration to Italy by sending her musical talent there to be educated. One of the most noted German masters of the seventeenth century was a pupil of the great Venetian school. Heinrich Schütz, pupil of John Gabrieli, was born in 1585. His decided musical talent led the Grand Duke of Hesse Cassel to send him to Venice to study. On his return to Germany he was called to Dresden and was appointed royal chapelmaster at that capital, a position which he held from 1617 till his death in 1672. Under his direction the music at Dresden won a high reputation. His character as a man and an artist exercised a great influence on his countrymen; he sent Germans to Italy to study, and attracted Italian masters to Germany, besides educating a number, being a successful teacher himself. Schütz was a thoroughly educated man; his sterling character, his uprightness, manliness, and sincerity in all his dealings with men, secured for him the admiration and esteem of all classes of society. His Italian education under Gabrieli rendered him a zealous participant in the new musical movement of the day, and, though his activity was exhibited chiefly as a composer of church music, he was the first to introduce the opera into Germany. He was a thorough master of the mediæval tonal system and studied profoundly the *a cappella* style of the earlier Venetians. He did not, however, remain fixed to the older school, but eagerly adopted the ideas of Monteverde and other progressive musicians. And, above all, he did not lose his own nationality in his admiration for Italian music. His works were Teutonic in character; they were the foundation of modern German

Heinrich
Schütz and
the opera at
Dresden

music. More than any other German master of the seventeenth century, he was the means of elevating the musical character of his country to the glorious height it subsequently reached in the mature works of Bach and Handel.

First opera
outside of
Italy Opera appeared for the first time in any foreign country under Schütz at the court of Torgau, on the occasion of the marriage ceremonies of the Landgraf of Hesse with Sophia Eleanor of Saxony in 1627. Rinuccini's "Dafne" was translated into German for this purpose, and set to music by Schütz, as the old composition of Peri could not be adapted to the translated text. Schütz's new music to this play has been lost. This beginning of the opera in Germany was not followed up, however, either by Schütz or others. It was not till toward the end of the century that the German opera was cultivated in a national style, under Keiser, Mattheson, and others at Hamburg. Henceforth the people enjoyed this entertainment, which formerly had been reserved exclusively for the rich and great; though it is true there existed for a long time previously a kind of operetta of popular origin. We read of such a dramatic musical play at Nuremberg in 1618, entitled, "A fine play of three bad wives who could neither do right towards God nor their husbands. To be acted personally by six persons."

Schütz's long life was productive of numerous compositions His chief works are in the sacred dramatic style. He composed music to the Passion of Christ as recorded by the Four Evangelists, to the Seven Last Words, and to the Resurrection. This music is decidedly in advance of all previous masters; Schütz, in a word, gave the sacred cantata its leading modern characteristics. The old-fashioned, monotonous psalmody or intoning disappeared, and was replaced by the modern recitative and arioso style. In the four Passions, however, Schütz did not make use of the recitative; the chief excellence of these works is due to the impressive dramatic character of the choruses. In his work entitled "Saul, Saul, was verfolgst du mich ? " and of which the theme is the conversion of Saul by the voice from heaven, Schütz has succeeded in representing the scene with remarkable power without the aid of visible means, but only by musical tones, through the combined voices and instruments. Schütz is the direct forerunner of Bach and Handel in these forms of the oratorio and passion music. Other German masters of his time who contributed to the growth of a new national style of dramatic sacred music were Johann Hermann Schein, Johann Rosenmüller, Andreas Hammerschmidt, and Heinrich Albert. The last-named master, the nephew of Schütz, was the author and composer of numerous airs or songs.

CHAPTER XVII

INSTRUMENTS AND INSTRUMENTAL MUSIC

Instrumental music is the most recently developed branch of the art. Previous to the foundation of the opera it consisted chiefly of simple pieces for the organ, clavichord, viola, and lute. The ancients had no purely instrumental music worthy of the name. In the Middle Ages the minstrels and others practised it incidentally in accompanying their songs and dances, but it had no character of its own, and was almost entirely subordinate to the vocal parts. The earliest instrumental pieces were, for the most part, mere copies of the vocal airs, in unison or in the octave. During the fifteenth and sixteenth centuries musical instruments, like the organ, clavichord, lute, and viola and other bowed instruments, were greatly improved, and the ground was prepared for the future orchestra, which, however, was not a well-organized combination of instruments before the time of Monteverde and Carissimi.

Develop-
ment of the
organ
The organ is the most important of ancient instruments. We owe its origin to the hydraulos, or water organ, of the ancient Greeks, which probably sprang from the syrinx, or Pan's pipe. The real construction of the water organ is not accurately known, yet undoubtedly it consisted of a row of pipes placed in the holes of a wind chest partly filled with water. By forcing more water into the chest the air was compressed, and thus the pipes were set in vibration under the control of the player, who operated on the keyboard.

The water organ was superseded by the organ with a wind chest and with bellows in place of water; but exactly when this great improvement was made is not certain. In the fourth century there were two small wind organs in the Temple of Jerusalem. Organs with bellows were used earliest in the East, especially at Constantinople, in the time of the Byzantine Empire. They were introduced into the Latin Church in the seventh or eighth century. In 756 Pepin received an organ from the Byzantine Emperor, Constantine Copronymus. Charlemagne in 812 received an organ from the East, which was placed in the cathedral at Aix-la-Chapelle. In the ninth century organs were used in Venice, Germany, and England. An organ was built in the church at Winchester in the tenth century, which had four hundred pipes and twenty-six bellows, and required seventy lusty men to blow it. Two organists played at the same time. There were only ten keys ; for every key, therefore, forty pipes sounded together, producing the effect of a mixture. In these early organs we find this so-called mixture, or harmonic tones, agreeing with and fortifying the ground tone by means of smaller pipes, tuned in fifths, octaves, and thirds. This combination was founded on an acoustical principle then unknown. Organ pipes have few overtones, and sound dull without the artificial production of the overtones by additional pipes. The mixtures, when properly used, give power and brilliancy to the organ tone. In early times, however, the art of combining mixtures was crude, and they are said to have shrieked shrill and loud.

These old organs consisted of a single row of pipes. For some time the keyboard had a very limited compass of twelve or thirteen keys, from B to e or f in diatonic order, according to the Dorian scale. The keys were a foot long and three or four inches wide, and required the fists and elbows in playing. The bellows were small and numerous, like ordinary blacksmith's bellows ; the intonation must have been very inaccurate. Subsequently a second keyboard, with separate pipes for the mixture, was introduced. The keyboard of the largest pipes was called the principal or prestant ; the second

The keys and keyboard

keyboard of mixture pipes was called the hintersatz. In 1361 Nicholas Faber built an organ for the cathedral at Halberstadt, which had three keyboards.

Pedal organ   A pedal organ is said to have been constructed by van Os, about 1120, which proves that Bernhard the German, of Venice (1470), was not the inventor of the pedal organ, as has been asserted. At first the pedals were attached by ropes to the manual keys, and were only eight in number — from B to b. Later large bass pipes were added to serve the purpose of an independent pedal, as nowadays. In the fourteenth century the compass of the organ was extended to more than two chromatic octaves. In the fifteenth century great improvements were made in organ building. The compass now embraced three chromatic octaves. The keys were made smaller, so that the fingers could be used in playing, and finally the seventh and octave could be spanned by the hand. In the sixteenth century the reed and stopped pipes were added to the diapason, and this enriched the tone color and gave an opportunity to contrast stops. Organ building continued to progress during the sixteenth, seventeenth, and eighteenth centuries until it has reached an ideal point as regards sublimity, grandeur, and power of the full organ with its mighty pedal bass. In the time of Bach and Handel such organs were common. Since then the organ has been greatly improved in action, mechanism, and tone variety; new solo stops have been added, and the art of organ building has greatly advanced; yet the organ in the time of Bach and Handel was a mighty instrument, and the true organ style reached its culmination in their works.

Organists and organ music   Organ building and organ playing reacted on each other during the many centuries of growth, but it is not until the fourteenth century that the names of organists are known. We read of Francesco Landino, the blind organist of Florence, who was crowned by the Doge of Venice in 1364 as poet and masterly organist. Owing to the mechanical drawbacks and limited compass of the instrument at that time, organ playing had only a very limited scope, and hardly deserves the name of "masterly." In the fifteenth century Bernhard the German was distinguished as organist. No examples of his music are extant. Antonio Squarcialuppi was a famous Florentine organist who died in 1475.

The oldest organ pieces preserved are by Conrad Paumann of Nuremberg, born in the early part of the fifteenth century, who was blind from birth. He was not only a master of the organ, but played the zither, harp, flute, violin, and lute. He was the inventor of the so-called lute tablature — a system of notation. The organ pieces of Paumann are commonly in two-part simple counterpoint. They have a flowing, instrumental style, and do not suggest vocal music, but they are crude.

Paul Hofhaimer (1459–1537) was a learned organist and composer, and trained numerous pupils. Germany preceded Italy in organ playing, and in composing for that instrument. The oldest organ pieces were published by Schlick in 1512, and about the middle of the century, organ compositions were frequently printed. Jacob Buus, the famous Netherland organist, published two books of ricercari; about the same time Willaert and De Rore published original fantasie e ricercari. Organ playing and composition were cultivated particularly by the Venetian masters of the sixteenth century. They gave an impetus to this branch of art. Their pieces were the germ of the highly developed form and style which reached an ideal height in the great organ works of Sebastian Bach.

The names of the Venetian organ pieces were capriccio, contrapunto, canzone, toccata, preludium, ricercare, etc. The principal Venetian organ masters were Willaert, De Rore, Bell' Haver, Guammi, Parabosco, Merulo, Andrea, and Giovanni Gabrieli.

Claudio Merulo was the first organist of his time; his toccatas are especially noted. The word "toccata" is derived from *toccare* (to touch), and suggests the idea of a piece for a

Conrad Paumann

Claudio Merulo

keyed instrument. The toccata is a brilliant piece, in which running passages alternate with contrapuntal figures in free style, as in a fantasia. The melody is not prominent. It does not suggest the vocal style, as is the case with the canzone. Merulo's toccatas were published in the years 1598 and 1604. The preludium and fantasia are very much like the toccata in form and style. The contrapunto and canzone were fugal in treatment. The ricercare in those days was a fantasia-like prelude, which in Bach's time became an elaborate master fugue.

Frescobaldi The height of Italian organ music was represented by Girolamo Frescobaldi, born 1591, whose complete works have been preserved. He is said to have studied in the Netherlands, where organ playing stood on a high plane. Frescobaldi was organist at St. Peter's in Rome. It is said that thirty thousand people once assembled there to hear him play. He had numerous pupils from various countries, including Froberger and Kerl, the famous German organists. He improved the various forms of organ music, — the prelude and fugue, fantasia, toccata, etc. He gave a definite form to the organ fugue, which reached ideal perfection in the great works of Bach. At Rome he was followed by Bernardo Pasquini, who stands next to Frescobaldi as an Italian organ master.

Jan Pieters Sweelinck was a celebrated organist in Amsterdam (1562–1621). Among his numerous pupils were several German organists, of whom Samuel Scheidt was the most noted.

Supremacy of German organists The Germans ultimately excelled the Italians as organists. They gradually developed organ style and technic during the seventeenth century to the time of Bach and Handel. The most prominent of these organists were Froberger, Kerl, Pachelbel, Reinken, and Buxtehude. The latter was born in 1669, and died in 1707. He was the model of the young Sebastian Bach, who imitated his style in his early organ composition. These German masters developed the forms which their Italian predecessors originated, — the fantasia, toccata, fugue, etc. They were thorough masters of the fugal style. We owe to them the art of choral variations (*Choral-vorspiele*) for the organ, in which the German chorals are used as themes for elaborate contrapuntal treatment. Sebastian Bach is the highest representative of this style.

The origin of keyed string instruments — the clavichord, spinet, harpsichord, and virginal — may be traced back to the old monochord and psalter of the Middle Ages. The original monochord is said to have been invented by Pythagoras in the sixth century B.C., though, according to Lepsius, its principle was used twenty-four hundred years before by the Egyptians. It was used by the ancient Greeks to measure the relations of the intervals of sound, and consisted of a sounding board on which was stretched a single string, with a shifting bridge. In the Middle Ages a number of strings were used. It was found more convenient to dispense with the shifting bridges, and at the points of division to adjust fixed bridges, raised by an apparatus resembling the keys of the organ, to press the strings and produce the required tones. This led ultimately to the invention of the clavichord, which, together with the spinet, played a great rôle in the seventeenth and eighteenth centuries, before the invention of the pianoforte. Keyed string instruments

In M. Steinert's admirable treatise on "Keyed and Stringed Instruments" (published by C. F. Tretbar, New York) there is a picture of a clavichord of the fifteenth century (see page 15). This instrument looks like a small square piano. It has no legs, and is placed on a table when played upon. It can be easily carried about. Mr. Steinert says, "In this instrument a small bit of brass, called a tangent, is fastened to the back end of the key, and, when raised by pressing the key, strikes the string and divides it, thus producing at the same time tone and pitch. This instrument has more keys than strings, and three different tones are produced upon each set of strings ; a system which is called in German *gebunden*, Clavichord and in English, fretted." In the eighteenth century Faber constructed clavichords which provided the semitones with their own strings, and were called *bundfrei* (string-free), to distinguish them from the *gebunden* or fretted system. Hitherto the instrument had had strings for the lower or natural tones, the semitones on the upper keys being tangents directed toward the strings of the lower. Thus C$\sharp$ was obtained by striking the C string at a shorter length.

The clavichord was the favorite instrument of Sebastian Bach. His great work, forty-eight preludes and fugues, is named the "Well-Tempered Clavichord." Mozart is said to have used the clavichord in composing his "Magic Flute."

Spinet, harpsi-chord, or virginal

From the psaltery sprang the spinet, also called harpsichord and virginal. The ancient psaltery, in triangular, square, curved, or harplike form, was carried by means of a ribbon round the neck, or when used, was placed on some piece of furniture. Its strings were operated by means of a plectrum, fastened by rings to the hand of the performer. It was the prototype of the spinet. It is not absolutely known when either the spinet or clavichord was invented, but it is surmised that they came into use during the second half of the fourteenth century.

The spinet has the same shape as the clavichord, but it uses plectra, or jacks, instead of tangents. "The jack action is derived from the psaltery plectrum. All instruments of the spinet, harpsichord, virginal, and clavicembalo family were on the plectrum principle. The strings were set in vibration by points of a quill or hard leather, elevated on wooden uprights, known as jacks, and twitching or plucking them as the depression of the keys caused the points to pass upward." Shakespeare refers to the spinet in Sonnet 128 :

> How oft, when thou, my music, music play'st
> Upon that blessed wood whose motion sounds
> With thy sweet fingers, when thou gently sway'st
> The wiry concord that mine ear confounds,

Do I envy those jacks that nimble leap .
To kiss the tender inward of thy hand,
Whilst my poor lips, which should that harvest reap,
At the wood's boldness by thee blushing stand !

There were three different shapes of jack instruments common in the sixteenth, seventeenth, and eighteenth centuries, — the spinet, or virginal, of oblong rectangular form ; the harpsichord, of trapeze form ; and the upright harpsichord, or clavicytherium. The harpsichord resembled the modern grand piano in shape. It had a compass of four to five octaves. The number of separate strings to each key varied from one to four, and sometimes included one tuned an octave or two above the others. Some harpsichords had two separate keyboards, one for soft effects, the other for loud. These large harpsichords were the most powerful of the jack instruments. In the eighteenth century the harpsichord was used in the orchestra for dramatic accompaniment, especially in recitatives, and in filling out the harmonies of the orchestra. The accompanist played from a figured bass. The conductor usually directed from his seat at a harpsichord in front, while the accompanist sat at a harpsichord behind the players. The harpsichord had a stronger and more brilliant tone than the clavichord, but was inferior to it in producing gradations of tone, — *crescendo*, *diminuendo*, etc. In power of expression the clavichord was superior. It had a sweet, silvery quality of tone, charmingly hesitating and tremulous.

It is an error to suppose that the piano was derived chiefly Pianoforte from the jack or tangent instruments. The dulcimer is the prototype of the piano, just as the monochord is that of the clavichord, and the psaltery of the spinet and harpsichord. The dulcimer and psaltery were nearly alike. They differed only in the manner of playing them. The strings of the psaltery were set in vibration by means of a plectrum, whereas the strings of the dulcimer were struck by small hammers held in the hands of the performer. The dynamic

effects of loud and soft could be produced by means of hammers, which was not possible with the plectrum or jack, and
this led to the invention of a keyboard applied to the dulcimer.
The new instrument, known since 1711, was called by its inventor pianoforte, and has retained this name ever since. The
Germans called it hammerclavier. The inventor was Cristo-
fori, born in 1653 at Parma. Sebastian Bach in 1737, and
Mozart in 1777, acknowledged the value of the invention of
the pianoforte, but it was not until toward the end of the
eighteenth century that the pianoforte fairly superseded
the older class of keyed instruments. Haydn, Mozart, and
Beethoven wrote for the piano, although they often played on
the clavichord in their younger days. With Beethoven the
pianoforte began its modern career. In his time the grand
piano had acquired its prominent features, though it has been
greatly improved since. There is a vast difference between
Beethoven's Broadwood grand and the modern grand.

Clavichord
masters
The earliest school of clavichord players and composers
was the English, in the time of Queen Elizabeth. I have
already given an account of Byrd, Dr. Bull, Orlando Gibbons,
and others. Great progress was made by the French masters
in the seventeenth and eighteenth centuries. Lully wrote
some pleasing compositions for the clavichord, and the Couperin family was particularly distinguished as clavichord composers. There were three brothers, Louis, François, and
Charles, but François Couperin, the son of Charles, excelled
them all. He was born in Paris in 1668 and died in 1733.
The style of these French composers is distinguished for its
elegance, finish, and expression. We owe many graceful adornments of style to them, but their use of turns, grace notes,
and trills is excessive. It reminds us of the wigs, queues, and
shoe buckles of the *ancien régime*. These composers gave
romantic and fanciful titles to their pieces. They are the first
so-called programme composers. Some of the titles are " La
Favorite," " La Ténébreuse," " La Bandoline," " La Bersan,"

" Le Reveil-Matin," " Les Papillons," etc. Another French clavichordist of the same school was Chambonnières (1620–1670), also the famous dramatic composer, Rameau, who excelled even Couperin. Among his charming pieces may be mentioned his " Deux Minuets," " L'Égyptienne," " La Poule," " La Timide," " Musette en Rondeau," etc.

Clavichord music was cultivated in Italy and Germany during the seventeenth century. The organists were generally skillful performers on this instrument. Froberger and Muffat, in Germany, and Alessandro Scarlatti and his son Domenico, in Italy, were famous clavichordists.

In the early stages of clavichord playing the application of the fingers to the keyboard was singularly restricted. We read that in 1571 the following fingering was used for the scale of F major:

	f	g	a	b	c	d	e	f	g	a	b	a	g	f	e	d	c
Right hand	1	2	1	2	1	2	1	2	1	2	3	2	1	2	1	2	1
Left hand	3	2	1	0	3	2	1	0	3	2	1	2	1	2	1	2	3

Systems of fingering

Praetorius says it does not matter at all what kind of fingering is used, and we may even use the nose if only we make everything sound clear and pleasing to the ear. Mattheson as late as 1735 used only four fingers in the scale of C major. He said it does not matter whether we use two, three, four, or five fingers in playing. What the player should do with his thumbs remained unsettled before the time of Scarlatti and Bach. Emanuel Bach declared that the thumbs of our forefathers seemed often to be in the way; they had too many fingers apparently.

The clavier suite was cultivated particularly by the French masters of the seventeenth and eighteenth centuries. It consists of a series of dance movements, generally all in one key, which contrast with each other more or less in rhythm and tempo. Most of the dances which were thus applied to the clavichord have long since become obsolete. Originally they were dances of the court or of the people. The favorite

The clavier suite

dances were the allemande, bourrée, anglaise, bransle, courante, gavotte, hornpipe, chaconne, giga (or gigue), minuet, sarabande, passacaglia, passepied, rigadon, polonaise, siciliano, etc. It was very natural to select a number of these dances and group them together as a series or suite of pieces. The suite form was used also in chamber and orchestral music even before its application to the clavichord. Some of the suites had an opening movement not in dance form, — an overture, prelude, toccata, etc. This is the case with the English suites of Bach. The partita was a kind of suite not composed exclusively of dances. The suite was sometimes called the *sonata da camera* and *sonata dei balleti*, to distinguish it from the *sonata da chiesa*, or sonata in general. The modern sonata is not derived from the suite directly. The name "sonata," now of such definite meaning, was at first represented by short Venetian organ pieces. In the seventeenth century Covelli, the Italian violinist, composed sonatas for violins and bass in several movements. The fugal style predominated, though dances were introduced. Purcell and Biber composed similar sonatas. The first application of the name to a solo for clavier was made by Johann Kuhnau, cantor of the St. Thomas School at Leipzig (1701–1722).

One of the greatest masters of the clavichord was Domenico Scarlatti (1683–1757). He carried clavier technic to a high point of brilliancy, and he was surpassed only by Emanuel and Sebastian Bach. Scarlatti's so-called sonatas are short, difficult, single movements, which resemble the modern étude in form rather than the sonata, — they are homophonous in style rather than fugal. One of his most famous compositions is the "Cat's Fugue," which is often played nowadays in the concert room. I shall consider Emanuel and Sebastian Bach as clavichord masters in later chapters.

Bowed stringed instruments The origin of the bowed stringed instruments is uncertain. They were not used by the ancient Greeks and Romans. Nero did not play the fiddle at the burning of Rome. Bowed instruments were in use in very ancient times in the East. The rebab and ravanastram were ancient Eastern bowed instruments. The crwth, or crowd, is one of the oldest bowed stringed instruments, and it is said to have come from India. It was used in Wales long before the thirteenth century. Similar to the crwth were the rebec, geige, rotte, etc. In the time of the troubadours an instrument appeared in southern France called the vielle, or viola. It was a hurdy-gurdy and viol in one, for the same instrument was played by plucking or bowing the strings, and sometimes by rubbing them with a wheel. Later the viola became a separate bowed instrument. In the fifteenth century viols were made in different sizes to correspond with the soprano, alto, tenor, and bass voices. There were two classes of viols, — viola da gamba and viola da braccio. In the course of the sixteenth century the art of viola making advanced greatly under masters like Gasparo di Salò and Andrea Amati. During the fifteenth and sixteenth centuries there were six kinds of viola da gamba (leg viol), three for the bass, and one each for tenor, alto, and soprano, all with frets on the finger board. The most common viola da gamba was the tenor, from which the modern violoncello was derived. It had five, six, or seven strings, tuned as follows :

Viola da gamba

There were also seven kinds of viola da braccio (arm viol), named great quint bass, bass, and tenor, and four smaller ones. Our modern violin is derived from the largest of these four smaller instruments. It bore several names (descant-viol, violetta, rebecchino, violino). The smallest of the violas was called pocchetto, and had three strings, tuned as follows:

Viola da braccio

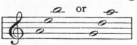

Other instruments belonging to the class of the viola da gamba were the viola bastarda, lira da gamba (a large bass instrument with twelve to fourteen strings) lira barbarina, and viola di bordone, or baryton. The latter had five to seven strings for the bow to play upon, and as many as twenty-four metal strings under the neck, played on by the thumb, "pizzicato." Haydn composed a large number of pieces for the baryton, as it was the favorite instrument of his patron, Prince Esterhazy.

Viola d'amore

The viola d'amore, or viole d'amour (love viol), is one of the best instruments of its class, and has a delicate, silvery quality of tone. It is rather larger than the modern viola. "It has seven catgut strings, the three lowest of which, like the C and G strings of the viola, are wound with silver wire. Below the neck and passing through the bridge, are seven more strings of metal, tuned in unison with the others, so as to vibrate sympathetically with them, giving a second resonance to the tone, full of sweetness and mystery." [1] The modern way of tuning the instrument is in thirds and fourths, as follows :

The viola pomposa was a large viola invented by Sebastian Bach, wherewith to execute his difficult basses, but it was discarded for the violoncello, and passed out of use.

Violin makers

The art of violin and viola making was greatly advanced in the sixteenth century under Gasparo di Salò, Maggini, and others at Brescia. Some of their instruments are highly prized nowadays. Ole Bull's favorite solo violin was a Gasparo di Salò. De Bériot played on a Maggini. The double basses of Maggini are still valued for practical use. However, the perfect model was not yet evolved ; it required the life work

[1] See Berlioz, Instrumentation, IV.

of successive men of genius to bring about this result. The early Italian violins are too small, the violas are too large. Cremona was destined to become the center of this wonderful evolution, under the famous Amati, Guarneri, and Stradivari makers.

The Amati family are generally considered as the founders of the Cremona school. Andrea, the eldest (1520–1577), may have been a pupil of Di Salò. His instruments have a clear and silvery tone, but are not powerful, owing to their small size. His sons Antonio and Geronimo worked much in their father's style. Nicolò (1596–1684), son of Geronimo, was the last and most eminent of the Amati family. He improved the model; the proportions of the instrument are better as regards thickness of wood and elevation of back and belly. The tone, therefore, is stronger and equally pure and clear in comparison with the earlier violins. He made also some larger violins, called grand Amatis, which are highly prized as well as priced.

The Amati family

"The violins of the Amati," says Paul David, "are the link between the Brescia school and those masters who brought the art of violin making to its greatest perfection, Antonio Stradivari and Joseph Guarneri. The tone of Di Salò's and Maggini's violins is powerful, but has a veiled character." Nicolò Amati's violins have a clearer tone, but smaller. Their successors perfected the model and tone of the instrument, and since their day there have been no improvements, even in trifling details. The Stradivari violins are still the perfect model.

The Guarneri family of violin makers were (1) Andrea, who worked with Stradivari in the workshop of Nicolò Amati, and developed an entirely original style from his master's model; (2) Giuseppe, son of Andrea, who also developed a style of his own; (3) Pietro, likewise a son of Andrea, commonly called Peter of Cremona, whose instruments are entirely different from those of his father and brother;

The Guarneri family

(4) Pietro, known as Peter of Venice, grandson of Andrea, whose violins have a rich, pure tone; (5) Giuseppe (Joseph), a nephew of Andrea, called del Gesù, from the I. H. S. added to his labels. He is the greatest maker of his family, and his only rival is Antonio Stradivari. Paganini's favorite instrument was a Joseph Guarneri, which is now in the museum at Genoa. The value of the best Joseph violins is probably twenty-five hundred dollars or more.

Antonio Stradivari

Antonio Stradivari (1649–1737), the greatest of violin makers, was a pupil of Nicolò Amati. During his long life he gradually improved the instrument in all its details. His productivity was remarkable; more than a thousand of his later instruments are still in existence. He also made a large number of violas, cellos, and basses, besides lutes, guitars, mandolins, theorbos, etc. His best violins excel all others in nobility and fullness of tone, and in beauty and durability. His perfect model has been copied by most violin makers to the present day; even the cheap fiddles we see in shop windows are copies of the Stradivari model. The superiority of the Cremona violins was not fully appreciated before the nineteenth century, if we judge by the low prices of the eighteenth century. A London dealer was not able to dispose of his Strads at the insignificant price of four pounds apiece! Now the best sometimes bring no less than ten thousand dollars.

Perfection of the bow

It is a singular fact that Stradivari and the other great makers who perfected the violin should not have devoted their genius to the perfection of the bow, which is just as important as the instrument itself; for without the perfect bow the highest technic, beauty of tone, and musical expression cannot be attained. It was reserved for François Tourte (1747–1835) to perfect the bow. The picture of the violin bow in Leopold Mozart's "violin school" gives one a vivid idea of the clumsy character of the old bow. Before Tourte's time the modern effects of staccato were quite impossible, and the dynamic effects of *piano, forte, crescendo,* and *diminuendo* were very limited. There must have been a roughness in tone and execution we should hardly tolerate nowadays. Tourte's improvements in the bow were made after 1775. Notwithstanding the imperfect bow prior to this date, famous violinists had arisen in Italy and Germany, who advanced the art of violin playing to a considerable extent, and prepared the way for great violinists like Viotti, Paganini, and others of the nineteenth century, who availed themselves of the perfected bow, and were thus able to carry virtuosity to a great height.

Although violin playing was practised in a rude manner as early as the thirteenth century, it was not until the middle of the sixteenth century that the domination of the lute was broken down. The earliest known composition for solo violin is a Romanesca by Marini, published in 1620. A marked improvement in violin composition was shown in the works of Farina, Merula, and Ucellini, written before the middle of the seventeenth century. During this period the rudiments of the classical violin sonata appeared. Its form consisted of alternate slow and quick movements. Among the earliest are the sonatas of Fontana and Neri. The so-called sinfonia and canzone, of similar form, were merged into the sonata about 1650, and sonata was henceforth the name of violin compositions with several movements. Neri made the distinction between *sonata da chiesa* (church sonata) and *sonata da camara* (chamber sonata). The former was in three or four movements : first, a slow prelude followed by an allegro in fugal style ; second, a slow movement ; third, a brilliant finale. The sonata da camera at that time was in reality a suite of dances, — allemande, sarabande, gigue, etc. The first distinguished master of the chamber sonata was Vitali (1644–1692). He was followed by Torelli (1657–1716), who originated the violin concerto, accompanied by string orchestra. But the most eminent violin master of the seventeenth century

Violin masters

was Arcangelo Corelli (1653–1713). He improved the technic of the instrument, and gave a classical style to the art of composition. His sonatas for one or more violins with bass served as models to his successors. They have conciseness and logical structure; his harmonies and modulations are in good taste; pathos, expression, and vivacity are the main characteristics of his music. He did not use the highest positions of the instrument. He was looked upon as the father of true violin playing by his contemporaries and followers. The violin sonatas by Purcell and Biber, the German composer, were suggested no doubt by those of Corelli, who is rightly considered as the founder of the classical chamber style.

The Venetian master Vivaldi (died 1743), though not so eminent as Corelli, exercised a decided influence on the further development of the concerto form. He gave the solo violin part more brilliancy, and improved the orchestration. Veracini (1685–1750), the Florentine violinist, was distinguished for his execution and passionate fire. His violin sonatas are noble in style and show harmonic and melodic originality. He used double stops and improved the bowing. He had a strong influence on Tartini.

Giuseppe Tartini (1692–1770), the greatest violin virtuoso before Paganini, was not only one of the most remarkable violinists who ever lived but a distinguished composer and writer on musical acoustical effects. He had a great command of the finger board and bow, and overcame all difficulties of execution with apparent ease. He had a fine tone, perfect intonation in double stops, and his trills and double trills were finished and brilliant. He played with deep feeling and expression. He used a longer bow than Corelli, and used it with greater skill and freedom. He was a remarkable teacher. His most prominent pupils were Nardini, Bini, Graun, Ferrari, and Manfredi. As a composer he surpassed his models, Corelli and Vivaldi. His sonatas and concertos are conceived in a freer and larger form; his melodies are broader and more expressive, and his harmonies and modulations are richer and more varied; his slow movements are passionate and emotional, and his quick movements are fiery and characteristic, being impressed with his own peculiar individuality. In this respect he reminds us of Paganini, the most extraordinary virtuoso who ever lived. Tartini's most famous work is the sonata called the "Devil's Trill," which holds a place among the most famous violin pieces in the modern repertory. His published compositions consist of over fifty sonatas and eighteen concertos with accompaniment of the string orchestra. Besides these there exist in manuscript forty-eight sonatas and one hundred and twenty-seven concertos. With Tartini "the exclusive classical Italian school of violin playing reached its culmination, and the pupils of Corelli and Tartini form the connecting link between that school and the schools of Germany and France." *[Tartini's compositions]*

Somis, Giardini, Lulli, and Pugnani were contemporaries of Tartini. Pugnani (1727–1803) was the teacher of Viotti (1753–1824), the founder of the modern Franco-Belgian school. The most prominent representatives of Italian violin playing directly after Tartini were Geminiani, Nardini, and Locatelli. Geminiani was the first to publish a "violin school" of any importance, but Leopold Mozart, the father of the illustrious composer, published a "violin school" a few years later, which ranks higher than his. Pietro Locatelli (1693–1764) was a pupil of Corelli. He was remarkable for his technic. In his sonatas and concertos he followed in the footsteps of his teacher. They are composed in a serious vein. His caprices and études, on the other hand, have little value except as experiments in developing execution. He has been called the great-grandfather of our modern "Finger-heroes." His caprice, "Le Labyrinthe," is a famous piece of eccentric execution, which only virtuosos are able to vanquish. *[Locatelli]*

Nicolò Paganini (1784–1840), the most noted of violin virtuosos, exercised a world-wide influence which has lasted to the present day. He was the genius *par excellence* of the violin. The story of the brilliant public career of this extraordinary man forms one of the most interesting chapters in the history of music. The wonderful effect of his playing did not depend on the perfection of his technic and mere *tours de force*, but on his flights of pure genius, which defied description. As soon as he began to play, the audience was spellbound. "There was in him — though certainly not the evil spirit suspected by the superstitious — a demonic element which irresistibly took hold of those who came within his sphere." He possessed in the highest degree originality and character. Though his tone was not powerful, its singing quality was intensely expressive and thrilling. "He made a great use of sliding his fingers along the strings — sometimes producing a most beautiful, at other times a most laughable, effect." He was fond of tricks and surprises; sometimes he made sounds "like the mewlings of an expiring cat." He made free use of flageolet tones and tremolo. "The main technical

features of Paganini's playing were an unfailing intonation, a lightning-like rapidity on the finger board and with the bow, and a command of double-stops, harmonics, and double-harmonics hardly equaled by any one before him or after him. He also produced most peculiar effects, which for a long time puzzled all violinists, by tuning his violin in different ways." He produced his staccato by striking the bow violently on the string and letting it spring upwards. He also made frequent use of pizzicato passages for the left hand. His compositions show originality, though for the most part they are now old-fashioned. His twenty-four caprices "Perpetual Motion" and the rondo "La Clochette" are still favorites. Schumann and Liszt transcribed the caprices for piano. Brahms composed twenty-eight variations on a theme of Paganini. The list of his works embraces two concertos, sets of variations, including

the " Carnival of Venice," caprices, sonatas for violin and guitar, and three quartets for violin, viola, guitar, and violoncello.

Germany followed in the path of the Italian masters of the German
violin. The most prominent German violin masters of the violin
masters
time of Corelli were Furchheim, Baltzar, Walther, and Biber.
Franz Heinrich Biber (died 1698) was a composer and violinist of high merit. He had great warmth of feeling and
considerable technic, as his works show. His sonatas for
violins and bass compare favorably with Corelli's. Many of
the pupils of Corelli and Tartini entered into the service of
German princes and exercised an influence on native talent.
A number of German violin masters arose in the eighteenth century, the most noted of whom are Pisendel, Graun, Benda,
Stamitz, Cannabich, and Holzbauer. The three last-named
masters were connected with the celebrated orchestra at
Mannheim, which was perhaps the foremost in Europe about
the middle of the century.

Although violin playing was practised in France at a very
early date, it was very elemental until the advent of Lully.
Baptiste Anet (c. 1700) was the first French violinist of note ;
he was the pupil of Corelli. He was greatly excelled, however,
by Jean Marie Leclair (1697–1764), also a pupil of Corelli.
His compositions rival those of the best Italian masters of his
time. They are characterized by vivacity, grace, and charm,
and often express seriousness and deep feeling. Other French
violinists of the eighteenth century were Pagin, Lahoussaye,
Berthaume, Gaviniés, and Boucher.

Giovanni Battista Viotti (1753–1824) marks a new era in Viotti
French violin playing. He was an Italian by birth, and a
pupil of Pugnani. He made his first appearance in Paris in
1782, and was acknowledged as the greatest living violinist.
He lived in Paris for a number of years, and his playing and
teaching exercised a potent influence on French and German
violinists. His most celebrated pupils were Rode and Baillot.
He is looked upon as the founder of the Franco-Belgian

school, which produced some of the greatest modern violinists — De Bériot, Vieuxtemps, Wieniawski, Sarasate, and others. Viotti ranks among the foremost violinists. He was one of the first to extend the classical sonata form to the violin concerto. He composed twenty-nine concertos, twenty-one string quartets, twenty-one string trios, fifty-one violin duets, eighteen violin sonatas, etc. The study of some of his concertos still forms a part of the regular training for students of the violin. His "Concerto in A Minor" is sometimes played in the concert room, but his works are for the most part antiquated.

The most eminent German violin masters of the nineteenth century were Spohr, Ferdinand David, Boehm, Ernst, Hellmesberger, Joachim, Ferdinand Laub, Lipinski, and Molique. Ole Bull belonged to no school. He was a player of decided originality and of great popularity, but was not free from a certain charlatanism, and exerted no influence on musical style.

The lute   During the sixteenth and seventeenth centuries the lute was a favorite instrument, and was in the hands of all artists and dilettanti. Its literature was enormous and widespread. Originally it had only four strings, but later as many as fourteen on the finger board, with frets, while from a second neck beside the finger board ten more strings were stretched. These strings were not shortened by the fingers, and had to be tuned over again every time the key changed. It was said that if a lute player lived to be eighty years old, sixty of them would have been spent in tuning his instrument. The theorbo, chitarrone, and Roman theorbo were large lutes which were used in the early opera as thorough-bass instruments to accompany the recitative, etc.

Wind instruments of the sixteenth and seventeenth centuries   The regal, positive, and organo di legno were small portable organs used in the early opera. There were two classes of flutes — flûtes à bec (or block flutes) and traverse flutes. The former had the mouthpiece at the end of the instrument, like the clarinet; the latter was played like the modern flute, sideways, with the lips applied to an embouchure. There were no less than eight sizes of block flutes, ranging from bass to soprano.

The cornetto was a wind instrument with a wooden mouth-piece, and had a hard but clear quality of tone. Its range was from a to g³. It was used in some of the church music of Gabrieli, and had a place in the orchestra till near the middle of the eighteenth century, when it entirely disappeared.

The fagotto or bassoon family of double-reed instruments were numerous. At first they were not played directly by the lips, as the mouthpiece was inclosed in a bag; in fact they were bagpipes, like the schalm, shawm, or musette. The shawm is said to have cackled like a goose. The oldest class of these instruments, called the pommer or bombardon, was in various sizes from bass to soprano. Later the bag was discarded and the bassoon was played by holding the double reed in the mouth, as nowadays. The oboe was derived from the shawm. It appeared in various sizes about 1700. The clarinet was invented in 1700, but did not find a permanent place in the orchestra until Mozart's later years (1791). The clarinet is a single-reed instrument, with an ebony mouth-piece. Its bore is different from that of the oboe, and this difference, combined with the single reed, accounts for its characteristic tone quality. The reed instruments

The trombone assumed its present modern appearance and tone characteristics during the sixteenth century. The trumpet is one of the most ancient instruments, familiar to the Jews, and often mentioned in the Bible. Rome adopted the trumpet under the name of "tuba" or "lituus." From the large-bored tuba sprang the bugle, serpent, horn, cornet, etc. The lituus was a small-bored cylindrical trumpet, from which came the trombone.

The horn (French horn, Waldhorn) was used originally to give signals in hunting. It was introduced into the orchestra before the end of the seventeenth century, and in the early years of the eighteenth century both Handel and Bach made The horn use of it. Gossec, in 1757, was the first French composer to employ horns. Gluck was the first dramatic master to produce tragic and thrilling effects by certain motives for the solo horn. Since his day the horns have played an important and characteristic part in the modern orchestra.

Orchestra of the time of Monteverde   The orchestra in the sixteenth century was in its infancy. It hardly deserved the name before the time of Monteverde. In a ballet performed in 1581 mention is made of oboes, flutes, cornets, trombones, viole da gamba, lutes, harps, flageolets, and violins. In the oratorio " L'anima e il corpo" by Cavalieri, performed in 1600, the orchestra consisted of a double lyre (or viole da gamba), a double guitar (or bass lute), a harpsichord, and two flutes. Monteverde, in his opera "Orfeo," employed an orchestra consisting of ten tenor viols, two bass viols, two little French violins, two viole da gamba, two harpsichords, one double harp, two large guitars, two organs of wood, one regal, two cornetti, one clarion, three trumpets with mutes, and four trombones. Monteverde made various combinations of these instruments to characterize the dramatic personalities. We owe the tremolo of the strings to him. The violin now gained its leading place in the orchestra. Cavalli, in 1649, accompanied an aria with two violins and bass. Scarlatti, in 1676, used a double orchestra consisting, first, of two solo violins and violoncellos; second, a large body of accompanying violins, tenors and basses. In Scarlatti's time the string band — first and second violins, viola, violoncello, and contrabass — was organized as nowadays, and constituted the real body of the orchestra. The wind instruments were accessory, and were available for giving variety of tone color and effect.

Orchestra of Bach and Handel   The wind instruments at that time were flutes, bassoons, oboes, horns, trumpets, and trombones; kettledrums were also used. After the middle of the eighteenth century the clarinets were added. The solo trumpet played an important rôle in the scores of Handel and Bach. It was then a high soprano instrument and capable of florid execution. Handel used an excessive number of oboes, and wrote passages for them quite in the style of the violin. He did not seem to appreciate their real character. Bach, on the other hand, composed some beautiful, pathetic, cantabile solos for the oboe, which express the true nature and function of this lyric instrument. He used also the oboe di caccia, which is a tenor bassoon, so to speak, and not to be confounded with the English horn, which is a tenor oboe. Bach's ideal of an orchestra was two or three first violins and as many second, two first and two second viols, two violoncellos, one double-bass, two or three oboes, one or two bassoons, three trumpets, and one pair of kettledrums. This limited number of strings was entirely inadequate to balance the wind instruments.

This orchestra was intended to coöperate with a choir of at least twelve singers! This small proportion of voices was characteristic of most choirs in those days. Haydn and Mozart are the founders of the art of modern orchestration, but in their early scores they employed few wind instruments. Haydn's first symphony is for strings, two oboes, and two horns. In their later orchestral works they used generally two flutes, two oboes, two bassoons, two horns, two trumpets and kettledrums, and sometimes clarinets and trombones. Beethoven's combination of wind instruments was about the same. Since his time the orchestra has increased in size and efficiency, but remains the same in its chief features; the string band is larger, and new wind instruments have been added.

The modern orchestra

In the course of the development of instrumental accompaniment in connection with the opera in the seventeenth century, the idea of independent concerted instrumental music was conceived; thus arose the concerto and symphony in three contrasted movements, suggested by the so-called Italian overture. Sammartini (born 1700) was one of the first to promote the symphony, but it was reserved for Emanuel Bach and Haydn to give it a classical form.

CHAPTER XVIII

HANDEL AND BACH — HAYDN

During the first half of the eighteenth century Italian masters reigned supreme; yet the musical scepter was destined to pass from their hands through the gigantic work achieved by Handel and Bach. Under their mighty genius the foundations were laid for the ultimate supremacy of Germany.

George
Frederick
Handel

George Frederick Handel was born at Halle on the twenty-third of February, 1685 (about four weeks before the birth of Bach). Handel's father was a surgeon, with the title of Kammerdiener. At a very early age the son showed a passionate love of music ; so much so that his father opposed his cultivation of the art. At the age of eight years the attention of the prince of Weissenfels was drawn to the boy's great talent, and he persuaded the father to withdraw his opposition, and to provide regular musical instruction for his son. He now became the pupil of Zachau, the learned cathedral organist, who gave him a thorough training in organ playing and counterpoint. Handel's remarkable skill was shown when he was only twelve years of age, on the occasion of his visit to Berlin, where he was introduced at court. The Italian composers, Bononcini and Ariosti, were favorites at court, and the latter recognized young Handel's remarkable talent. Bononcini ignored him at first, and then tried to puzzle him with the difficult task of thorough-bass reading, but Handel acquitted himself well. Years later, when Handel was in his maturity, he met Bononcini as a rival in London in the field of opera, and vanquished him. Handel's esteem for his father's wish that he should study law was evinced after his father's death (1697), by having his name entered at the university for five years, but at the same time he continued his musical studies and became organist at one of the churches of his native town.   His absorption in music, however, finally led him to abandon the study of law and to leave home at the age of eighteen to seek his fortune as a professional musician.

He directed his steps first to Hamburg, where he remained from 1703 to 1706, and then set out for Italy. His four years' stay in Italy was spent with the utmost advantage to his musical development. On his return to his native land he went to Hanover, where he made the acquaintance of Steffani, the director of music at the court, whose chamber duets served as a model for his own. In 1710 he was appointed Steffani's successor at Hanover, but was restless in this narrow sphere ; he visited England several times, and finally remained there altogether. The duke of Chandos, who lived in regal grandeur at Cannons, engaged Handel in 1717 as his chapelmaster. A number of grand anthems, his first oratorio "Esther," and the lovely pastoral "Acis and Galatea" were the fruits of the three years of service to this nobleman. In 1720 the new opera house was established at the Haymarket by a company of leading noblemen, under the name of the "Royal Academy of Music," and Handel was engaged as composer and director of music. The next twenty years were very eventful in the life of the composer. During this period of his connection with the Italian opera he entered on an heroic struggle with the cabal of Italian singers, who were backed by the whole nobility. At the outset all went harmoniously and gloriously ; Chrysander calls these first eight years "the golden time." During this epoch Handel wrote twelve operas ; then came in 1728 the popular English "Beggar's Opera" and ballad plays, which gave a new turn to the public taste, and emptied the benches of the Italian opera. This led to a new opera academy, and Handel went to Italy to engage singers.

Director of music at the Haymarket

In 1732 Handel's first oratorio " Esther " was performed
on the stage with action, followed in the next year by his
" Deborah." This was a step toward breaking the chains
which the Italians had already imposed upon him. Now
succeeded a period of strife in which Handel undertook to
govern the singers; but they were incorrigible, and rose in
rebellion. Supported by the nobility, they set up an opera
in opposition to Handel, who soon found himself deserted by
the public and was obliged to carry on an unequal contest.
At last he decided to give up the opera; he retired from the
stage in 1737, ruined in purse and broken in health; but in
abandoning this degenerate field to his enemies he was destined
to achieve an honorable triumph in a new field of art, and
through his former trials he came to be the means of developing the oratorio to the highest point, and also of enriching
the lives of untold generations of men, as well as to be the
direct benefactor of the poor and needy of his day. He devoted himself during the remainder of his life to the composition and performance of his unequaled oratorios, and died
on the fourteenth of April, 1759.

Sebastian Bach was born at Eisenbach on the twenty-first
of March, 1685, and was consequently twenty-seven days
younger than his contemporary. His family before him had
been for generations distinguished for their musical talent,
and one has only to consult the genealogical table to marvel
at the number of musicians in the Bach family, — descendants
of Hans and Veit Bach, who lived in the second half of the
sixteenth century. Indeed, there is no second case on record
of a particular artistic talent or faculty running through so
many generations and branches of one family. Sebastian was
a son of the court musician Johann Ambrosius Bach. On the
death of his father, which occurred in Sebastian's childhood,
he lived with one of his older brothers, Johann Christoph
Bach, organist at Ohrdruff, and received his first musical
instruction from him. His brother appears to have been

overstrict with him. It is related that Sebastian was forbidden
to use a book of organ and harpsichord pieces which were
the object of his desires. But he managed to reach through
the lattice of the bookcase where the pieces were locked up,
and spent six months in copying them out secretly on moonlight nights, whereby he is supposed to have hurt his eyes,
and caused the blindness with which he was afflicted in his
later days. His brother discovered him in this and was mean
enough to take away the copy he had so patiently transcribed.

In his boyhood he possessed a fine soprano voice, and sang   Positions
in the choir of the St. Michael's School at Lüneburg, where   held by
he was pursuing his education at the gymnasium. In 1703   Bach
he was appointed court musician at Weimar, and occupied
successively the position of organist at Arnstadt, Mühlhausen,
and Weimar, and the office of chapelmaster to the duke of
Anhalt-Cöthen, until his call to Leipzig in 1723, on the death
of Kuhnau, whom he succeeded as cantor and director of
music at the St. Thomas School. He held this honorable
office until his death.

Bach led a very quiet, uneventful life. He was hardly ever
absent from his post, except now and then in response to the
invitation of some princely patron. In his younger days he
was invited to Dresden to meet the celebrated French organist
Marchand in a trial of skill. The company was assembled,
Bach was ready, but the Frenchman did not make his appearance ; he had prudently left Dresden by the early morning
post. A few years before Bach's death he received a pressing
invitation from Frederick the Great to visit him at Potsdam.
On Bach's arrival he was ushered into the king's presence
without having time even to dust his coat. His majesty was
so desirous of meeting the great musician that after a cordial
reception he was taken from room to room by the king to try
his Silbermann pianofortes. Frederick gave him the theme
of a fugue to improvise upon, which he did in a masterly
manner to the astonishment of the listeners ; on his return

home Bach wrought out a number of remarkable movements on this theme which he engraved with his own hands and dedicated to the king, under the name of " Musical Offering." During his latter years Bach was afflicted with total blindness. He died on the twenty-eighth of July, 1750.

Lives of Handel and Bach contrasted

" Handel and Bach," says Rochlitz, " were born almost at the same moment and died in the ripe years of manhood. They were both Saxons, and were large, powerful men of iron constitution. Their eminent genius for music urged them irresistibly onward, and both acquired · in early life a strict and thorough knowledge of the theory and practice of music from distinguished organists. They both found a much more extended and elevated sphere, and became celebrated far and wide. They were honored by the mightiest princes of their age; but while they thankfully acknowledged these attentions of the great, they were not allured one hair's breadth from their unceasing activity in their calling. They both exercised their gifts in every noble form of composition, and, more than all else, dedicated their art to the pure and sublime themes of religion. As men, they were upright, straightforward, and firm, heart and soul, in the Christian faith. Although both were blind in their old age, they still continued to pursue their beloved calling to the last; and now they rest in peace and blessedness. They were but little understood by their contemporaries, though honored and respected; but now the world pays them universal homage. Yet with all these apparent similarities they were very unlike. Handel's restless, passionate spirit impelled him while still a youth to seek his fortune in the turmoil of the world, which he accepted as his lifelong field of action, whether it was to struggle or to love, to conquer or to maintain his rights. He sought to know everything that was uncommon in men, all that moves and commands them in art as well as life, without showing himself arbitrary, but winning much for the growth of his own mind and character.

He preferred to have intercourse with the mass of the people
among whom he lived, yet he moved freely among the great
who governed the people. He would allow neither the one
nor the other to govern him, however, though he was ever
willing to serve all classes faithfully. His courage never
deserted him ; he carried out his undertakings against the
most persistent and powerful opposition, and with many
joyful and painful experiences remained ever true and faithful
to his principles. In his maturer years he began to hold an
account with persons and things, and selected the path best
adapted to his whole nature, which he pursued to the end of
his days, and accomplished what no one before or since has
done. He was never married ; he died rich. His body rests
in Westminster Abbey among splendid monuments. His life
throughout was heroic !

" What a contrast to Bach ! From the time when Bach was
so fortunate as to receive the appointment of organist at Arnstadt, with an annual salary of seventy to eighty dollars, his
desires apparently were fulfilled. He sought for no higher
post, and only when a new one was offered him did he accept
it thankfully as the gift of Providence. In every new position
it was his only aspiration to do his duty faithfully, and accordingly he made his gifts serve his place ; so that as an organist he composed organ pieces ; as the Weimar chapelmaster,
psalms and sacred cantatas and chamber music ; and as the
musical director of the St. Thomas School, his great, polyphonic, difficult, and learned vocal works. Kings and princes
not infrequently commanded him to play to them. He did
their will modestly, and, fully satisfied, returned to his simple home. He must have known that he was the greatest
organ virtuoso in the world, and at that time a great master of this instrument was well rewarded. He was highly
esteemed in France, England, and Holland, but was never
known to express the wish of setting his foot on foreign soil.
He married young, brought up a whole colony of children,

Simplicity
of Bach's
character

died poor, and rested in the churchyard, no one knew where, until accidentally his bones were discovered near the St. Thomas Church. His life was patriarchal."

Corresponding contrast of style, form, and expression

These well-drawn contrasts in the character and worldly career of the two masters have a parallel in their works. We discern corresponding differences of style, form, and expression. We perceive in Handel's works the decided influence of his worldly career on his music. He unites three nationalities, so to speak; he is a German in his creative originality and learning, an Italian in his rare vocal style, and an Englishman in his clear, solid, and simple expression. Although he was a thoroughly trained musician before leaving his home at Halle, he learned much in Italy. He studied the best masters, Scarlatti, Steffani, and others, and formed his vocal style on their models. His long life in England made a still greater impression on his musical creations. Without sacrificing one iota of his principles as an artist in order to gain the popular ear, he was able to hide his learning and reserve his strength, and thus please the uncultivated and learned alike. He gave up as much as he could of skill and learning to reach all hearts and minds, and accomplish the difficult success of pleasing the many without offending the few. Like Mozart he was a universal master, although he did not exercise his genius in so many and diverse forms of the art.

Handel's long career as an opera composer served as an admirable school for his talents; and when, by free choice rather than by absolute force of circumstances, he set out on a much higher and more fruitful path, he was so well equipped that his triumphs were but the natural result of his former discipline. He founded his later works on the grand subjects of the Bible,—on its sacred text and historical record; not, however, in a narrow, literal sense, but in a broad, universal spirit for all mankind. His sincere religious faith and principles, his many trials, and his strength of character under trial rendered him fully worthy as a man, as well as artist, to create such works as " The Messiah " and " Israel in Egypt." These masterpieces are more than lyrical and dramatic ; they have a grand objective character, and are comparable to Greek tragedy or the great romantic tragedies of Shakespeare.

The operas of Handel are not musical dramas in the sense of the present day. The musical element predominates greatly over the dramatic action; the characters, as actors, are generally trivial and insipid. It was reserved for Gluck and Mozart to combine harmoniously the musical and dramatic elements. The former fulfilled the French ideal of a declamatory and musical play ; the latter created universal opera, in which French, Italian, and German styles and ideas were marvelously combined. Handel was content to avail himself of the conditions of the opera as he found them. He accepted the pedantic, conventional forms then in vogue, and sought only to beautify rather than to enlarge or transform them. As pure music his opera airs and pieces represent the highest artistic style of his period, and express clearly and definitely the characters that utter them ; but they demand no powerful dramatic action, for their subject-matter requires none. These are the very conditions of his oratorio solos. Each voice — soprano, contralto, tenor, or bass — is selected as the type of certain personal ‘characteristics, without suggesting any dramatic action on the part of the performer.

Of Handel's forty operas not one is on the modern stage, and we shall probably never witness their revival. Notwithstanding the long and furious opposition with which Handel had to contend during the twenty years of Italian opera in London, he was not defeated as an opera composer, but as an opera manager. He retired, broken in health but unconquerable in spirit. He had already succeeded beyond expectation in educating the English public to his style, and thus eventually it was prepared to appreciate his great work in the field of oratorio, which was, in fact, much more akin to the

Handel's oratorios

English mind. In the first place, the oratorios were sung in English, which was an immense advantage. Then again, the sacred subjects which he selected were more interesting to that pietistic age, which knew no middle ground but only extremes, —- either an orthodox belief or a total abandonment and frivolity. These characteristics were more or less reflected in the manners, literature, and drama of that period. Before the resignation of his position at the London Opera, even as early as 1732, he brought out his first oratorios, " Esther," " Deborah," and "Athalia " ; he had written his " Coronation Anthem," " Alexander's Feast," and the " Funeral Anthem." In 1737 he retired from the opera, and went abroad to Aix-la-Chapelle to try the baths for his health. His speedy cure appears almost miraculous ; in a few weeks he returned to England, fully restored, and ready to take up his work again with redoubled zeal. His productivity at this time was astonishing. In the summer of 1738 he composed the oratorios of " Saul " and " Israel in Egypt " in the incredibly short time of three months. Two months were given to " Saul," and on its completion he immediately went to work on " Israel," which he finished in twenty-eight days. In 1740 he composed " L'Allegro." But these works did not find immediate appreciation ; he had yet to live down personal spite and enmity.

" The Messiah " In the summer of 1741 he composed " The Messiah " in twenty-four days, and, seeing no prospect of success in London, he accepted an invitation to go to Dublin. He would fain try his fortune there, and see whether prejudice and hatred would follow him. This was the turning point in his career. " The Messiah " met with a glorious reception, and the composer was greeted everywhere with cordiality. Victory had perched on his banner, and on his return to London at the end of nine months he found the public eager to hear his great work. It was performed in London for the first time at the Covent Garden Theater in Lent of 1742. Not long afterwards " The Messiah " was heard in all parts of the kingdom, and Handel's fame was now established as firmly as a rock. This greatest of all oratorios stands far above the changes of taste, and so long as Christian faith and modern civilization endure it will maintain its place in the hearts of men. Whatever opinions may be held with regard to the Bible, — whether they be orthodox, rationalistic, elevated, or worldly, — it is certain that this oratorio will remain unaffected by them. This is because the sublime sacredness of the theme and the consummate choice and skill exhibited in the selection and combination of the various scriptural texts have found their appropriate and adequate expression in lofty and inspired strains. " In 'The Messiah' there are no personalities, but only voices to express the religious feelings of all humanity; for real personations would appear too insignificant to represent the grandest and most universal facts of human history." "The Messiah" has become a part of the religious life of England. "It has fed the hungry," says Burney, "clothed the naked, fostered the orphan, and enriched succeeding managers of oratorios more than any single musical production in this or any other country. This sacred oratorio, as it was at first called, on account of the words being wholly composed of genuine texts of Scripture, appearing to stand in such high estimation with the public, Handel, actuated by motives of purest benevolence and humanity, formed the laudable resolution of performing it annually for the benefit of the Foundling Hospital, which resolution was constantly put in practice to the end of his life, under his own direction, and long after his death by others, and in consequence of these performances the benefactions to charity in less than twenty years amounted to over £10,000."

Handel composed nineteen English oratorios: Esther (1720), Deborah (1733), Athalia (1733), Saul (1738), Israel (1738), Messiah (1741), Samson (1741), Joseph (1743), Hercules (1744), Belshazzar (1744), Occasional (1746), Judas Maccabeus (1746), Alexander Balus (1747), Joshua (1747), Solomon

Handel's compositions

(1748), Susanna (1748), Theodora (1749), Jephthah (1751), Triumph of Time and Truth (1757).

His five great Te Deums are Utrecht (1713), Chandos (1718–1720), Queen Caroline's (1737), and Dettingen (1743). He composed two Italian oratorios, one German passion, six psalms, twenty anthems, four odes, twenty-four chamber duets, ninety-four cantatas, nineteen English songs, sixteen Italian airs and canzonets, seven French songs, two Italian and two English serenatas, the finest of which is "Acis and Galatea."

Subjects of oratorios   Handel's oratorios hold the middle ground between the the secular and church styles of his time. He was the mediator between these two styles, as embodied in the operas of Scarlatti and his school, and the church music of Italian composers after Palestrina. Biblical history furnished the most universal and popular subjects for his genius. The older oratorios of German composers, like Isaac, Senfl, and Schütz, were conceived in the strict church style, in which the chorals sung by the congregation formed an indispensable part. The subjects were almost invariably taken from the New Testament, and were directed to the Passion of Jesus. This is the case with the great sacred works of Bach; the church style characterizes them throughout.

Handel took a wider range. His "Hercules" and "Alexander Balus" are secular oratorios, and his sacred oratorios are drawn from both the Old and New Testament. The heroes of Jewish history,—Judas Maccabeus, Samson, Joshua, Saul, etc.,—are represented in a combined narrative and dramatic form. They are musical epics. Dramatic representation and portrayal of character predominate, as in the epic poem; whereas lyric expression, devout prayer, and worship are more characteristic of the older form of passion music. "The Messiah" belongs to the latter class. In this, his greatest work, there are no personalities, but ideal voices to express the religious and devotional feelings of the Christian

world ; real personations were impossible, owing to the selection of isolated texts from all parts of the Scriptures. With
the exception of " The Messiah " and " Israel in Egypt " his
oratorios are musical dramas. In " Samson," for instance,
the characters are Samson, Delilah, Micah, Manoah, the
chorus of Israelites in opposition to the chorus of Philistines,
the heathen priests of Dagon against the maidens of Delilah.
All these are treated dramatically and are sharply defined by
the music.

Notwithstanding the lyric beauty, pathos, and brilliancy of **Importance**
his solos, the most important element of his oratorios is the **of the**
choruses. In grandeur, sublimity, and dramatic fire and **chorus**
effectiveness they have never been equaled. In " Samson,"
" Israel in Egypt," " Judas Maccabeus," and others, it seems
as though the whole Jewish people were giving united voice
to their sentiments. His choruses are elemental, like the
forces of nature, — the ocean surge or Niagara. They sweep
onward with irresistible power, yet do not destroy us, but lift
us up to a sublime height. His choruses are the only effective ones for a very large mass of voices. They have been
impressively sung by four thousand voices or more in the
Crystal Palace at the Handel festivals.

Handel composed three German operas : Almira (1704),
Nero (1705), and Florindo und Daphne (1708), all of which
were produced on the Hamburg stage. Among his thirty-
nine Italian operas, the following are the most prominent :
Rinaldo (1711), Radamisto (1720), Serse (1738) (containing
the popular aria " My Plane Tree," known under the name
of " Handel's Largo "), and Deidamia (1740).

Handel stood next to Bach in the field of instrumental
music. He was a great organist, not on account of his technical skill but of his inspired improvisations and contrapuntal
facility. He composed twenty-one organ concertos. For the
clavichord (harpsichord) he composed two sets of suites
(which contain the popular variations called " The Harmonious

Blacksmith" and the superb "Fugue in E minor"), four minuets and a march, and fourteen "pieces." His orchestral works are his "Water Music" in twenty-one movements, written for his patron George I, concertante, twelve grand concertos, fireworks music, forest music, overture, hornpipe, and six concertos for oboe, etc. His chamber music consists of twelve sonatas, thirteen trios, two sonatas for violins, a sonata for oboe, violin, and viola, and a sonata in five parts.

Handel's influence on instrumental music was far less than his great contemporary's, but as a choral master he reigns supreme. "In his breadth and flow of melody and the picturesqueness of his grand yet simple conception he was the glorified apotheosis of the purely contrapuntal vocal music. . . . The whole tone of his mind and genius were singularly attuned to the best features of English character." He lived in England most of his life, and became a naturalized Englishman in 1726. A German in his learning, an Italian in his vocal style, and an Englishman in his simplicity, independence, and healthy understanding, he was yet more than a cosmopolitan. Like Mozart he had his own individuality, his own distinctive style ; the essence of the Handelian style is simplicity and majesty. His choral works are conceived on a majestic and colossal scale. The fame and popularity of Handel became universal before his death. He is one of the grandest personalities in the history of music.

Sebastian Bach represents, in his famous passions, the highest attainment of church music, and marks the culmination of the older forms of instrumental music. He was the forerunner of Beethoven and of the modern romantic school of instrumental composition, — the first great master in this branch of the art.

Delay in the recognition of Bach's genius

The influence of Handel's music was immediate and universal, but more than three quarters of a century elapsed after Bach's death before his influence was fully felt. Mozart and

Beethoven had only a limited acquaintance with the epoch-making works of Bach. Even Bach's own sons and pupils did not, and could not, appreciate his true significance as a great representative musician. They wondered at his organ playing, his vast learning, his inexhaustible creative ability, but they were too near to view him in the full light of history, as we are better able to do. Had his sons and disciples understood him, they would have taken better care of his manuscripts ; it is known that those which are preserved are only a portion of all that he produced. Of the five passions which he composed only two are at hand. A century elapsed before the " Passion according to St. Matthew " was performed for the first time after the composer's death, and this revival inaugurated a new era in the musical life of Germany. The Bach Society was organized for the purpose of publishing his works. This laudable undertaking has accomplished lasting results for musical art. Through these printed works the master has at last become known to the best intelligence of the musical world, and his music has taken an indispensable place in the minds and hearts of the most earnest and enlightened musicians and of the public. There is no longer any excuse for ignorance and prejudice to belittle the genius of Bach, to deny him equality with Handel and other great musicians. Popularity and an easy comprehension of a master's works are not always the infallible criterion of merit. Full appreciation sometimes comes only after years, generations, and even centuries of neglect.

As Palestrina is the representative master of mediæval church music, so Bach is the highest representative of Protestant church music. In this field he is not only the most profoundly subjective artist, but is equally remarkable for the richness and wonderful range of his imagination, and for his consummate mastery of musical form. He was one of the most intellectual musicians who ever lived, yet made his skill and learning subservient to his emotional nature, which his

Bach the highest representative of Protestant church music

religious fervor ennobled and intensified. Those who find his music cold and passionless are simply ignorant of his style, which must first become familiar, or else they are incapacitated by nature from being moved and elevated by his music. His sacred music is founded in a large degree on the Lutheran chorals. This old custom of introducing melodies into the higher forms of church music reached its perfection in his cantatas. Many of the cantatas are founded on some particular choral, which is wrought out in varied forms of solo and chorus. One of the most splendid specimens of this choral art is the cantata on "A mighty fortress is our God" (Ein' feste Burg). The simpler chorals, harmonized in four parts, which Bach intersperses in all his church music except his masses, are the best types of the class, and will always stand as a monument to his genius. The melodies, however, were not original with him — only the harmonies. The most prominent of Bach's sacred works are the passions according to St. Matthew and St. John, the "Christmas Oratorio," the "Magnificat in D," and the "Mass in B Minor." "The Passion according to St. Matthew" has no rival in its special form. It is the highest representation that has ever been conceived in music of the trials and death of Christ. Among hundreds of similar works before and during Bach's day, his are the only ones that have lived.

Passion and oratorio compared   The oratorio has replaced the passion, but the older form, as completed by Bach, possesses a certain reality and intensity of religious ardor and belief that not even the grandest oratorios of Handel, except "The Messiah," can rival. The St. Matthew passion music is a more deeply subjective conception, more intensely lyrical and dramatic than "The Messiah"; but the latter work will, nevertheless, always be more popular and universal, for it is more general in its text and treatment. Handel's long experience with the public, his early Italian training, and consequently his vocal art have rendered his music more easy to be caught by the ear and understood and appreciated by the great public. In their choruses they are equally grand, but Handel has one advantage, — his music is not hard to sing. Handel expresses more frequently simple grandeur and sublimity; Bach, deeper pathos.

As a contrapuntist Bach is acknowledged as the foremost of all masters. No one has shown a more subtle and consummate knowledge of the relation of chords. His bold use of dissonances found no parallel in his own day; his ever new and striking harmonic progressions render the study of his works invaluable to the student. As an original harmonist he stands beside Chopin, Wagner, and other modern masters, while as a contrapuntist he towers above them all. All the voices of his counterpoint are perfectly melodious, and so natural that it seems as if the complex structure of his polyphony created itself, and as if the parts could flow in any direction as freely as water. Within this sphere he shows infinite variety and originality. No two fugues of his are treated alike; each one has its individual, characteristic theme and is worked out in accordance with it. Bach could do this because his calm and simple life made no demands on him; he could pursue his own gropings and reflections in peace; he could make new discoveries in the domain of musical sound without being arrested halfway by external affairs or practical considerations. He did not write for a public, but for himself and his ideal critic; his music, therefore, is free from conventionalities, and his best works cannot grow antiquated. He appears modern now, and must remain so, because he stood above fashion. As an instrumental composer he marks an important turning point in musical history. The various older forms of the suite, fugue, etc., found their ideal in his works; at the same time, he gave a new impetus to this branch of music through his teaching, and his unequaled performances on the organ and clavichord. There is no doubt, also, that the modern sonata acquired its first definite form in some of his compositions, as, for instance, the Italian concerto.

Bach as a contrapuntist

Sebastian Bach is the founder of modern instrumental music, and can be compared with Beethoven in this branch of art, as he has been with Handel in vocal music. Bach, like Beethoven and Schumann, was one of the most deeply subjective poets. He reveals the full psychological meaning of sounds; the various, individual moods find their characteristic expression, and music reaches at last its essentially modern stage, in which the spiritual life of the artist is revealed to us. We crave no deeper intimacy with men like Bach, Beethoven, Chopin, or Schumann than is offered to us through their works. Marx says:

> No one has ever equaled Bach in depth and truthfulness of characterization. In the recitatives of the St. Matthew passion not a single tone is uttered otherwise than with the aim of giving characteristic expression to the words, by means of significant harmonic and melodic progressions. This is also true of his airs and choruses, and of many of his instrumental compositions. It was under the influence of this deep insight into the spiritual life of the world of sound that this master developed harmony so fully, rightly, and significantly, and all that later musicians have discovered and created, except wild fancies and transient whims, may be traced back to that epoch in which it was given to Father Bach to reveal the truthfulness and deep spiritual significancy of his art in connection with the word of God.

His compositions

Bach's vocal works are: first, his church cantatas (some have been lost, but the Berlin Library contains over two hundred, of which the greater part has been published) and his passions according to St. Matthew and St. John; second, his double motets, " Magnificat in D," masses, and other church music, and several secular cantatas. His instrumental music consists: first, of orchestral suites, concerted pieces for various orchestral instruments, and solo concertos, sonatas, fugues, etc., for solo violin and violoncello — among which are some of the most interesting and difficult pieces for these instruments; second, his clavier (piano) concertos for one, two, and three claviers, with stringed accompaniment; third, his many clavier chamber compositions, consisting of preludes and fugues (including "The Well-Tempered Clavichord"), suites, partitas, toccatas, sonatas, etc.; and finally, his numerous organ works,—choral variations, preludes, fugues, toccatas, fantasias, etc.

Bach reconciled the long uncertainty of treatment of the old church modes in relation to the modern harmonic system. In his choral harmonizations and organ preludes (*Vorspiele*) he often makes use of the church modes, but the modern harmonic system is largely predominant in his works. He was one of the first to adopt equal temperament in tuning (with his own hands) the clavichord. His unique and monumental work, "The Well-Tempered Clavichord" (Das Wohltemperirte Klavier), was written to test the system of equal temperament in tuning. This system renders available all the twelve major and minor keys comprised within the chromatic octave. Before his time the system of tuning was such that only a certain number of keys were available. We rarely find compositions that used a signature of more than four sharps or four flats, for the extreme keys were thrown out of tune by the unequal system of tuning.[1]

"The Well-Tempered Clavichord" is in two parts, each containing twenty-four preludes and fugues, through all the major and minor keys of the octave chromatic scale; as, for instance, C major, C minor, C♯ major, C♯ minor, D major, D minor, and so on. The first part was composed in 1722, the second part in 1744. "The Well-Tempered Clavichord" is one of the great monuments of modern music, not on account of its key-scheme, but as an ideal representation of the form and spirit of polyphonic art, which Bach's genius carried to the highest point ever reached in the history of music. In this art Bach is the musician of musicians. "The Well-Tempered Clavichord" has been called the "Bible of Musicians." Schumann said, "Let it be your daily bread." Beethoven, it is said, always had a copy of it on his pianoforte.

[1] Grove, articles on "Temperament" and "Wohltemperirtes Klavier."

Influence of the work   Bach had a great influence on technical execution in organ and clavichord playing. He had his own system of fingering, which made equal demands on all the fingers and thumbs, and in organ playing also on both feet, heel, and toe. All the faculties of the mind, soul, and body are required of the performer to do justice to his master works. "The Well-Tempered Clavichord" may be termed the epitome of Bach's genius. The sovereign master of the fugue reveals all the wealth of his creative imagination in this work. His astonishing technical command and severe logic of method are lost sight of in our enjoyment of the music as the expression of his emotional nature. Some numbers are character pieces in as full a sense of the term as Schumann's "Novelettes" and "Fantasiestücke." Some are full of religious pathos, such as (Part 1) the preludes and fugues in C♯ minor and B♭ minor, the prelude in E♭ minor and (Part 2) the fugue in E major. Other examples are lively, gay, or energetic, such as (Part 1) the fugue in C minor, preludes and fugues in D♭ major and D major, fugue in E♭ major and (Part 2) fugue in F minor. The lighter phases of Bach's genius are displayed in his English and French suites, partitas, inventions, etc., for the clavichord. The old dance forms were raised to an ideal point by him; though contrapuntal in treatment, they are free and buoyant in spirit and charming in effect. The English suites in G minor and A minor are particularly pleasing. The "Chromatic Fantasia and Fugue" is one of the most brilliant and remarkable of his clavier compositions. His Italian concerto is also a noteworthy example of the older sonata. His six sonatas for violin and clavichord are one of his noblest works. His chaconne in D minor for solo violin is unique.

His most important orchestral work is the suite in D, which contains the popular "Aria." Bach began his career as a great organ master; and from this starting point he developed an entirely original style of vocal music, based on instrumental principles. He stands in marked contrast to

Handel, who represents the culmination of the old vocal style, based on true vocal principles.

Notwithstanding Bach's wonderful achievements in church, chamber, and clavier music, the very soul of his genius is embodied in his unequaled organ pieces. He may be termed the Shakespeare of the organ. He stands above all others. Among his numerous organ compositions may be mentioned his passacaglia in C minor, toccata in F, fantasia and fugue in G minor, preludes and fugues in A minor, B minor, E minor (" Wedge Fugue "), G major, E♭ major (" St. Ann's Fugue "), and six trio sonatas. Bach's activity was unending, as composer, performer, director, teacher, music engraver, and inventor of musical instruments. He was a model paterfamilias, and lived only for his art and his family. Bach was a well-educated man himself, and paid especial attention to the education and musical training of his sons. Among his pupils were Altnikol, Agricola, Doles, Vogler, Marpurg, Kirnberger, and Krebs, — all musicians of distinction. Of Bach's twenty children several became famous musicians. His third son, Karl Philipp Emanuel, was in his time more celebrated than his father.

Organ compositions

The genius of the Bach family centers in Sebastian. He is the typical representative of this long line of musicians, who were also distinguished for their moral and religious traits of character. The Bach family is often cited as furnishing most remarkable proof of the law of heredity, — the transmission of certain traits of character and talent from generation to generation. " In this family," says Maczewski, " musical talent was, as it were, bequeathed, and it seems almost like a law of nature that the scattered rays of the gift should after a hundred years finally concentrate in the genius of John Sebastian." The progenitor of the musical branch of the Bach family is traced back to Hans Bach, who lived at Wechmar about 1561.[1] The most prominent of the nineteen

Heredity of musical genius in the Bach family

[1] See Grove for genealogical table of the Bach family.

musicians of the Bach family prior to Sebastian were the brothers Johann Christoph and Johann Michael, who ranked among the most worthy composers of the seventeenth century.

Wilhelm Friedemann Bach (1710–1784), styled the Halle Bach, was the eldest son of Sebastian. He was considered as the most gifted of all his brothers, and his father built great hopes on him, and bestowed the utmost care on his musical training. He entered the University of Leipzig, where he distinguished himself as a talented mathematician. Afterward he became organist at Dresden and Halle. In 1767 he resigned his position, as his disorderly life made him careless and irregular. From this time forth he led a wandering life, and finally died in great degradation and poverty. He was the black sheep of the family, and his life exhibits the melancholy spectacle of a ruined genius. Friedemann had a profound knowledge of the theory of music; he was a great organ player and a wonderful improviser. His few published compositions are stamped with originality and power.

Johann Christoph Friedrich Bach, known as the Bückeburg Bach, was the ninth son of Sebastian. His numerous compositions do credit to the family.

Johann Christian Bach, known as the Milan or English Bach, was the eleventh son of Sebastian. He was influenced by Italian music. His operas achieved popularity. His clavier compositions were brilliant, and made him a favorite with piano players.

Emanuel Bach

Karl Philipp Emanuel Bach (1717–1788), called the Berlin or Hamburg Bach, was the third son of Sebastian. His remarkable intelligence led his father to give him an academic training; and at the same time to have him thoroughly instructed in music, especially in clavichord playing. He studied law at Leipzig and Frankfort, and had hardly completed his university studies when he received an invitation from the Crown Prince of Prussia, afterwards Frederick the Great, to accept a musical position at court. He remained in this service for a number of years, but resigned his place in 1767, being invited to succeed Telemann as musical director at Hamburg, where he continued to live until his death. By his daily practice in extemporaneous playing Emanuel Bach acquired a freedom and elegance of style matched by no other of his time. His position and intercourse with high society were not without good influence on his music. He possessed hardly a tithe of the genius of his father, but as he lived more in the world, he became a man of fashion and popularity; his name was far better known than his father's, and leading musicians looked up to him as the great authority. Even young Mozart said of him, "He is the father, we are mere children. Those of us who can do anything right in music learned it of him."

As a vocal composer Emanuel Bach was inferior. It was chiefly as a clavichord player and composer that he took the first rank. His refined style and finish of execution were unequaled. Burney paid him a visit at Hamburg, and thus describes the man and his performance:

Burney's visit to Emanuel Bach

> After dinner I prevailed upon him to sit down again to a clavichord, and he played with little intermission till near eleven o'clock at night. During this time he grew so animated and possessed that he not only played but looked like one inspired. His eyes were fixed, his underlip fell, and drops of perspiration stood on his countenance. He said if he were to be set to work frequently in this manner, he should grow young again. His performance to-day convinced me of what I had suggested before from his works, that he is not only one of the greatest composers for keyed instruments who ever existed but the best player in point of expression; for others, perhaps, have had as rapid execution; however, he possesses every style, though he chiefly confines himself to the expressive.

Emanuel Bach's celebrated treatise "On the true art of playing the clavichord" contains the principles of all good piano playing.

Emanuel Bach produced numerous works in all branches of music. His vocal works comprise two oratorios, sanctus for two choirs, twenty-two passions, cantatas, and songs, nearly all of which are forgotten. His instrumental works are more interesting, especially his clavier sonatas, which have historical value as marking the transition between the older and modern styles. Emanuel Bach is the connecting link between Sebastian Bach and Haydn. He wrote two hundred and ten solo pieces for the clavichord, consisting of sonatas, fantasias, and rondos; fifty-two concertos with orchestral accompaniment; eighteen symphonies, etc. He gave a lighter and freer form to the sonata. The older strictness of thematic treatment was abandoned; the homophonous style predominates throughout. Though his music lacks depth of feeling, it is brilliant, graceful, elegant, and finished; it furnished the germs which under the influence of Haydn's genius sprang into life and bore rich fruit.

Franz
Joseph
Haydn

Franz Joseph Haydn, "the father of the symphony and quartet," was born in 1732, at Rohrau in Austria, of humble parents. As a mere child he astonished people by the correctness of his ear and the beauty of his voice. He soon learned to play most of the instruments then in use. In 1740 he entered the Cantorei of St. Stephen's at Vienna as boy singer. He now received instruction in Latin, writing and arithmetic, singing, clavier and violin playing. But, strange to say, no instruction was given him in musical theory and composition, yet he began to compose by instinct. When his voice broke he lost his place in the choir, and was thrown on the world, penniless and friendless, until he found one friend in a singer, who gave him shelter. Subsequently he obtained a few pupils, and was enabled to rent an attic. Secluded there he devoted himself to study and composition. Unaided by a teacher he mastered the principles of fugue contained in the " Gradus " of Fux and studied at his worm-eaten clavichord the sonatas of Emanuel Bach. Haydn is perhaps the only great composer who was entirely self-taught. Under this drawback we marvel at his rare mastery of counterpoint and technical skill in composition. No doubt his self-reliance aided his inventiveness, for he was the creator of the classic form of the symphony and quartet.

The young Haydn had the good luck to make the acquaintance of Porpora, who proposed that he should become his accompanist. His association with this distinguished vocal master proved to be of great service to him, for he thus acquired the Italian vocal style.

Under the patronage of a wealthy amateur, von Fürnberg, Haydn wrote his first string quartets. In 1759 he was appointed musical director to Count Morzini, who had a good orchestra at his country seat. Here Haydn composed his "First Symphony" in D, — a small work in three movements for violins, viola, cello and bass, two oboes, and two horns. His happy, playful nature is expressed in this first symphony, as in all his later works.

In 1761 Haydn received the most important appointment of his life, as chapelmaster to Prince Esterhazy, one of the foremost of the Austrian nobility. This position exerted an important influence on his career. He now produced numerous compositions — symphonies, quartets, operas, and church music — and his reputation grew year by year. He remained in this service until the death of the prince in 1790. These thirty years with Esterhazy were of inestimable value to Haydn's development as a composer, but the crowning work of his life was not yet accomplished. This period, like Handel's long service as an opera composer, prepared him for a higher sphere of action; and in both instances this change seemed to be more the result of circumstances than of selection. It is very doubtful whether Haydn would have fulfilled his high mission if he had always stayed in Vienna and had not made his memorable and eventful journey to England. Salomon, who was connected with the Hanover Square concerts in London, had long besought Haydn to visit England, but with no success, until he happened to be in Vienna at the moment when Haydn had lost his position

Chapelmaster to Prince Esterhazy

by the death of Prince Esterhazy. He persuaded Haydn to take this step in December, 1790, and on his arrival in London he was surrounded by enthusiastic friends. In England a new world was opened to Haydn; he was honored beyond all others of his profession, and reckoned the years spent there, in which he composed his noblest symphonies and quartets, as among the happiest of his long life. The twelve symphonies written for the Salomon concerts are his best, and are the principal ones heard nowadays. Haydn often declared that he became famous in Germany by means of his triumphs in England. His oratorios "The Creation" and "The Seasons" are rightly considered as the fruits of his English experiences, though he did not compose them until his return to Vienna after his second visit to England. The appreciation and admiration which now greeted him at home as well as abroad strengthened his enthusiasm and elevated his musical conceptions. "The Creation" was composed in 1797, and its first performance capped the climax of his fame. Haydn died in 1809 at the age of seventy-seven years.

His indefatigable industry is shown in the immense number of works he produced. The list embraces one hundred and twenty-five symphonies, seventy-seven string quartets, thirty-five string trios, thirty-one concertos, sixty-six wind and string compositions, fifty-three piano sonatas, one hundred and seventy-five pieces for the baryton, and capriccios, divertimentos, fantasias, etc., for various instruments. His vocal works consist of five oratorios, nineteen operas, fifteen masses and other church music, songs, and canons.

Haydn's genius was displayed in almost every form of music. No German master ever surpassed him in vocal technic and style. His operas are forgotten, but his masses live, and rank among the best church music. They are performed more frequently than any others in the churches of Germany. His "Stabat Mater" is a beautiful work, full of religious sentiment. His oratorio "The Creation" rivals "The

Messiah" and "Elijah" in popularity. It is as fresh and
charming to-day as when it was first written. Though not
so profound and sublime as "The Messiah" and the St.
Matthew passion, it has qualities they do not possess ; the
orchestral part is far more artistic, and the solos and concerted numbers are more modern in style. His "Creation,"
"Seasons," and other vocal works are distinguished for charm
and beauty of melody, finish of style, tasteful ornamentation,
and variety of form. Like all his music they reflect the
happy, genial nature of the artist.

As an instrumental composer Haydn holds a position of
the highest importance in the history of music. His creative
originality cannot be overestimated. He is justly considered
as the real inventor of the modern symphony, sonata, and
string quartet ; for though the general outlines of these forms
existed before his time, it is he who made them classical
for all time. The symphony and concerto sprang from the
old Italian overture in three movements, — fast, slow, fast.
Sammartini was one of the first to compose orchestral symphonies. The early symphonies of Haydn are in three-move-
ment form, but his mature symphonies have four movements,
the additional movement being the minuet, which is introduced before the finale. Haydn extended the several movements in their larger and smaller divisions. He developed a
highly important means of giving unity and variety through
the so-called free thematic treatment of a musical idea or
motive. In Haydn's instrumental music we observe this evolution of a long movement out of little motives, the smallest
members of a musical thought, which recur again and again
under constantly changing conditions of key, melody, harmony, position, rhythm, and instrumentation; ever expressing
new meaning, beauty, and variety, without losing the central
idea of the piece. This free form reflects vividly and precisely all the emotions of the tone poet, — joyful or sad, humorous or gloomy, playful or grotesque. Every mood of feeling

Inventor of the modern symphony

is expressed more directly and subjectively in these free
thematic compositions than by the older and stricter forms of
counterpoint. In the fugue, canon, and other forms of imitative counterpoint, the several voices or parts are treated alike
as individual, melodious members, the bass being as melodious
as the soprano, the tenor as melodious as the alto. The theme
and counter-theme never cease to assert their importance,
though they may be relieved by new motives and recurring
digressions. The network of polyphony continues throughout.

Treatment of the theme In the sonata or symphony, on the contrary, the motive or
theme does not usually appear in all the parts alike in imita-
tion, but may be confined to a particular part, as the air or
melody, while the other parts merely contribute their accompaniment to enhance the effect, having no independent character of their own ; just as in a song the accompaniment may
consist of full or broken chords or parts of chords, introduced
to enrich the melody. In a word, this is homophonous music.
But this song form is only one form of free thematic music.
The polyphonic element also pervades it more or less ; and so
the sonata or symphony is a mixture of the polyphonic and
homophonic styles. In other words, it is the harmonious
union of the melodious style, which the Neapolitans cultivated
so extensively, with the old contrapuntal style. As a matter
of course, if the melody be given wholly to a single part while
the other parts are held strictly subordinate to it, the emotion
of the composer can be expressed more directly and intensely
through such a single melody than when all the parts are made
equally melodious, for, in the latter case, the individual movement of the several melodies must be prescribed by the
demands of the harmony, of which they are equal members.
But in this latter case what is lost in individual expression is
compensated for by the architectural beauty of form.

Analysis of the sym-phony Haydn's later symphonies generally open with a short, slow
introduction that leads into the first allegro movement, which
is always composed in the so-called sonata form. The following tabular view will exhibit this first movement in detail :

A. — PART I

Principal theme	Transition: Composed of new motives	Side Theme: Reminiscence of principal theme, leading to new motives	Conclusion: New phrases or periods worked up to conclusion
Tonic key	Modulation	Dominant, — or relative major, if movement opens in minor	Dominant, — or relative major

B. — MIDDLE PART, OR FREE FANTASIA

This contains materials from the first part, according to the fancy of the composer. Reminiscence of principal theme, side theme, transition, and conclusion may be employed as well as new motives and passages, but the keys of the first part must be avoided. Free modulation is largely employed. The middle part does not end with a cadence, but leads into the third part generally by a passage with pedal point on the dominant.

C. — PART III. REPRISE

Repetition of Part I, — principal theme, transition, side theme, and conclusion in tonic key.

The second, slow movement is either (*a*) in large song form, with two extended and repeated divisions, or (*b*) a theme with variations, or (*c*) in slow rondo form, in which a recurring melody, often changing from major to minor, is contrasted by intermediate digressions or episodes.

The third movement (minuet) is in the following form:

Part I		Trio	
Principal theme	Middle part .	Principal theme .	Middle part .
Tonic key	Modulatory	Relative key	Modulatory

Repetition	
Principal theme	Middle part
Tonic key	Modulatory

The finale (fourth movement) is usually in rondo form, though some of Haydn's finales are in sonata form. His rondos are not so highly developed as Beethoven's. They generally consist of a light and piquant principal theme which often recurs, being relieved by intermediate episodes. They are very characteristic. Here Haydn displayed his wit and humor, playfulness, and jollity. It is not positively known whether he was the first to introduce the minuet into the symphony and string quartet, but "it is he," says Otto Jahn, "who gave the minuet its peculiar and typical character. It was the dance of the polite world, and cannot be listened to nowadays without reminding us of powdered wigs and knee breeches, or the dainty little porcelain figures and engravings of that age, which provoke a smile in spite of our appreciation of their graceful merit. Haydn did not parody the minuet of his time, but divested it of its genteel dignity ; he took it up as the citizens danced it, and knew how to throw into it popular gayety and humor, originally foreign to this dance. He was inexhaustible in conceits, surprises, and witticisms." He idealized the minuet as Chopin did the mazurka and other Polish dances.

Influence of Haydn on instrumental music

The influence of Haydn on instrumental music was universal. He first prepared the way for Mozart and Beethoven, and later in life he was in turn influenced by them. The great symphonies and quartets of Beethoven mark the culmination of classical form ; yet the best of Haydn's, especially those composed in London, will always claim our admiration and interest. It is true we miss in Haydn the grandeur of thought, dramatic fire and passion, deep pathos, and massive orchestration of Beethoven, yet we are fascinated and delighted with the joyousness, simplicity, and playfulness of his musical nature. One master is the complement of the other ; Beethoven's symphonies are like tragedies, Haydn's are like comedies.

The modern art of orchestration begins with Haydn, so far as the effective treatment of the string band is concerned.

He worked out the problem of individualizing the different
parts of the harmony and combining them so as to produce
unity of effect. In making the string band the heart and
center of the orchestra he set the example for Mozart and
Beethoven, but the true nature and function of the wind
instruments were better understood by them. Even Gluck
made a freer use of solo wind effects than Haydn, who
declared that he did not learn how to write well for the wind
orchestra until his old age. Haydn was the creator of the
string quartet, and in certain respects he has never been surpassed in this form of music, which was his natural mode of
expressing his feelings. Quartets were composed before his
day by Stamitz, Jommelli, Johann Christian Bach, Boccherini,
Pleyel, and other contemporaries, but Haydn surpassed them
all, and gave a new character to the quartet. He established
for all time what is designated as the "quartet style." His
first quartets were thin and insignificant compared with the
wealth of thought and beauty of his later ones. He individualized the four solo instruments, and gave them greater scope
and variety of effect, so that they appear like four persons
holding conversation with each other. His best quartets em-
body the very essence of his genius; they possess inimitable
charm and fascination. Mozart declared that from Haydn he
first learned the true art of writing quartets.

The creator of the string quartet

Haydn also left his mark on the piano sonata; he far
excelled his model, Emanuel Bach. Several of his sonatas,
as for example the two in E♭, go beyond Mozart's, and fairly
stand beside the early sonatas of Beethoven in beauty and
instrumental effect. The trio, for piano, violin, and violoncello, was introduced by Haydn, but it was reserved for
Beethoven to create immortal works in this form.

The position which Mozart holds as an instrumental composer is a relative one between Haydn and Beethoven. He
was in many respects the teacher of both. Haydn in his last
symphonies shows the influence of Mozart, just as Beethoven

does in his early works. Both learned of him a richer art of instrumentation. Mozart's wonderfully musical ear and sensibility comprehended the very nature of the instruments; no one ever knew how to treat them singly or in combination better than he did. His wind-instrumental parts are distinguished by the exquisite beauty of their cantabile. It was this appreciation of the peculiar nature of each instrument that rendered Mozart the indispensable teacher of Haydn and Beethoven, and a necessary member of the group. Mozart did not enlarge the general form of the sonata and symphony, for the thematic periodic structure of these forms was already thoroughly wrought out; but he rounded and beautified the separate parts and made a movement now and then more massive. This is true, however, only of his last three symphonies.

CHAPTER XIX

GLUCK

Before the ascendency of Gluck and Mozart, the opera in Italy and France had developed certain national characteristics, without reaching a perfect ideal in either country. The Hamburg opera of Keiser and others was a short-lived attempt to establish native German opera; nor did Purcell live long enough to build up English opera. For a long time all Europe was, blinded by the dazzling light of Italian opera. The trills and runs, the freaks and caprices of the virtuosos of the stage, held the ear-entranced public in subjection. This wide departure from the original idea of a pure musical drama led Gluck, who had a long experience as a composer of conventional Italian operas, to return to first principles and to attempt to reform dramatic music.

Christoph Wilibald, Ritter von Gluck, was born at Weidenwang, Austria, on the second of July, 1714. He received early training in singing, violin, violoncello, organ, and clavichord playing. His parents belonged to the household of Prince Lobkowitz, and the son found appreciation and encouragement from this nobleman. At his residence in Vienna, Gluck had the good fortune to meet Prince Melzi of Lombardy, who was so much pleased with his performance on the violoncello and his talent for music that he appointed him chamber musician and invited him to Milan, where he received musical instruction from Sammartini. After four years of study he produced successfully his first opera, "Artaserse," at Milan in 1741. His reputation soon spread, and he was invited to compose other works for the Italian stage, — Demofoonte (Milan, 1742), Demetrio

Birth and early training

245

and Ipermnestra (Venice, 1742), Artamene (Cremona) and Siface (Milan, 1743), Fedra (Milan, 1744), and Poro (Turin, 1745).

Visits to
London
and Paris
In 1745 Gluck accompanied his patron and friend, Prince Lobkowitz, to Paris and London, where he brought out several operas ; but he did not find English soil favorable to his music, for the Italians exercised absolute control there. During his stay in London he met Handel, whose music made a lasting impression on him. Handel consoled him for his want of success in London, saying, "You have taken too much trouble with your operas for this place, for Englishmen require everything to be beaten out on drumheads to please them." He, however, did not praise Gluck's music, which he considered detestable, declaring that Gluck knew no more of counterpoint than his cook. Gluck's English experience exercised an important influence on his career. His visit to Paris gave him an opportunity to hear the operas of Rameau, whose noble choruses and recitatives stood in marked contrast to the florid and insipid Italian opera arias. These foreign experiences led him to reflect on the nature of his talents and ultimately to change his style. On his return to Vienna in 1746 he devoted himself to the study of musical æsthetics as well as literature and language. Two years later Gluck produced his " Semiramide " in Vienna with brilliant success. In this opera he showed decided progress over his earlier works, for it contains the germ of his distinctive dramatic and musical qualities. In 1754 Gluck was appointed director of the royal opera, and held this position for ten years ; during this period he composed a number of operas, the most noted of which are his " Clemenza di Tito " and "Orfeo." Meanwhile he went to Rome where he enjoyed high appreciation. The pope conferred on him the title of Chevalier. It was not until almost the end of his career as director at Vienna that he disclosed to the public his plan for a reform of the opera, which had gradually formed in his mind.

The production of his "Orfeo" in 1762 marked the open- Reforms in the opera
ing of the most eventful period of Gluck's life. Hitherto he
had followed the beaten path of the Italian opera. Even after
this date he composed more or less in the traditional Italian
style, and it was not until his opera "Alceste" appeared that
he turned entirely aside from the old course, henceforth to
obey no master but himself. "Alceste" was published in
1769. In his dedication to the Grand Duke of Tuscany, Gluck
sets forth the new principles which he so earnestly aspired
to spread abroad, as follows:

When I undertook to set "Alceste" to music, I resolved to avoid all
those abuses which the vanity of the singers and the far too great com-
plaisance of the composers had introduced into the Italian opera, —
abuses which have rendered the finest and grandest plays tiresome and
ridiculous. I sought to lead music back to its true object, that of second-
ing the poem in order to intensify the passion it expresses, and add
interest to the dramatic situations, without interrupting the action or
marring it by superfluous ornaments. I believed that music should be
to poetry what the liveliness of the colors and a happy mixture of light
and shade are to a well-ordered drawing, which animate the figures without destroying their outlines. I have for this reason taken particular care
not to interrupt the actor in the fire of his dialogue in order to introduce a tedious ritornelle, nor to stop him in the middle of a phrase on
a favorite vowel for the purpose of exhibiting the flexibility of his voice,
or that the orchestra might give him time to exhaust his breath on a
long-holding note. Furthermore, I have not thought it right to hurry
through the second part of an aria, when it might be precisely the most
passionate and interesting moment, in order to repeat the words four
times invariably or to finish the aria where the sense did not permit it
to end properly, merely to allow the singer to exhibit his skill and grace
in varying the passage at pleasure. In short, I wished to banish all those
abuses against which good taste has long protested in vain.

My idea was that the overture ought to indicate the subject and
prepare the spectators for the character of the piece they were about to
see ; that the instruments should be introduced in proportion to the
degree of interest and passion in the words ; and that it was necessary
above all to avoid making too great a disparity between the recitative
and the air of a dialogue, so as to break the sense of a period or
awkwardly to interrupt the movement and animation of a scene. I also
thought that my chief endeavor should be to attain a grand simplicity,

and consequently I have avoided making a parade of difficulties at the cost of clearness; I have set no value on novelty as such, unless it was naturally suggested by the situation and suited to the expression; in short, there was no rule which I did not consider myself bound to sacrifice for the sake of effect.

The full force of these principles applied only to the degenerate *opera seria* of his time; they were not entirely original with him, for they had already been accepted and realized in part by other musicians.

The invitation to Paris
The doubtful success of "Orfeo" and "Alceste" in Vienna led Gluck to seek honor and appreciation in Paris, which was then the center of the intellectual and artistic world. He had an ardent admirer in Du Rollet, a French writer, who adapted Racine's "Iphigénie en Aulide" as an opera text for him. On its completion Du Rollet made an effort to interest the French public in the matter. Gluck himself directed an article to the *Mercure de France*, in which he wrote, "It is my cherished desire to create music which shall respond to the taste of all nations, and remove all the ridiculous differences of national music." During the same year (1773) Gluck was invited to Paris through the influence of his former royal pupil Marie Antoinette. Without her all-powerful influence Gluck would probably have failed to get his work on the stage. "Iphigénie en Aulide" was brought out in Paris in 1774, but it had only a divided success at first; party spirit ran high, and it was not until after repeated performances of the work that opposing voices were silenced. The battles between the admirers of comic opera, or "Buffonists," and the adherents of Lully and Rameau, or "Antibuffonists," were now renewed with fiercer fury than ever. The old French opera party believed that they had found a champion in Gluck, as one who represented in part the traditional ideas to which they were so firmly wedded; but while Gluck laid great stress on perfect declamation and dramatic action, he far surpassed Lully and Rameau in the tragic depth

of his characterization, dramatic power, beauty of melody, choral effects, and richness of orchestration.

In 1774 Gluck's "Orfeo ed Euridice" was produced at the Académie, and made a profound impression. He never wrote anything greater than the second act of this immortal work; time has proved it to be the most popular of all his operas. Gluck rearranged his "Alceste" for the French stage and produced it in Paris, in 1776, with brilliant success. He then returned to Vienna to work on the texts of "Roland" and "Armide" by Quinault. During his absence the Italian party left no stone unturned to advance their own interests, and invited the celebrated Italian composer Piccinni to Paris as their champion. French society was now divided as to the merits of these rivals, and the music they were supposed to represent. In polite circles it was no longer asked, "Is he a Jansenist, a Molinist, a philosopher, or a pietist?" but "Is he a Gluckist or a Piccinnist?" The first literary men in France took part in this war of opinion, armed with their pens. Rousseau, Abbé Armand, and other able writers stood on Gluck's side; Marmontel, La Harpe, and others, on the Italian's side; while Baron von Grimm tried to be neutral, but was evidently Italian in his sympathies. Marmontel adapted Quinault's "Roland" for Piccinni to compose — the same subject that Gluck was at work upon. As Piccinni did not understand a word of French it went hard with him, and he began to fear that his star was not in the ascendant; but at last his "Roland" was finished and ready for performance. When he started for the theater he took leave of his family as though he were going to execution. They were in tears, and his friends were in a state of despair, but he consoled them with the words, "Come, my children, this is unreasonable. Remember we are not savages. We are living with the politest and kindest nation in Europe. If they do not like me as a musician, they will at all events respect me as a stranger." His "Roland" had a brilliant success; even

Rivalry with Piccinni

Piccinni's enemies had to admit that this opera was good music, although they rightly held that it lacked dramatic strength. For a time Gluck's light was obscured. Piccinni's opera held its place on the stage and the disputes still continued.

The climax of Gluck's career was reached by his " Iphigénie en Tauride" in Paris, May 18, 1779. This epoch-making work marks the highest attainment of his genius, the complete fulfillment of his artistic principles. Piccinni's opera on the same subject was cast into oblivion, and French opera in the sense of Lully and Rameau no longer existed. Gluck was the first German dramatic composer to conquer the French; not long after his death he was claimed by them as a national composer.

"Iphigénie en Tauride" contains many thrilling dramatic effects and musical beauties. Among them are the airs of Thoas and Pylades ; "and beyond all, the sleep of Orestes — the heart-breaking remorse of the deceitful parricide, the spirited choruses, and the barbarous Scythian dances."

Gluck's latest opera was " Echo et Narcisse " ; it was produced in Paris, in 1779, without much success. Gluck retired to Vienna in 1780, where he passed the rest of his days in the enjoyment of fame and fortune. He died November 15, 1787.

Gluck's music superior in dramatic power to the librettos The subjects of most of the operas of Gluck are drawn from Greek tragedy as represented by the French dramatists. Their plays are not comparable to the ancient prototype in general conception nor in the treatment of special details. Gluck showed himself greatly superior to the French poets in endowing the characters with tragic grandeur, nobility, and pathos. He had a keen understanding and profound appreciation of dramatic characterization ; though, like most opera composers, his plots are not developed so as to hold our interest fast until the climax and solution of the conflict have been reached. They are rather a series of situations, connected with one another from necessity, in order merely to furnish the composer with a text. It is remarkable that Gluck, who stood out so boldly against the musical inconsistencies and defects of his time, should not have tried to improve the construction of the librettos. But his characters live, like Shakespeare's. Above all, we are struck by the simple grandeur and nobility of his musical conceptions, though in the librettos which were furnished him not a trace of grandeur is discernible. " As Winckelmann was able to recognize the genuine spirit of Greek art from the works of art of a later period," says Jahn, "so Gluck grasped the true grandeur that lay hidden in the principal situations of his operas, which the poet had been unable to bring to light, and while he believed he was merely following out the idea of the poet faithfully, he reproduced out of his own nature something new and great. The truth and simplicity of his representations, the elevated bearing and noble pride that animate the figures of his operas, in short, all the traits of artistic grandeur are what constitutes his imperishable fame."

Gluck was a great master of the recitative; he carefully allotted every syllable its proper time and accent, and his declamation, therefore, is faultlessly perfect. The French language favored him in this respect. He did not allow the air the same prominence that the Italians did; he would not sacrifice one iota of dramatic truth to sensuous charm and beauty of melody. His airs are in simple form, divested of all richness of ornament. Many of them are noble and beautiful in their simplicity, but in general they lack the full inspiration of a divine musical nature like Mozart's. Gluck's thoughts evidently did not flow easily and spontaneously. He was not well skilled in polyphonic writing. This is plainly evident in those places where the several dramatic characters are made to declaim or sing in concert with each other; he then found it difficult to preserve the musical individuality of each, as Mozart did with such wonderful art.

Masterly treatment of recitative and chorus

Gluck gave great prominence to the chorus in his operas; it fulfilled in a measure its original function in the ancient tragedy. Impressive examples are the chorus of the Spirits of Rage and Hate in "Armide" and the chorus of Furies in the second act of "Orfeo." No dramatic master before or since has written more tragic and thrilling choruses.

Orchestral effects

In dramatic orchestration Gluck was the foremost master of his time and had a strong influence on Mozart. He removed the harpsichord from the orchestra, and introduced the harp, trombones, and clarinets. He gave more importance and interest to the overture, and employed, with magic effect, the artifice of momentary pauses to vary or emphasize speech in music. The dramatic and lyric effect of some of his instrumental solos has never been surpassed; as, for instance, the pathetic flute solo in D minor in the scene in the Elysian fields of the "Orfeo." In the words of Berlioz, "It is the sublime lament of a suffering and despairing departed spirit." What is more touching and expressive of poignant grief than the oboe solo of Agamemnon's air in "Iphigénie en Aulide"! What is more graphic, terrible, and suggestive than the repeated motive of the contrabasses, — the hoarse barking of Cerberus in the infernal scene of "Orfeo"! No wonder that Hector Berlioz, the great modern orchestral colorist, raved over the poetic and dramatic strokes of Gluck's genius.

To sum up our estimate of Gluck — he aimed at a simple, grand style, and "preferred the Muses to the Sirens." In simplicity and dignity he approached the Greek ideal. His characters live, his declamation is perfect, his choruses are beautiful and dramatic, his orchestration is graphic and tragic. "In a word, all his French operas show him to have been a noble musician, a true poet, and a deep thinker." He was the forerunner of Mozart, and anticipated Wagner to some extent in his dramatic aim.

CHAPTER XX

MOZART

Wolfgang Amadeus Mozart, born January 27, 1756, in Salzburg, was the son of Leopold Mozart, the noted violin master. The story of the child's precocious genius transcends by far any other case on record of musical "wonder" children. His musical nature was evinced almost in infancy; when he was but three years old he showed a fondness for striking thirds and other harmonious intervals at the clavier, and took great delight in listening to his sister Marianne's performances. His father now gave him lessons, and he began to compose. When he was only five he composed a minuet, which is given as his first work in Köchel's catalogue. Two years later he began to compose for instruments in combination, knew the effect of sounds as represented by notes, and had overcome the difficulty of composing unaided by an instrument. Before he had received any lessons on the violin he astonished his father and friends by playing the second violin part in some new trios that they were trying for the first time. The child's remarkable intelligence was shown in other ways than in music. His disposition was characterized by an extreme sensibility and tenderness. His only sister, five years his senior, was also gifted in music, and at the age of nine years was a remarkable player on the clavichord. The father decided to bring his wonderful children before the eyes of the world, and so the whole family started on a journey. They visited Munich, Vienna, Paris, London, The Hague, and Amsterdam, where they created universal wonder and admiration, and were presented at court. Mozart's first serious work, two sonatas for piano and violin, was published when he was

Early evidences of genius

253

but seven years old. On their return to Salzburg in 1766, Wolfgang's interrupted studies were resumed. During the next two years he composed two cantatas, a Latin comedy, and his first piano concertos.

In 1768 they visited Vienna and were presented at court. Mozart now composed his first opera, "La finta semplice," by command of the emperor. At the time he was only ten years old. The work was in three acts, yet Mozart worked so bravely at it that it was soon finished; but the jealousy and opposition of certain musicians, and the duplicity of the manager of the opera, prevented it from being produced. Soon after this he composed a German operetta "Bastien und Bastienne," which was produced in the private theater of Dr. Mesmer, a friend of the Mozarts. In 1769 father and son set out for Italy, and visited all the principal towns. Wherever they went the boy excited great wonder. Padre Martini, Farinelli, Hasse, Jommelli, and many other famous musicians marveled at his miraculous gifts as performer and composer. During this first visit to Italy he composed a number of works, among which was the opera "Mitridate," performed successfully in Milan under Mozart's direction. It was repeated twenty times to crowded houses. In 1771 the travelers returned home to Salzburg, the tour in Italy having been of the highest service to Mozart's musical and worldly prospects. His genius was in a state of exaltation in that land of music and art. In 1772 they visited Milan again, where Wolfgang produced his new opera "Lucio Silla," which was repeated again and again before enthusiastic audiences. On his return to Salzburg in 1773, Mozart composed four symphonies, three divertimenti for wind instruments, a mass, a string quintet, a piano concerto, and a concerto for two violins. During the summer he composed in Vienna a grand serenata and six quartets. In 1774 Mozart was very busy with his studies and composition. The fruits of this period were two masses and other church music, four symphonies, two serenatas, a bassoon

concerto, a divertimento, and piano variations. The father and
son then visited Munich, where Wolfgang composed "La
finta giardiniera." It was brought out in January, 1775, and
was received with great favor. During the next two years in
Salzburg he was wonderfully productive in almost every form
of composition; masses, serenades, cassations, divertimenti,
sonatas, concertos, variations, etc., followed one another in
rapid succession.

In reviewing the early achievements of this precocious
genius Otto Jahn says :

Universal-
ity of his
talents

As a youth of twenty-one years Mozart not only stood alone as a
virtuoso on the clavier, organ, and violin, but far excelled the first masters of his time as a composer. From his earliest childhood onward we
find no contradiction between ideas and execution, the form and con-
tents of his works. We see how he went on step by step and mastered
every form naturally and completely. All the elements of a musical
nature were united harmoniously in Mozart. We witness in him the
organic development of a rare artistic nature, which cannot be arrested
by any obstacles, but rather makes everything bend to it. It is the
greatest success which a youthful artist can have that at the very
threshold of manhood he should thus gain complete control of all the
materials and technics of his calling.

All that schooling and discipline could furnish, Mozart had
acquired, and now he was ready to go out into the world,
fully armed and equipped to fight his way against all opposition. He could not, in self-respect, remain any longer at
Salzburg, for the manner in which he was treated by the
Archbishop Hieronymus, in whose nominal employ he stood,
was outrageous, and has given this unworthy man an undesir-
able notoriety in musical history; otherwise his name would
have been entirely forgotten long ago. In 1777 Leopold
Mozart resolved to send his son away to seek his fortune.
Wolfgang and his mother accordingly left home, and directed
their steps first to Munich and then to Mannheim, where they
remained a number of months. Mannheim possessed a good
opera and one of the foremost orchestras in Europe. It was

Attempts
to establish
himself at
Mannheim
and Paris

here that young Mozart learned the value of the clarinet as an orchestral instrument. He found admiring friends among the distinguished musicians and poets of Mannheim, and fell in love with the singer Aloysia Weber; but his romance was nipped in the bud by his father, who wrote to him, "Off with you to Paris, and that immediately." Leaving Mannheim in March, 1778, he arrived in Paris on the twenty-third. But his father's anticipations of success were not fulfilled. Mozart found little encouragement in Paris. He failed to produce any opera on the stage, and the only important work composed and performed during his stay was the symphony in three movements, called the "French, or Paris, Symphony." His artistic hopes were crushed by the illness and death of his mother, and overcome with grief he hastened to leave Paris in September, 1778, and returned to Salzburg, where he was consoled by the warm welcome of his father and old friends. In all the situations and experiences of life Mozart was an indefatigable worker; from his childhood to the day of his death he exercised his creative faculty to the utmost. "In mourning for his mother, disappointed in his first love, and with all his hopes falsified," he settled down for a year in Salzburg (1779–1780), and devoted himself to composition, producing three masses, two vespers, a vocal trio, songs and canons, two symphonies, two serenades, a divertimento, four sonatas for piano and violin, sonatas for four hands, variations for piano, a piano concerto, etc.

"Idomeneo" performed at Munich

His dislike for Salzburg, however, determined him to turn his steps elsewhere. Through the influence of his friends in Munich he was invited to compose a grand opera for the carnival season. The subject was "Idomeneo, re di Creta." He lost no time in completing the score, and went to Munich to conduct the rehearsals. The initial performance took place in January, 1781, and won a triumph. Though "Idomeneo" has never been as popular as "Figaro" and "Don Giovanni," it is Mozart's first important dramatic work. His previous

operas were composed in the conventional Italian style.
They rank among the best of that period, but were doomed
to be forgotten. It was not so with his "Idomeneo," which
marks the turning point in his career as a dramatist; he no
longer follows the Italians blindly, but takes the serious and
noble Gluck as his model. In "Idomeneo" the chorus element is prominent, the declamation dramatic, and the orchestration more varied and effective than ever before.

Mozart now took up his abode in Vienna, where he was
destined to accomplish his great life work. From this time
onward he appears as a mature master; his individuality is
stamped on all his numerous and beautiful works. If any
music can be called divine, it is Mozart's. In 1781 he composed "Die Entführung aus dem Serail," by command of the
emperor Joseph II. It was brought out with brilliant success
in the following year. A month later Mozart married Con-
stanze Weber, the younger sister of his first love. The felicity
of their married life was marred by the want of resources; they
began housekeeping with little or nothing. Mozart, though
already famous, had many trials to contend with; his talent
did not meet with substantial reward. He had no prospect
of a fixed appointment and was obliged to give lessons and
concerts. It was a disgrace that the emperor, who was so loud
in his praise of Mozart's music, did not bestow on him a good
position. He earned more by his subscription concerts than
by his lessons or his compositions. The programmes of his
concerts usually consisted of his own works, — a symphony,
two piano concertos, etc., and an improvisation; he composed
a new piano concerto for each concert. Mozart was the
creator of the modern piano concerto; his piano playing is
described as wonderful in the singing quality of his touch,
and in the elegance of his running passages and ornaments.
Clementi declared that he had never heard anybody play with
so much mind and charm as Mozart. Haydn said, with tears
in his eyes, that as long as he lived he should never forget

*Establish-
ment at
Vienna and
marriage*

Mozart's playing; it went to the heart. It was said that those who never heard him improvise could have only the faintest idea of his inspiration.

Mozart's life in Vienna was one of ceaseless activity; work followed work with astonishing facility. He composed his three immortal symphonies in E♭, G minor, and C major within six weeks (1788). The following works were the fruits of this last period : Così fan tutte (1790), Figaro (1786), Don Giovanni (1787), La clemenza di Tito, and Die Zauberflöte (1791); six string quartets (dedicated to Haydn); a string quintet in G minor; his best piano concertos in D and C minor, C major, etc. ; piano fantasia and sonata in C minor, and his unfinished Requiem. These masterpieces will endure as long as musical art itself.

Mozart's worldly affairs were far from satisfactory; even the wonderful triumph of his " Don Giovanni " did not relieve him of his pecuniary difficulties, and he was obliged to borrow money for his household expenses. He applied to his friend Puchberg for immediate assistance, but up to the last he suffered from want. Mozart was naturally of a sunny disposition, but during his last days he was weighed down with deep melancholy. The story of his " Requiem " might be cited in this connection. He died, probably from brain fever, December 5, 1791, at the age of thirty-five years.

Character
of Mozart
　　　As a man, Mozart was distinguished for his naïve simplicity, geniality, honorable openness, and freedom from the least taint of falseness or intrigue. His extremely affectionate nature and sensibility characterized him from early childhood. If not one of the grandest personalities in musical history, he was one of the most lovable and amiable. He was one of the most charitable and forgiving of men; to the poorer brethren of his profession he was liberal to excess of his time and labor. Many of his finest concertos and sonatas were written to oblige his friends, or to help them in distress. His own pecuniary embarrassments were not due to reckless

extravagance, as many have supposed, but to his generosity
and want of self-interest in making professional engagements.
A great artist is rarely a good business man. His friendly
generosity was often cruelly abused by seeming friends. It is
no exaggeration to say that Mozart was the victim of unprincipled music sellers and managers of theaters, who gained possession of his manuscripts in an underhanded manner to
reap pecuniary advantage from them. " Die Zauberflöte "
brought him no remuneration, owing to the perfidious conduct
of Schickaneder, the opera manager, who well knew the desperate circumstances of the man he was cruelly defrauding.
But Mozart, who seemed incapable of resenting an injury,
when made fully aware of his treachery, simply exclaimed,
" The wretch ! " and dismissed the matter from his mind. His
resentment of very grave injuries extended no further than
the exclamation, " The wretch ! "   He was always ready to
return good for evil. Mozart's only serious fault seemed to
be a love of pleasure and gay company ; he had a passion for
dances and masquerades, and would not willingly forego an
opportunity of attending them ; late hours combined with
overwork must have had a bad effect on his health. But this
gay life never became a vice, as is proved by his preserving to the last his earnest and unfailing attachment to his
home. His wife ever possessed his full love and confidence ;
to her he confided everything ; he never engaged in any
important undertaking without consulting her. This love of
company was, in fact, only a virtue carried to excess. He
loved to have his friends about him when he worked, and
many of his finest airs and themes were composed when he His method
was playing at billiards, a game of which he was very fond, of compos-
or in a traveling carriage, when on a journey. Mozart's manner of composing well shows his wonderful endowment. In
early boyhood he formed the habit of mental composition,
and he was able to finish the most elaborate piece, even an
orchestral score, in his mind, before writing out a note of

it. On one occasion he deferred the composition of a sonata for piano and violin until the day before the concert. As he could find no opportunity to put his own part on paper, he executed it without notes or rehearsal with the violinist, to the delight of the audience. His power to remember what he had conceived was as astonishing as his ability to work out the score without any instrument. On the evening before the presentation of " Don Giovanni " the overture was wanting. Mozart wrote out the score before the next morning. Unless he had conceived and memorized the parts of the score beforehand, such a feat as this would not have been possible. Mozart is rightly considered as the universal mas-

ter. This unparalleled universality is displayed not only in his complete mastery of every kind of musical composition from a popular air to a grand symphony, from a simple dance to a solemn requiem, but in the rare adaptation of different national peculiarities of style to his own individuality. It was his mission to unite and beautify the national elements of music, which hitherto had remained distinct. European music attained its concentration for the first time in history in his works ; no other master was endowed so peculiarly with the power of appropriating, so to speak, what other great musicians had conceived, without slavish imitation of them. It was the intense appreciation of a kindred spirit. He was always a willing learner; but all that he learned from others did not tend in the least to efface the bright impression of his own individuality. As a boy he composed operas in the conventional Italian style, and church music in the style of German contemporary musicians like Michael and Joseph Haydn, Eberlin, and others. The strong impression which Gluck's operas made on Mozart is shown in his " Idomeneo," which was produced after his second visit to Paris. On his memorable visit to Leipzig and Berlin in 1789, Mozart learned to know Bach's eight-part motets and some of his organ works. " Here is something from which one may still learn," he exclaimed. The influence of Bach's wonderful polyphony is shown in Mozart's last string quartets, the grand fugue-finale of his C major symphony, the overture to " Die Zauberflöte," the four-hand fantasia in F minor. Other examples might be cited to show that Mozart never ceased to learn from others and still show his own originality everywhere.

As an instrumental composer, Mozart holds the interme- Mozart as
diate place between Haydn and Beethoven. He had a potent an instrumental com-
influence on both masters. Mozart owed the general form poser
and style of the symphony and quartet to Haydn, but later he had the great advantage of hearing the best orchestras in Europe — at Mannheim, Munich, and Paris — while Haydn was entirely restricted to his own small band. Mozart thus learned how to write for the wind instruments in a much freer and more effective manner than Haydn. He did not enlarge the general form of the symphony and quartet, — this was the mission of Beethoven, — but he rounded and beautified the details ; his themes are poetic, beautiful, and emotional. There is a deeper pathos and sensuous charm in the best works of Mozart than in those of any of his predecessors. They have the divine harmony and perfection of form of the Madonnas of Raphael or the poems of Milton. Ambros, the musical historian, says of Mozart's last three symphonies, " Considered as pure music, it is hardly worth while to ask whether the world possesses anything more perfect." The " Symphony in G Minor" is the very epitome and essence of his divine genius.

In reviewing Mozart's numerous instrumental works — three hundred and seventy-eight out of six hundred and twenty-six — we are struck with their diversity of form : sonatas, fantasias, variations, rondos, etc., for piano; violin and piano sonatas ; piano trios, quartets, and quintets ; string duos, trios, quartets, and quintets ; divertimentos, cassations, and serenades for wind and stringed instruments ; symphonies, marches, and dances for orchestra; concertos for piano, violin, and other instruments.

Certain of these forms owe their classical character to Mozart. His divertimentos, cassations, and serenades, composed in six to eight movements for wind and stringed instruments, were intended to be played in the open air. They number collectively thirty-three. In Mozart's time they were great favorites, and are still interesting on account of the complete mastery displayed in the treatment of the wind instruments.

Piano concertos

Among Mozart's most important works are his piano concertos. The solo instrument and the orchestra are combined and balanced so as to form an organic whole. In his treatment of the piano he introduced no mere bravura passages; his passages are founded for the most part on the scale and broken chords. In playing them, clearness, taste, and the power of singing on the instrument are required. The grace, sweetness, and tenderness of these finished works give them an irresistible charm. Their perfect workmanship and beauty of form render them classical models, although the concerto and all forms of piano music have been greatly developed since Mozart's time.

Haydn was the founder of the quartet, and in certain respects has never been surpassed in this form of music; yet Mozart, through his rare mastery of polyphony and lyric melody, revealed new beauty in his quartets. In the six dedicated to Haydn he individualized and beautified each of the four voices to the utmost. When these quartets first appeared, however, they were severely criticised, and declared to be "hideous stuff." The only one that has anything startling to modern ears, accustomed to the dissonances of "Tristan," is the famous introduction to the "Quartet in C," with its false relations of harmony. This quartet, in spite of the unhappy critics, is now considered as Mozart's finest.

His preeminence in dramatic music

While Mozart stands beside Haydn and Beethoven as an instrumental composer he is preëminent in the field of dramatic music. He was endowed by nature and favored by opportunity to bring this to ideal perfection, at least as regards the musical element of the opera. He first learned of the Italians and Gluck, and then beat them with their own tools. "Don Giovanni" and "Figaro" are the greatest of all Italian operas. The century and a half of previous cultivation reaches its climax in these masterpieces. Mozart fully appreciated the Italians; his musical instinct led him to them, at first, as naturally as he sought society and friends; but while he adopted their melodious style and warmth of coloring, giving singing its full rights and place, he did not rob the opera of dramatic action. He made the music express to the utmost the force and truth of the diction and define the full outlines of the characters of the play, without depriving it in turn of sensuousness and beauty. For the overture, recitative, air, concerted pieces, chorus, and orchestral accompaniment, he employed a more elaborate development of themes and motives, according to the artistic requirements of each form as placed in the drama. No one has ever united more perfectly than Mozart, precision and energy of dramatic expression with the richest and purest melody. His characters are musical revelations, — they think, feel, and act in tones. Music is their natural organ and native speech. Every one appears on the stage before us, and remains true to his or her individuality in all situations, in every phase of passion, true and consistent throughout. This is exhibited just as vividly in his exquisite trios, quartets, and other concerted music, as in his arias. In the famous sestet in "Don Giovanni" the several voices maintain their characteristic individuality during the most complicated interweaving of the parts. Voices introduced merely to fill up the harmony do not exist in his ensembles. For this purpose Mozart exercised his perfect command of technical vocal composition with rare mastery of counterpoint. The great symphonist and contrapuntist joined hands with the great dramatist. Before his time the treatment of the orchestra remained comparatively

Union of dramatic expression and melody

insignificant as a means of dramatic expression and coloring, though Gluck pointed the way, especially in the use of solo wind instruments. Dramatic orchestration under Mozart became more symphonic and massive in character. The solo instruments are refined organs of feeling, which intensify the dramatic fire and give color and sensuous beauty to the vocal parts, while they support and relieve them from beginning to end.

In his operas every feeling of the heart finds utterance; pathos and passion, humor and tenderness, love and hate — every emotion is expressed in beautiful tones. Mozart never oversteps the boundary line which separates beauty from cacophony. A divine harmony and classic purity of form distinguish his dramatic music, as, indeed, all his music, from the little minuets which he composed as a child to his immortal "Requiem," which he left unfinished. He has well been called the "Raphael of music."

Otto Jahn's estimate of Mozart Mozart died too early to reach the highest aim of his transcendent genius. The texts of his operas are for the most part trivial and frivolous, yet the nobility and purity of his own nature rendered even the subject of "Don Juan" religious and spiritual music. "Of all composers who have lived since his time," says Otto Jahn, "there are none who have not been affected by his mind and soul, none who have not inherited something from him. For like all truly great creative minds he belongs to two periods, whose union he was destined to effect. While he absorbed and transformed all that his time and surroundings could bestow, he reproduced from his own nature the germ of a new art life. All that his senses granted him, all that his mind could grasp, all that moved his heart, every experience of life was transformed into music, which lived and stirred within him. From this inward life the artist created works of imperishable truth and beauty. And while our gaze is uplifted in reverence and admiration to the great musician, it may rest with equal sympathy and love upon the pure-hearted man. We can trace in his career, lying clear and open before us, the dispensation which led him to the goal of his desires; and, hard pressed as he was by life's needs and sorrows, the highest joy which is granted to mortals — the joy of successful attainment — was his in fullest measure. 'And he was one of us!' his countrymen may exclaim with just pride; for wherever the highest and best names of every art and age are called for, there among the first will be the name of Wolfgang Amadeus Mozart."

CHAPTER XXI

BEETHOVEN

Early
training

Ludwig van Beethoven, the greatest of all instrumental composers, was born at Bonn, December 16, 1770. His father was a singer in the electoral chapel. Before Ludwig was four years old he was obliged to practise his daily task of exercises at the piano, and was often urged by blows. His father soon placed him under the tuition of Pfeiffer, an opera singer, who was a good musician. At school he learned to read, write, and cipher, and a certain Zambona taught him some Latin, French, and Italian. This limited education was a source of mortification to Beethoven throughout his life, and no doubt strongly influenced his character. He learned organ playing from van den Eeden, court organist, and subsequently composition from Neefe, who predicted that his pupil would be a second Mozart. At the age of eleven Ludwig played the preludes and fugues of "The Well-Tempered Clavichord" with energy and fluency, and had composed variations, bagatelles, and sonatas for the piano. His remarkable talent attracted the attention of the elector, and at the age of fifteen he was appointed assistant organist of the court chapel. In 1787 he was sent to Vienna to study with Mozart, probably at the elector's expense, but the illness and death of his mother soon called him home. The habits of his father had become so bad that the duty of supporting his younger brothers devolved in a measure on Ludwig.

During the next four years he earned a small salary as organist, viola player, and teacher, and felt keenly the hardships and sorrows of life. A happier episode was the appreciation and sympathy he received from his devoted friends

Count Waldstein and the von Breuning family. The widow von Breuning was cultivated and kind-hearted, and had a good influence on the young genius. Her daughter Eleonore became his pupil, and in turn acquainted him with Homer, Shakespeare, and the German poets. He became a great reader, and gradually acquired a very good intellectual training. His passion for Shakespeare and Plutarch was lifelong. Beethoven exercised the same charm on these noble friends that he did later on the proud aristocracy of Vienna. This youthful period of development came to an end in 1792, when Beethoven was free to accept the elector's kindness, and went to Vienna to study, with the intention of returning to his native place; but he never saw it again. He was destined to remain in Vienna for the rest of his life, except for an occasional absence on a journey. The list of Beethoven's compositions up to this time consists of the trio for strings, op. 3, two easy sonatas, serenade, op. 8, some sets of variations, songs, and other pieces, — very little compared with what Mozart, Schubert, and Mendelssohn accomplished in their youth.

At Vienna Beethoven first attracted attention by his piano- **Life at** forte playing, and was soon recognized as a pianist of the **Vienna** first rank, especially on account of his wonderful improvisations, in which he had no rival. He pursued his studies in composition with Haydn and Albrechtsberger, but was not satisfied with their instruction, for the former was not sufficiently systematic, and the latter sought to bind his genius to pedantic rules. Beethoven considered his first five years at Vienna as the happiest of his life; he had kind and devoted friends among the best society, and was a favorite with people of the highest rank. The Archduke Rudolph, Prince Lobkowitz, Prince Lichnowsky, and other noblemen were his lifelong friends, who tolerated his eccentricities and defects through everything. This shows what a fascination there was in the man as well as in his music. During his first years he often played at the houses of his noble friends and patrons, but as time went on, he became more and more absorbed in composition, and ultimately withdrew from society and the public, except on rare occasions when concerts of his new works were given for the first time.

It is not clearly ascertained how many of his earlier works were written in Bonn and during the first years in Vienna. It is certain, however, that before the end of the century he had composed more than twenty piano sonatas, three sonatas for piano and violin, three sonatas for piano and violoncello, three piano trios, the quartet for piano and stringed instruments, the quintet for piano and wind instruments, the piano concertos in C and B♭, five trios, six quartets, the string quintet in C, the septet, his First and Second symphonies, the ballet music to " Prometheus," and a number of songs and

Period of despond-ency variations. During this exceedingly productive period deafness had already begun to afflict him. In 1802 he had a dangerous illness which brought him almost to the grave. It was during this crisis of his life that he wrote his will, in the form of a letter to his brothers, in which he paints a vivid and touching picture of his trials and suffering. " Born with an ardent, lively temperament," he writes, " fond of social pleasures, I was early compelled to withdraw myself, and lead a life of isolation from all men. When I at times have determined to rise superior to all this, oh! cruelly have I been again cast down by proofs of my defective hearing, and yet it has been utterly impossible for me to say to people, ' Speak louder, shout, for I am deaf!' " On the recovery of his health he became more resigned, and devoted himself with redoubled zeal to composition. The powerful will and character of the man could not succumb to despair; he proudly and patiently endured his fast-increasing deafness, the coldness and jealousy of his brothers, the sneers and cavilings of unfriendly rivals, and never in the course of his life sought to defend himself against attacks on his professional abilities. Although he had

warm friends among the nobility, he would not bow down to
rank and wealth; he looked on it as a degradation of his
genius. The prince held no higher place in his estimation   Political
than the private citizen. He was a stanch republican in his   ideas
political ideas, and did not hesitate at any time to avow his
principles; and it required no little courage to do this in
Vienna. His love for the writings of Plutarch and Plato may
account for his political belief. " Plato's ' Republic ' was
transfused into his flesh and blood," says Schindler.

Beethoven not only had a great heart but a powerful mind.
He did not limit himself to music, but reasoned and reflected
on the great events of his time. He was an insatiable reader,
especially of history, and the all-absorbing interest he felt in
the great events which were then taking place, his sympathy
for struggling humanity, mark him distinctively as a representative man as well as musician. He welcomed Napoleon
as the liberator of nations, and fondly believed at first that
he had no other ambition than to found a free republic and
inaugurate the happiness of the world. This enthusiasm
prompted Beethoven to compose the grand " Heroic Symphony" in honor of the First Consul, a work which well represents the new form and spirit of modern music. When the
composer heard that Napoleon had been proclaimed emperor,
he threw the score of his symphony on the floor with exe-
crations. Years afterwards, when the " man of destiny " had
come to his tragic end at St. Helena, Beethoven sarcasti-
cally remarked that he had composed appropriate music to
this event, alluding to the " Funeral March," which had been
introduced into the symphony before its publication.

The first fifteen years of the nineteenth century was the   1800–1815
most fruitful period in Beethoven's life. The mature and
original works which he produced during this time extended
from op. 30 to op. 117, with the exception of a few numbers.
This list embraces many sonatas, concertos, trios, quartets,
and other chamber music, the Third, Fourth, Fifth, Sixth,

Seventh, and Eighth symphonies, the oratorio of " The Mount of Olives," the " Mass in C," the opera " Fidelio," the music to " Egmont," the overtures to " Coriolanus," " King Stephen," and " Ruins of Athens," the fantasia for piano, orchestra, and chorus, songs, and other vocal pieces. After this period the remaining works of Beethoven appeared in less rapid succession. He became engaged in a lawsuit that robbed him of his peace of mind. His brother Karl, who had been unfortunate in marriage, died in 1815 and left his son to the care and protection of the composer, but the widow, an unprincipled woman, would not give up her son, and Beethoven was forced to bring the case before the courts. It was very mortifying to Beethoven's proud, upright nature to have to prove the bad character of his sister-in-law, but this was imperative, as the will of the father was not sufficient ground by law for removing the child from the mother. It was not till several years had elapsed and the case had been carried from court to court (because Beethoven was not a *von*), and a new action brought, that it was decided in his favor. This nephew, on whom Beethoven lavished all his affection, afterwards proved to be a worthless fellow. For three years Beethoven did not compose any important works ; yet during the few remaining years of his life he produced some of his grandest masterpieces, — the " Mass in D," the " Ninth Symphony," his last overtures, pianoforte sonatas, and quartets. These colossal works may be said to have been wrung from the very agony of his mental and bodily sufferings. He was neglected by the public, who were bowed down in Rossini worship ; he was estranged from his friends ; he was frequently ill, and totally deaf ; he was cursed with bad relations ; and he had the care of his nephew, who capped the climax of ugliness by shooting himself in the head, and who was imprisoned in consequence of his attempt at suicide. Yet Beethoven's lofty soul rose superior to the tragedy of life, and sang the glorious strains of joy and " love embracing the millions."

Lawsuit
with his
brother's
widow

During his last three years he composed incessantly, yet he thought that all he had accomplished was but a mere prelude to what he was yet to do. " I feel," he said, " as if I had written scarcely more than a few notes. I hope to bring a few great works into the world, and then, like an old child, to end my earthly career somewhere among good people." But his wish was not fulfilled. His C♯ minor and F major quartets were his last works (dated 1826). On his return from the country to Vienna in December he caught a violent cold in his stomach ; this was the beginning of the end. After a painful illness he died, on the evening of March 26, 1827, in the midst of a sudden storm of rain, hail, and lightning. It would seem as though Nature, whom he had loved so much, sympathized with the sorrow of the moment.

" Beethoven was below the middle height, broad across the shoulders, and very firmly built. His head was large, the forehead high and broad, with abundant hair, in earlier years black, in his last years quite white. His face was pockmarked and his complexion so dark that he looked very much like a Moor. Though his face was ugly it was wonderfully expressive. When lost in thought his look was gloomy and stern, but when he recognized a friend his smile was peculiarly genial. His eyes were the most attractive feature of his face, and the earnestness and sincerity of his character beamed forth from his glance. His manners were abrupt and often rough, and his deafness made him suspicious." His troubles with his family embittered him and he shunned society, yet beneath the outer crust of pride and obstinacy and bearishness there beat a warm, generous, and sympathetic heart. Beethoven was immensely fond of a joke, and some of his humor was hard to tolerate. His brother John, who was a rich proprietor, called on the composer and left his card, " Johann van Beethoven, Landed Proprietor." Beethoven immediately returned it after writing on the back, " L. van Beethoven, Brain Proprietor." His simplicity and independence of character gave an irresistible force to everything he said or did, but made it very hard for his friends to bear. He was always in difficulties about his lodgings and domestics. He said of a servant who told a falsehood that she was not pure at heart, and therefore could not make good soup. He hired apartments in different parts of the city, and moved from one place to another as the whim seized him. He was a great walker, and spent much of his time in the open air; many of his finest ideas came to him while walking in the suburbs of Vienna or the country with his notebook in hand. No man loved the country more; his summers were spent there, and he looked forward to his escape from the city with all the delight of a child. He said, "Woods, trees, and rocks give the response which man requires. Every tree seems to say, Holy, Holy." As he sat by some tree, inspiration would come to him, and among such surroundings his "Fidelio," "Heroic Symphony," "Mount of Olives," and in fact the majority of his great works were sketched in his notebooks and afterwards erased and rewritten again and again until they finally reached perfection. His many notebooks, where all the ideas were written down as they occurred to him, afford a precious insight into Beethoven's method of composing. There is hardly a bar of his music which was not rewritten again and again: a work grew like a plant or tree, a gradual and organic process. The theme of the "Hymn of Joy" in the "Ninth Symphony" is found in one of his first sketchbooks, when he was a young man; it was years before it was developed and incorporated into his greatest work. Whole years of reflection were comprised in his works, but when a composition was once done he would never alter a note.

Deafness   Who can conceive what a source of unhappiness and suffering was the deafness which afflicted Beethoven during the greater part of his life? Think of a blind painter, and one may imagine the deaf composer, unable to hear a note of his divine music. It seems hard to believe that the creator of the "Seventh Symphony" and the "Choral Symphony" was doomed to receive no delight or happiness from their actual sound. We read in a letter of Rellstab, who visited Beethoven in his latter days, that the composer struck a chord softly. "Never will another fill me with such melancholy. He had C major in the right hand, and struck B in the bass, and looking at me steadily repeated the wrong chord several times that I might hear the sweet tone of the instrument; yet the greatest musician on earth did not perceive the discord."

Yet this fatal deafness befriended him, as it were, when it closed the doors of sense behind. In his ideal world he unburdened his sorrows, hopes, joys, and aspirations. They became the companions of his solitude. Beethoven has vindicated the true spirituality of music; the deaf musician has proved that the ancient, poetical significance of music as the divine art is true. This inward life accounts for the composer's early inclination for instrumental music. The wide range opened to his imagination and emotions by the modern orchestra, with its unlimited resources of instrumental color and technical means, enabled Beethoven to speak in the "language of a thousand souls," and move the world with his impassioned eloquence.

Beethoven owed much to Haydn and Mozart, but he was not content to be a mere imitator. He began where they left off. Through his originality and daring he carried the classical forms of instrumental music to the culmination point. In his first works, from op. 1 to op. 30, or thereabouts, Beethoven shows the influence of his predecessors to some extent; and yet in his very first work — three trios — striking originality and independence are asserted on every page. And it was not long before he left all far behind in his lofty flight of genius. It was his peculiar and remarkable character as much as his great musical gift that impelled him on the path of progress.

Originality and independence

Many writers have divided the works of Beethoven into
three periods, but they are not to be so sharply defined ; in
general they correspond to the life periods of youth, maturity,
and old age. In his earlier works he followed the path of
Haydn and Mozart to some extent ; in his middle period he
went his own way, and appeared in all his originality and
strength ; in his last period he revealed himself as a prophet
and dreamer of heavenly things. He soon outgrew the limits
of previous musical construction. What a contrast between
his " Heroic Symphony " and all that had been conceived
before! Beethoven was destined to develop the art of thematic
treatment to a point never reached before nor surpassed since.
The several movements were laid out on much broader foundations, the musical periods expanded to their utmost limits.
The so-called middle part (*Mittelsatz*) of the movement was
made more impressive and more elaborate ; also the coda
(*Schlussgruppe*) was much extended, worked up, and made
the very climax of the whole movement. Splendid examples
of this kind are the opening movements of the Heroic and
Fifth symphonies.

In the art of motive building Beethoven followed Haydn
and Mozart, but with new results. We are astonished at the
never-ending variety which this thematic play brings forth.
The opening allegro of his "Fifth Symphony" is often cited as
a wonderful example of the development of the great dramatic
movement from a single motive of four notes. He intensified
the character of every movement. The scherzo owes its origin
to Beethoven, who developed it from the slower minuet, transforming its nature, and rendering it highly poetical, imaginative, and humorous.

In the adagio, or other slow movement, the master gives
utterance to his pathetic, solemn, and religious feelings.
Here he speaks the language of his inmost soul ; we feel
that "he was a man of sorrows, and acquainted with grief."
The finale assumed much greater importance than formerly.

Under Haydn and Mozart it usually consisted of a light rondo, which conducted the work to a gay and pleasing conclusion. Mozart, however, in his "Jupiter" symphony, gave an example of a broad, noble, and masterly finale. Beethoven extended the finale, and made it the climax of the whole work. What is there grander or more inspiring in all art than the last movement of the "Fifth Symphony"?

Beethoven's music, more than any other before his time, is characterized by vivid contrasts in the themes and passages, rhythmical effects, bold dissonances and modulations, dynamic expression, varied and massive instrumentation. This is true not only of the several movements as a whole but of their subdivisions. The movements are held in close relation by contrast of emotions, by elevated or depressed, passionate or calm, moods. If the first movement is conceived in a powerful or fiery or tragic spirit, the feelings after a time are rendered all the more susceptible to the calm mood of the slow movement, which may lead through sadness and longing to the vivacity and jocoseness of the scherzo, and this in turn to triumphant joy in the finale. Each is thus employed with its special æsthetic problem, and contributes its share to the total effect of the work. This same æsthetic law of contrast applies also to the divisions of each movement with its several themes.

Beethoven broke down the restrictions that governed transitions of key. He made sudden progressions into remote keys. His bold modulations were unprecedented. Before his time the composers of symphonies and sonatas had generally confined themselves to a narrow range of keys, especially between the several movements. In eighty-one works of Beethoven in sonata form the second movement occurs in the dominant only three times; in the subdominant nineteen times; in the submediant, or third below, thirty times. This latter was his favorite change. Beethoven was the greatest master of the variation. Witness the finale of the "Heroic *Character of his work*

Symphony," the *andante con moto* of the Fifth, the adagio of the Ninth, the slow movements of the trio in B♭, the Appassionata and "Kreutzer" sonatas. His variations are not exhibitions of skill and learning, or of musical embroidery, but are full of beauty and feeling. Each variation is a character piece or tone poem.

The dramatic and intensely emotional character of his ideas impelled him to use a great number of dynamic nuances. If we compare him with his predecessors, we are impressed with the great number of marks of expression. The cavatina of his B♭ quartet .is sixty-six measures long, and has no less than fifty-eight marks of expression.

Orchestration
Beethoven advanced the art of orchestration to its essentially modern stage. His orchestra is practically the same as Mozart's, but the instruments are used with greater freedom and technical execution. He employed more massive combinations. His tuttis are more powerful, his solo and chorus effects more varied than ever before. He works the orchestra up to grand climaxes by extended rhythmical passages in ever-growing crescendo. An intense dramatic spirit and tragic fire are characteristic of his symphonies and overtures. Witness his "Fifth Symphony," the overtures to "Leonore, No. 3," "Egmont," and "Coriolanus." Even the orchestral preludes of Wagner are not so great in tragic pathos.

Beethoven did not introduce unusual instruments except in very few works. He was too reserved in his employment of trombones. None are used in his symphonies, except in the finale of the Fifth, the "Thunderstorm" of the "Pastoral," and the choral part of the Ninth; but he used them freely in the overture to "Leonore" and in the opera "Fidelio." On a few occasions he employed the contra-fagot and the basset horn. He first raised the kettledrum to the importance of a solo instrument. In his Eighth and Ninth symphonies they are tuned in octaves. Since his time the orchestra has been enriched by the addition of the English horn, bass clarinet, bass tuba, valved horns and trumpets, harp, etc., and a larger string band. Nowadays the full orchestra employs also a larger chorus of wood and brass instruments.

Music cannot express verbal ideas, but as a spiritual language it transcends all words in expressing intense moods of feeling. Beethoven is its greatest poet. His works are genuine tone poems that are clearly understood and felt by every musical listener who has learned the language of tones, — a language which cannot be translated into words, as has been so often attempted by Wagner, Lenz, Marx, and others, who waste labor and thought in trying to explain Beethoven's poetic intentions.

One striking feature of Beethoven's works is their difference of style. He is the least of a mannerist of all the masters. Each work has its own peculiar character; each is a type by itself. He may be compared with Shakespeare in this respect, as well as in the power of expressing so vividly and intensely every phase of human emotion. The operas of Wagner may also be cited as being wholly unlike each other in style and treatment. They, too, show wonderful progress in musical growth and characteristic variety. Only a few of Beethoven's works have titles to indicate their practical intention, yet each one impresses its meaning as clearly as daylight. The "Fifth Symphony" means more to us than the "Pastoral Symphony," — his one great piece of programme music. Even in this he aimed at the "expression of emotions rather than at tone painting" according to his own words. His "Egmont" and "Coriolanus" overtures and his Appassionata and Farewell sonatas have only general titles to characterize them, but they do not need more. The First and Second symphonies suggest the style of Haydn and Mozart, and yet they were considered daring when they first appeared. The beautiful and tender larghetto and the spirited scherzo of the "Second Symphony" are thoroughly Beethovenish. But with the Heroic he laid the cornerstone of the modern symphony. Here he revealed

The symphonies

himself in all his power, originality, and character. The tradi-tional form of the slow movement is replaced by the " Funeral March" on the death of a hero, which is the most impressive of all dirges. The scherzo is Shakespearean in humor and fascination, and the finale crowns the whole work. The Fourth is on a lesser scale, but has an Italian melodiousness and artistic finish which contrast with the heroic quality of the Third and the dramatic fire and pathos and triumph of the Fifth. The Pastoral is full of the joy of life in the contem-plation of nature.

The
"Choral
Symphony"
The Seventh is full of great contrasts of mood, — joy and sorrow alternate with humor and exulting passion. How different in character from the Fifth, though equally grand and intense! It is more truly romantic than the symphonies of the so-called romantic composers who have followed in this path. The Eighth is the most concentrated and concise of all his symphonies. It is distinguished for its joyousness, though mingled with strains of pathos. The Ninth or " Choral Sym-phony" stands alone in the history of music. The first three movements are instrumental, and have reference to the follow-ing choral part, which is set to Schiller's " Ode to Joy." The first movement typifies the tragic struggle of the soul, the scherzo suggests the grotesque humor and fantastic phases of life, the wonderful adagio expresses holy aspirations, and pure sentiments of the heart laden with sorrow. But these unheard-of accents of the instruments are not enough. The human voice now takes up the burden with the words, "O friends, let not these tones but happier ones inspire us!" Then follows the sublime hymn, with its theme of joy, love, and brotherhood for all mankind, or that charity which is the true essence of Christianity.

Beethoven employed the sonata form in all his important instrumental works; but we lose sight of the constructive outlines entirely in our appreciation of the poetical ideas and moods of feeling which dominate his music. What is true of

his symphonies applies with equal force to his piano and
chamber compositions. He developed instrumental technic
and expression to a much higher point in his piano sonatas,
trios, and concertos, and in his chamber music. The most
famous of these — the Moonlight, Appassionata, Farewell sonatas, the great B♭ sonata, op. 106, the last three sonatas in
E major, A♭, and C, the "Kreutzer Sonata" for piano and
violin, the B♭ piano trio, the piano concertos in G and E♭,
the violin concerto in D, the three quartets, op. 59, the harp
quartet, and the last transcendental quartets — are the greatest of their kind and are immortal.

As a vocal composer Beethoven was not preëminent. He
treated the human voice too much like an orchestral instrument. It is remarkable that while he often consulted orchestral musicians with regard to instrumental technical effects,
he apparently did not ask the advice of singers as to vocal
treatment. His disregard for the capabilities of the voices
was painfully exhibited in the "Choral Symphony" and in the
"Mass in D." On the other hand, in his beautiful song cycle,
"To the Absent Loved One," and in his most popular song,
"Adelaide," he showed an appreciation of the principles that
govern vocal art, — the *bel canto* of the Italians is combined
with German sentiment and feeling. "Fidelio" also contains
much that is vocally effective, though in this work, as in the
"Choral Symphony" and "Mass in D," the orchestra domi-
nates. "Fidelio," his only opera, holds an equal place with
Mozart's "Don Giovanni" and "Zauberflöte" and has one
great superiority over them in its noble subject. The dramatic
intensity of the great dungeon scene is hardly equaled by
Wagner or any other dramatic composer. It is heartrending
and thrilling, like the last scene of "King Lear." The dramatic interest of "Fidelio" ends with the dungeon scene. The
last scene is an anticlimax. Like most of the operas of that
time, "Fidelio" has spoken dialogue and conventional solos
and concerted numbers. The quartet, "Mir ist so wunderbar,"

Vocal com-
positions

is a great favorite, the prisoners' chorus is very impressive, and the duet of Leonore and Florestan at the end of the dungeon scene expresses delirious joy. Yet the orchestra is master everywhere. "There is not an instrumental note that has not its passionate, dramatic meaning; there is not an instrument that is not a party to the drama. The overture, No. 3, is the whole story of the agony and the womanly devotion of Leonore in concise and tragic form, just as the overtures to 'Egmont' and 'Coriolanus' are the summing up of the tragedies of Goethe and Shakespeare."

Beethoven considered the "Mass in D" as his greatest work. In composing it he did not think of the Roman Catholic service. It is not church music so much as the direct, subjective expression of a religious heart, which cannot be restrained by the barriers of mere form and ritual. The composer consecrated his whole heart and energy to the creation of this great mass. In the manuscript is written over the Kyrie, "From the heart! May it go back to the heart!" Beethoven was brought up in the Catholic faith, but he did not set much value on church forms and observances; yet he was religious, as his life and works prove. He was too much affected by the liberal spirit of the age to follow blindly in the footsteps of tradition; he dared to think for himself. It was remarkable that he would never converse on religion or thoroughbass. He had written with his own pen two inscriptions, which were framed and placed on his writing table. They were said to have been found in an Egyptian temple, and were as follows: "I am all that is, all that was, and all that shall be. No mortal hath uplifted my veil." "He is One, self-existent, and to that One all things owe their existence." This was an epitome of the loftiest and purest religion to Beethoven. His mass is inspired with a new spirit of religious consciousness. It is as profoundly religious as Palestrina's "Marcellus Mass" or Bach's "Mass in B Minor," and much more akin to our modern sentiments, taste, and feeling.

Beetho-
ven's "Mass
in D"

" In his mass Beethoven, wherever he is most imposing, is intensely dramatic, and when he follows tradition, he is least himself. Notice, for instance, the change from the passionate entreaty that is almost a defiance in the Kyrie to the ineffable tenderness in the Christe eleïson, the wonderful Incarnatus and Crucifixus." In the fugal movements, on the other hand, where he follows the traditional formulas, he is less impressive. But what is there in all music more beautiful and celestial than the lyric Benedictus, with the obligato violin solo !

"The religious element in Beethoven's music is not confined to works which have a sacred text. The yearning after heavenly rest, sublime hope, and thanksgiving" are found in his last quartets, and in almost all his mature works. His Choral Symphony is raised above the secular and church styles by the grand motive that inspired it. The struggle to overcome the world, and convert its temptations, trials, and disappointments into the eternal blessings of joy and love, is the text of a sermon whose grandeur and eloquence ought to move all mankind.

Beethoven is a world poet, like Shakespeare. There is an element of popularity in all his creations, yet his mature works were not understood by many cultivated musicians at first; even his earlier compositions were harshly criticised. We read with astonishment nowadays the following criticism, in the *Allgemeine musikalische Zeitung*, of Beethoven's three sonatas for piano and violin, op. 12 : " It is well known that Herr van Beethoven is a finished pianist, but judging from the compositions before us, it is a question whether he can be considered as favorably as a composer. It is not to be denied that he goes his own way, but what a bizarre and wretched way ! Learned, learned, and always learned, but with nothing natural — no melody. Nothing but materials without a good method," and so on in this strain. In his maturer years his great symphonies were received by many as the product of a man half insane. Even von Weber

Contemporary criticism

declared, when he heard for the first time Beethoven's "Seventh Symphony," that the composer was ready for the madhouse. Spohr had a poor opinion of the finale of the "Fifth Symphony." What a contrast to the endless rhapsodies that were published in a later generation in the futile attempt to explain his tone poems and translate their meaning into words!

His last five quartets have been called mystical and transcendental. They are the last utterance of a man who was nearing the end of his life tragedy. "Yet it is not a longing for death that here finds expression," says Nohl, "but the intense and joyful feeling of something eternal and holy that speaks to us in the language of a new dispensation. The nature of the four combined instruments was the only vehicle of this pure, ethereal, and spiritual music. The melodies move freely in a wide compass, the voices cross each other freely, giving wonderful etherealness and spirituality to the effect of the strings by their thinness and delicacy of tone when thus separated by long intervals between the several parts of the chords." While many consider these quartets his greatest tone poems, others call them "charcoal sketches," and talk about Beethoven's deafness. Fétis held them to be "the aberrations of a genius that goes out in darkness," and others "wrench the dictionary in the expression of their delight." But here "all criticism is blind and impotent."

Estimate of Beethoven

To sum up our estimate of Beethoven: it was his mission to spiritualize all forms of music; his great ideas have a religious tone and elevation that seizes the soul of the true listener. His great symphonies and quartets are like tragedies in their deep import and struggle of emotions; the different movements have as close a connection as the several acts of a tragic drama. He revealed a new and higher world, and spoke a language never heard before. The moral tone of his music will always exert a powerful influence for good on humanity wherever the wonderful art of music is known. In the Pantheon of art Beethoven holds a foremost place beside the greatest poets and artists of all time, beside Æschylus and Dante, Michael Angelo and Shakespeare. Like these inspired men he has widened and ennobled the mind and soul of humanity. "In his last works," says Dannreuther, "he passes beyond the horizon of a mere singer and poet, and touches upon the domain of the seer and prophet, where, in unison with all genuine mystics and ethical teachers, he delivers a message of religious love and resignation and release from the world." "A trace of heroic freedom pervades all his creations," says Ferdinand Hiller. "The expression 'Im Freien' (liberty) might serve as the inscription of a temple devoted to his genius." May the spirit of his immortal works dwell in the hearts of the lovers of freedom everywhere, and may men learn the lesson of patience, unceasing work, endurance, and faith which he exemplified in his life and taught in his works!

In the time of Haydn, Mozart, and Beethoven, Vienna was the capital of the musical world. All classes of people cultivated music; amateur orchestras and quartet clubs abounded, and noblemen emulated each other in having private opera and orchestral establishments. Among the many minor musicians who flourished then were several who deserve mention. *Contemporary musicians*

Ignaz Joseph Pleyel (1757–1831) was the favorite pupil of Haydn. He was a talented composer. His symphonies quartets, and quintets for a time rivaled Haydn's in popularity. Even Mozart, at first, thought that Pleyel's quartets might replace Haydn's; but time proved them to be only the reflection of Haydn's style without his inspiration, and they soon died a painless death.

Andreas Romberg (1767–1821) was one of a very musical family. His cousin, Bernhard Romberg, was a noted violoncellist and composer. Andreas composed operas, symphonies, and chamber music. His cantata, "The Lay of the Bell," has been popular in England and America.

Adalbert Gyrowetz (1763–1850), the most brilliant of these epigones, was prolific in all forms of music. He composed thirty operas (the most noted of which were his "Augenarzt," "Agnes Sorel," "Prüfung," and "Helene"), Singspiele, ballets, nineteen masses, and other vocal music. He wrote over sixty symphonies, and many quartets, overtures, serenades, dances, piano sonatas, etc. In his younger days he had a brilliant reputation in England and France. For twenty-seven years he was conductor of the imperial opera in Vienna. Although a thoroughly trained master, yet he lacked the one thing needful for a composer, — individuality; he was an unconscious imitator of Haydn and Mozart. He witnessed the entire rise and culmination of Beethoven's genius, for he was born seven years earlier and outlived him by twenty-three years.

Gyrowetz presents the melancholy spectacle of a composer who outlived his own fame. His works are entirely unknown at the present day, and his name is hardly remembered. His sad fate is that of many other minor composers, among whom the law of the "survival of the fittest" rules as in the animal kingdom. Of the majority it may briefly be written, as the abstract of the historian's page : they lived — and died.

When the pianoforte superseded the clavichord a number of masters arose, besides Mozart and Beethoven. The most famous were Clementi (whose "Gradus ad Parnassum" is still indispensable in the training of pianists), Steibelt, Sterkel, Kozeluch, Dussek, Woelfl, Hummel, Cramer, Tomaschek, and Field. Hummel was a pupil of Mozart, and was distinguished for his beautiful touch, finished execution, and elegance of style. His concertos and sonatas were once popular. His septet in D minor is a brilliant and charming work, and holds a place among the best chamber music. He also composed two noble masses. Johann Baptist Cramer was a pupil of Clementi. His numerous sonatas, etc., are shelved, but his piano studies live as classical models.

CHAPTER XXII

SCHUBERT

The most gifted of all the younger contemporaries of Bee- Early train-ing thoven was Franz Peter Schubert, born in Vienna on January 31, 1797, and died November 19, 1828, one year after the death of Beethoven. His whole life as a musician, therefore, was passed under the dominant influence of the great tone poet. Schubert's father was a schoolmaster, and of his nineteen children, the two oldest sons, Ignaz and Ferdinand, followed their father's calling. They were musical, and were taught the violin by their father. Franz was the thirteenth son. The members of this large family were devoted to each other, and it is evident that there was a general love of music among them. This talent centered in the little Franz, who began to pick out melodies on the old piano. When he was seven years old his father gave him violin lessons and his brother Ignaz, piano lessons, but as he soon outstripped them, he was placed under the tuition of Michael Holzer, in singing and harmony, and in violin, piano, and organ playing. "When I wished to teach him anything new," said Holzer, "he always knew it already." Holzer used to give him themes on which to extemporize, for he showed wonderful facility in this art, and had harmony at his fingers' ends. Before the completion of his eleventh year Franz became the leading soprano of the Lichtenthal choir, and was noted for the beauty of his voice and expressive manner of singing. He also played violin solos in church, and began to compose little songs, and pieces for the piano or for strings. Like the prodigy Mozart, the genius of Schubert bore early fruits. In 1808, when Franz was in his twelfth year, he was admitted into the Imperial school, or "Convict," as it was called. Here he received instruction in mathematics, history, French, and Italian, as well as in music. Though he had plenty of food for his mind, his body was nearly starved; he had but two wretched meals a day, more than eight hours apart, and in the winter time nearly perished from the cold. But little pains were taken to give him systematic instruction in musical theory and composition, although Salieri, the nominal conductor of the choir, gave him advice. Nevertheless Franz began to compose in almost every form of music, large and small. He was brimming over with musical thoughts, and was only hindered by the lack of means to provide himself with music paper.

The school orchestra An orchestra was formed by the boys of the choir, in which Franz distinguished himself from the outset. Their leader was Joseph von Spaun, a big boy, well known as an amateur musician. A warm friendship sprang up between him and Franz, and he soon discovered the rare creative talent of the little fellow, as well as his need of music paper. He determined that he should suffer this privation no longer, and henceforth Franz's consumption of music paper was astounding. His experience in the orchestra was very useful. Symphonies and overtures of Haydn, Mozart, Kozeluch, Cherubini, and others were practised diligently. Franz played first violin and sometimes conducted. He also delighted to play string quartets. Beethoven was the early object of his reverence, though the style of Schubert's juvenile works reminds us more of Haydn and Mozart. His sympathies were especially manifested for those compositions which may be termed poetical and imaginative; thus he gloried in the G minor symphony of Mozart, which he declared was like the songs of angels. The earliest known composition of Schubert is the four-handed fantasia for piano, composed in 1810. It contains twelve movements, each ending in a different key from that in which the piece begins. It is interesting to note that the first song of the first of all song composers, written in 1811, shows decided marks of originality. The boy was father of the man. This formless kind of song cycle is called " Hagar's Lament." It consists of twelve numbers of a fragmentary character. Probably many of Franz's early compositions are lost, but from this time forth he had the good habit of signing his manuscripts, and an unbroken record has thus been preserved.

Before leaving the Convict in November, 1816, Schubert had composed his "First Symphony" in D, several string quartets, overtures, a piano trio, variations, two fantasias for piano, songs, and other vocal pieces. Before the end of the year these were followed by an octet for wind instruments, three string quartets, a piano fantasia for four hands, thirty minuets, eight canons, and many songs and other vocal pieces. One of his great qualities was his astonishing spontaneity and productiveness. In his short life of thirty-one years he composed over eleven hundred and thirty-seven works. This fecundity of thought often betrayed him into prolixity and defective form. It is a pity that his early teachers did not guide him and give him a thorough training in counterpoint, but they were dazzled by his wonderful talent. *Early compositions*

During his apprenticeship at the Convict he had made great progress as a practical musician, and had had ample opportunities to hear his music constantly performed at school and at home. On leaving the Convict, when his voice broke, he was cast adrift on the world, with the absolute necessity of earning his daily bread, for the poverty of his family rendered this imperative. His only immediate opening was to become an assistant in his father's school. For three years he now settled down to an existence of unspeakable dreariness in teaching the children of the poorer classes the alphabet and the rudiments of arithmetic. The spectacle of so gifted a youth tied down to such tedious drudgery is melancholy indeed ; and yet these years were among the most prolific of his life. Other *Schoolteaching* men of genius have been obliged to submit to similar discipline, which in most cases has served as a spur to their creative powers. Some of his immortal works were written during this slavish routine. His whole being centered in music, and the most trying experiences of life could not render him unhappy and misanthropical. His disposition was naturally cheerful and even jovial, and he soon formed friendships of the most romantic nature with genial spirits of his own sex. These friends became warmly attached to him, for he was faithful and true, simple-minded and affectionate. Among them was Johann Mayrhofer, ten years his senior, and a gifted poet, whose words Schubert often set to music. Another friend was Franz von Schober, who was already acquainted with some of Schubert's songs, and had conceived an enthusiastic admiration for the composer. "When he found that he was a boy of about his own age, wearing out his nerves in a schoolroom, he determined to interpose." He offered Schubert a home with him, and became his chum. Subsequently he found another friend in Johann Michael Vogl, the imperial opera singer, who was twenty years the senior of Schubert, and was distinguished as a dramatic artist of rare ability.

From 1814 on we find a steady improvement in the character of Schubert's music, and we are astonished at his versatility ; he exercised his genius in almost every form of music. During that year he composed his "Second Symphony" in B♭, five string quartets, an overture in the Italian style, eleven dances for horns and strings, twenty-two songs, including the famous "Gretchen am Spinnrad" to Goethe's words, and his "First Mass" in F,—a work conceived in the true church style and full of melodic beauty.

Extraordinary productivity

In 1815 he composed the "Second Mass" in G, the "Third Mass" in B♭, the "Third Symphony" in D, one opera and six operettas, a Stabat Mater and a Salve Regina, four piano sonatas, a string quartet in G minor, thirty pieces for piano, and one hundred and thirty-seven songs. Some of these songs are among the most characteristic and famous : " Wanderer's Nachtlied," " Rastlose Liebe," the charming "Heidenröslein," the beautiful " Nähe des Geliebten," the Ossian songs, and the intensely dramatic and impressive " Erlkönig." Schubert happened to come across Goethe's ballad, and no sooner read it than he was seized with a " fit of wild inspiration, and was dashing the music upon paper when his friend Spaun came in and found him. It was all done in a short time, the rushing accompaniment and all ; and that same evening it was sung at the Convict before his old teachers and fellow-pupils." Strange to say, it was received rather coldly at first.

In 1816 he wrote the " Tragic Symphony," the " Fifth Symphony " in B♭, an overture, a concerto for violin and orchestra, a rondo for violin and orchestra, a string quartet, a string trio, a number of piano pieces, four cantatas, an unfinished opera, a Magnificat, Salve Regina, and other church music, including his beautiful " Stabat Mater," one of his best early compositions, and besides these no less than one hundred and thirty-one songs, of which ninety-nine have been preserved, among them the famous " Wanderer," Mignon's song, — " Kennst du das Land," — " Der König im Thule," " Der Fischer," and " Jäger's Abendlied," — songs that are stamped with the seal of Schubert's unique individuality and lyric genius. The record of his productivity during these three years of teaching is marvelous, and all accomplished in the intervals of school drudgery ! That a youth of nineteen should have accomplished such wonders shows that he was inspired. No wonder that his friend Vogl considered Schubert's songs the utterance of a musical clairvoyance, — the direct inspiration that sprang up unbidden in his soul from a divine source. Unlike Mozart he did not carefully perfect his works in his head before he wrote them down ; and unlike Beethoven he did not sketch his ideas in notebooks, and then gradually build up great works by a slow and careful process of selection,

Works composed in 1816

compression, and elaboration. This wonderful facility was often Schubert's weakness. It is remarkable that during this third year of his school-teaching he should have produced a greater number of compositions than in any subsequent year of his life. Among the eighty-six productions of the following year (1817) are fifty-two songs, many of them set to Mayrhofer's words. The list includes the famous "Lob der Thränen" and "Die Forelle," and of large works, his "Sixth Symphony" in C, three overtures in the Italian style (prompted, no doubt, by Rossini's triumphant visit to Vienna the same year), several piano sonatas, and miscellaneous piano pieces.

The next year, 1818, witnessed an episode in Schubert's life. He was engaged as teacher of music to Count Esterhazy, and went to stay at his country seat in Hungary for the summer, where he gave lessons to the little daughter Caroline. All the family were musical, and Schubert's intercourse with them was very pleasant. He became a favorite with the household, and from this time until his death he was always welcome whenever he chose to come. He returned to Vienna, however, in the autumn, and early in 1819 we find him sharing a gloomy and ill-furnished room with the poet Mayrhofer, with whom he led a thoroughly Bohemian life.

During the three years 1818–1820 Schubert composed about one hundred works: the "Mass in C," the "Mass in A♭," "Salve Regina," the "Twenty-third Psalm," the Easter cantata "Lazarus," and other sacred music, the operetta "Die Zwillingsbrüder," an overture for orchestra, quartets, quintets, dances for piano, and many songs.

The year 1821 may be considered as the turning point in his career, for his enthusiastic friends succeeded at length in bringing his name before the public in the most favorable light as a song composer. Among his admirers were the Sonnleithner family, who were cultivated musicians. At their house Schubert's music was constantly performed. Leopold

von Sonnleithner tried in vain to get a publisher for the
" Erlkönig "; finally it was printed by subscription, and the
sale was so rapid that Schubert was able to pay his debts
from the proceeds. A concert was also given, and his friend
Vogl sang the " Erlkönig " with rapturous applause. This
distinguished and highly cultivated singer was captivated
with Schubert's songs, and used his influence to make them
known to the public. On this occasion was sung, also, one
of Schubert's happiest inspirations, the double quartet for
male voices with string accompaniment, " Song of the Spirits
over the Waters " of Goethe. It is strange that this beautiful
composition failed to please the audience. We smile at the
following criticism of the *Allgemeine Zeitung:* " The eight-
part chorus of Herr Schubert is a farrago of all sorts of
modulations and vague departure from ordinary form, — no
sense, no order, no meaning. The composer resembles a big
wagoner who drives a team of eight horses, and turns now to
the right, now to the left, getting at one time out of the road,
then upsetting, and pursuing this game without once making
any honest headway."

During the same year eighteen of Schubert's songs were
published, and his name became generally known to the
public. Social reunions, under the name of " Schubertiaden,"
were organized by his friends and admirers. At these lively
meetings songs, dances, and conviviality were combined.
The music always consisted of Schubert's compositions.
Here he was in his element, and enjoyed every moment,
utterly oblivious of the past and future.

The " Schu-
bertiaden "

Schubert was now twenty-three years old, and the light of
his genius was dawning on the musical horizon. Every month
was fruitful in works that are now prized as among the richest
possessions of musical art. In 1821 appeared the beautiful
songs, " Geheimes," " Suleika," " Sei mir grüsst," " Lob
der Thränen"; in 1822, "Alphonso und Estrella" (his first important opera), the " Mass in A♭," his wonderful " Unfinished

Symphony" in B minor, and the exquisite song, "Frühlings-glaube," by Uhland. Then followed in 1823 the operas "Fierabras" and "Der häusliche Krieg," and the music to the drama "Rosamunde." These operas were unsuccessful, owing partly to poor librettos, but more perhaps to Schubert's lack of stage instinct. We find everywhere a wealth of beautiful melody, but his lyric genius and easy inventiveness proved a stumbling block; yet much of the music will always be welcome in the concert room. The overture and entr'acte music of "Rosamunde" are special favorites. His piano sonata in A minor, op. 143, was also composed in 1823, and several of his most charming songs, "Vergissmeinnicht," "Du bist die Ruh," "Der Zwerg," "Barcarolle," "Lachen und Weinen," and his celebrated "Die schöne Müllerin," — a set of twenty songs to the words of Wilhelm Müller. We read in Kreissle's biography of Schubert that at this period the clouds of destiny first gathered thickly around him; repeated disappointments, a monotonous existence, and bodily weakness contributing to produce a state of extreme depression. In Schubert's diary kept at this time we read, "No one fathoms another's grief, no one another's joy. People think they are ever going to one another, and they only go near one another. Oh, the misery of him who knows this by experience! My productions spring from my sorrow, those which are the product of pain seem to please the great world most. The loftiest inspiration is but a step from the absolutely ludicrous, just as the deepest wisdom is so near akin to crass stupidity." One is here reminded of King Lear's ravings. Schubert writes to a friend, "Picture to yourself a man whose health can never be reëstablished, whose most brilliant hopes have come to nothing, whose enthusiasm for the beautiful threatens to vanish altogether — and then ask yourself if such a condition does not represent a miserable and unhappy man.

Despond-ency

Meine Ruh ist hin, mein Herz ist schwer,
Ich finde sie nimmer und nimmer mehr."

This morbid state of mind, however, did not prevent him from composing, and his noble and cheerful octet in F was produced at this time. In writing to his brother Ferdinand in July he draws the picture of the tone poet finding consolation for the disappointments of life in the exercise of his art, and in the next year he became once more himself, jovial and buoyant. This happy mood was brought about by a long excursion which he made with his friend Vogl in the beautiful region of Upper Austria.

The only romantic passion which Schubert is known to have had was for Caroline Esterhazy, who now was a lovely young lady of seventeen. " That she was aware of his passion cannot be doubted, and one day she asked him, with pretended feelings of earnestness, why he never dedicated any of his pieces to her. He replied, 'What would be the use? All that I do is dedicated to you.'" His love, however, was not reciprocated. She admired him, as did the rest of her family, but he was too far removed in station and in personality to be attractive to her. No doubt some of the romantic beauty of his later music may have been inspired by this one tender passion of his life. His visit in 1824 to the Esterhazys at their country seat in Hungary certainly had an influence on the music composed about that time. We find an unmistakable Hungarian flavor in his " Divertissement à la Hongroise " for four hands, the quartet in A minor, the variations in A♭, his waltzes, and the superb sonata in C for four hands. Among the vocal compositions written at the Esterhazys was the famous quartet, " Gebet vor der Schlacht." This furnished an example of his wonderful readiness. " One morning, at breakfast, the countess begged him to set De la Motte Fouqué's poem to music. In the evening he presented the quartet, and it was practised at once."

In 1825 he finished his " Ninth Symphony," but it is lost. He also composed three piano sonatas, the one in A minor, op. 42, being altogether the best he ever wrote. Among

Romance

the twenty-two songs of this year are the " Die junge Nonne,"
" Allmacht," and the group of seven to Scott's " Lady of
the Lake," of which the most noted is the " Ave Maria."

Among the works of 1826 are the Shakespearean songs,
" Who is Sylvia?" and " Hark, hark, the Lark"; sonata
fantasia for piano in G, " Marche héroique " for four hands,
rondo for piano and violin, and, most important of all, the
string quartets in G major and D minor (the so-called posthumous quartets). The latter stands beside Beethoven's, and
has never been surpassed by any composer.

Poverty   In 1827 Schubert hoped to receive the appointment of
vice-chapelmaster, but this post was conferred on Josef
Weigl, the composer of the opera " Swiss Family "; thus
Schubert was disappointed in this chance of obtaining a
regular income and an honorable position. The small sums
which he received from his works were insufficient for his
humble wants; all through his short life he was pinched by
poverty. In no one year of his life did he have an income of
five hundred dollars. Perhaps the largest fee he ever received
was a purse of one hundred gulden from the Gesellschaft
der Musik-freunde in 1826, in reward for the " Twenty-third
Psalm " and " Gott in der Natur " written for them. In return
for this compliment he presented to them in 1828 the score of
his symphony in C, but at the time they were unable to
appreciate the wonderful character of this monumental work.
No doubt he would have had a better chance of general
recognition if he had not stood in the shadow of Beethoven's
commanding genius.

It is a pity that Beethoven and Schubert did not live to
become intimate. The great symphonist was too much pre-
occupied to seek out the shy and modest younger master.
During Beethoven's last illness some of Schubert's songs
were shown him, and he expressed his great admiration for
their originality and beauty: " Some day he will make a
noise in the world." Schubert and others went to Beethoven's

house during his last hours, and stood by his bedside. The
dying man made signs to his visitors with his hand which
they could not comprehend. Schubert was deeply moved, for
he worshiped Beethoven as a superior being. Among the
torch bearers at the grave was Schubert. Afterwards he
went to a tavern with a friend, filled two glasses with
wine, and drank the first to the memory of Beethoven, and
the second to him who should be the first to follow him,
little thinking that he himself would be summoned in less
than two years, and that he would be buried near the great
man whom he revered.

During the same year, 1827, Schubert composed his Last com-
profound and pathetic "Winter Journey," a cycle of twenty- positions
four songs, which, together with his fourteen "Swan Songs"
of a year later, mark the culmination of his lyric genius.
Among these masterpieces are the "Serenade," "Am Meer,"
"Aufenthalt," "Ihr Bild," and "Das Fischermädchen."

In the last year of his life, 1828, he composed the noblest
of all his church music, the "Mass in E♭." "His four masses"
says Frost, "are superior in refinement and true religious
style to any of Haydn or Mozart, the Requiem of the latter
excepted, and may worthily take rank with Beethoven's
setting of the sacred office in C. Schubert's "Mass in F," composed at the age of seventeen, is as remarkable an evidence
of early genius as any of the better-known works of Mendelssohn's boyhood. During the last year he also composed his
string quintet in C, which among his chamber music is only
surpassed by the quartet in D minor. He also wrote three
of his finest sonatas for piano, in C minor, A, and B♭, and his
only oratorio, "Miriam's Song of Triumph," a splendid work
which labors under the disadvantage of having the vocal
score supported only by piano accompaniment. But above all
these last works stands the "Tenth Symphony" in C major. The "Tenth
This glorious manifestation of his genius he did not live to Symphony"
hear. As soon as it was finished the score was presented to at Leipzig

the Gesellschaft der Musik-freunde. The parts were copied
out and the symphony rehearsed, but its extreme length and
exceeding difficulty (for that time) raised insurmountable
obstacles in the way of its performance, and it was returned
to the composer. In 1838, ten years later, Schumann rescued
this great masterpiece from oblivion. It was produced at the
Gewandhaus in Leipzig, on March 22, 1830, under Mendelssohn's direction. It made a profound impression, and was
recognized at once as the most remarkable work since
Beethoven's "Ninth Symphony." It was not heard in Vienna
until 1850, and then met with a cold reception, which shows
that Leipzig was far more cultivated in music at this time
than the city that gave him birth. "A prophet is not without honor save in his own country."

Schumann's
praise of
the sym-
phony
Schumann thus expressed himself after the first triumphant
performance : " We are transported into an unknown region.
Life in all its phases, color in exquisite gradations, the
minutest accuracy and fitness of expression are here, while
permeating the whole work is that romantic feeling so characteristic of Schubert's music. This heavenly long-drawn-out
symphony is like some thick romance of Jean Paul in four
volumes that we wish would never end. . . . A delicious
feeling takes possession of us, like that we get from some
lovely legend or fairy tale.

" Schubert's easy and brilliant mastery over the resources
of the orchestra would be unintelligible if one did not know
that six (nine !) other symphonies had preceded this. The
instruments converse with one another like human voices in
solo and chorus. Except in Beethoven I have nowhere found
such a striking resemblance to the organs of the human
voice. The complete independence, however, in which this
work stands with respect to Beethoven's, shows its mascu-
line originality."

A few months before Schubert's death a private concert
was given for his benefit, which shows that the musical

people of Vienna were growing more appreciative. The programme consisted entirely of his own compositions, among
them the noble trio in E♭ was played in public for the first
time. He received one hundred and sixty dollars from the
receipts of this concert, — a princely sum in his estimation.
This signal success inspired the idea of another concert, but
alas! the next programme of his works was not performed
until the master was cold in his grave.

Schubert's health now began to fail. He was troubled with **Last illness**
weakness, severe headache, and vertigo. The eleven hundred **and death**
and thirty-seven compositions which he had produced in nineteen years, combined with poor living, were more than enough
to sap his energies and overtax his brain. Cerebral excite-
ment caused an excessive rush of blood to his head. In Oc-
tober he made a short excursion into the country with his
brother and friends, to improve his health, but soon after
his return to Vienna, his appetite entirely failed him and he
soon took to his bed. He wrote a last letter to his lifelong
friend Schober, as follows:

Dear Schober: I am ill. I have neither eaten nor drunk anything
for eleven days, and shift, weak and weary, from my chair to my bed
and back again. . . . If I attempt to eat anything it will not stay by
me. Will you be so kind as to console me in this desperate condition
by the loan of some more books? I have read Cooper's "Last of the
Mohicans," "Spy," "Pilot," and "Pioneer." If you have any more of
his, I implore you to send them to me, . . . or anything else.

Your friend,
SCHUBERT.

His condition soon became worse, and the doctors thought
he was threatened with typhus fever. He asked his brother
Ferdinand, "What is going to happen to me? What are they
doing to me?" His brother and his physician replied hope-
fully, but in vain. He said solemnly: "No, no, here is my
end. . . . I entreat you to carry me to my own room, and
don't leave me in this hole in the earth. What! don't I deserve
a place above ground?" His brother tried to convince him

that he was lying in his own bed, but Franz replied, " No, no, it is not true; Beethoven is not laid here." This was taken as evidence of his desire to rest near Beethoven, and the wish was reverently respected. " On the next day," writes John Fiske, " there passed away one of the sweetest and truest souls that ever looked with human eyes."

Appearance
and char-
acter If the portraits of Schubert are true, his face is the mirror of his soul and character. Simplicity, kindness, truthfulness, fidelity, modesty, and amiability were his distinguishing traits. He was short in stature, round-shouldered, with plump arms and hands. His face was full and puffy and homely, yet when he became animated his eyes betrayed the sacred fire of his soul. In general society Schubert was awkward and shy, and shunned people of rank, but he was very companionable among his intimate friends, and it was his greatest pleasure to discuss music over a glass of wine in some cosy tavern.

Schubert was in truth a child of nature, whom to know was to love and esteem. His faults may be summed up as a general incapacity to understand his own worldly interests. All his friends agreed that he was entirely free from envy and hatred; he was high-minded and true in all the relations of life. Like Beethoven he was an enthusiastic lover of nature. His industry and power of work were marvelous. Usually he began to compose in the early hours of the morning as soon as he was awake; sitting on his bed he would write incessantly until breakfast time. He was generally absorbed in musical creation for the greater part of the day, but often gave up the afternoon to the pleasures of social intercourse. In facility of composition he has hardly been equaled by any one. He had only to read a poem through once or twice and it had composed itself in his mind, so to speak, with a characteristic melody, clothed with an appropriate accompaniment, and expressing vividly the true meaning of the words. It was impossible for him to evolve beautiful ideas from worthless words, and therefore it is not strange that among his six hundred and fifty songs we find some which are insignificant and weak.

"If fruitfulness," says Schumann, "be a characteristic of genius, Schubert is certainly one of the greatest; by degrees he might have set to music the whole body of German poetry. In whatever direction he wished his music to flow, it gushed forth in streams, and Telemann, who demands of a good composer ability to set a door-plate to music, would have found his man in Schubert. Æschylus and Klopstock, both so hard to set to music, yielded to his treatment as easily as the flowing strains of Wilhelm Müller and others."

Schubert was the greatest song composer that ever lived. He is the representative master here as Beethoven is in symphonic music. He was the creator of the modern German Lied, for the few songs of Haydn, Mozart, and Beethoven did not serve as models to him, except, perhaps, the one song cycle of the latter, "An die ferne Geliebte." *Preëminence as a song composer*

From time immemorial the Germans had their popular songs (Volkslieder). The minnesingers, mastersingers, and the Lutheran Church gave a powerful impulse to popular music in Germany, and prepared the ground for her great composers. During the sway of Italian opera, however, in the eighteenth century, the Volkslied was neglected. Then came a reaction, and a multitude of vocal pieces, called odes, were in fashion.

Lessing marks the new birth of German literature. Herder, the poet, revived the feeling for the poetry of the old Volkslied, and with the advent of Goethe, Schiller, and Heine a new and glorious era dawned on lyric poetry. Schubert flourished at the right moment to avail himself of the beautiful songs of Goethe, Heine, Uhland, Byron, Scott, and other contemporary poets. Married to the inspired music of Schubert, their words acquired deeper feeling and higher poetic meaning.

Among the multitude of song composers who have followed the path of Schubert there are several who are worthy of a place beside him. Many songs of Schumann and Franz are as full of pathos and poetic beauty, and sometimes show more refinement in the choice and careful treatment of the words and the accompaniment, but in spontaneity, variety, wealth of imagination, dramatic fire, and ear-haunting, characteristic melody, Schubert surpasses them all. His wonderful melodies are enhanced by an endless variety of rhythmical accompaniments full of rich and daring modulations. " He could make one believe that C major and F♯ minor are twin sisters."

Genius in
adapting
music to
poetry
What song is there by any other composer that matches the " Erlkönig " in dramatic intensity? This was published as opus 1. The famous "Miller" songs, " Winter Journey," and " Swan Songs " possess a certain ease, freedom, and spontaneity that later song composers have not equaled. What is more beautiful and fascinating in all music than his " Sei mir gegrüsst," " Du bist die Ruh," " Frühlingsglaube," " Die junge Nonne," " Tod und das Mädchen," " Barcarolle," " Geheimes," " Suleika," " Trockne Blumen," " Am Meer," and " Serenade "? These songs awaken in us an irresistible longing, a homesickness of the soul. His series of connected songs are distinguished by their subtle affinities with each other, presenting a complete psychological development of poetical and emotional ideas, a continuous flow of representative images. All the contrast of moods — joy, sorrow, hope, longing, love, hate, comfort, and submission — follow one another in harmonious sequence. Schumann's enthusiasm for Schubert knew no bounds. " There was a time," he says, " when it gave me no pleasure to speak of him. I could only talk of him by night to the trees and stars. Who amongst us at some time or another has not been sentimental? Charmed by this new spirit, whose capacities seemed to me boundless, deaf to everything that could be urged against him, my thoughts were absorbed in Schubert.

" He will ever be the prime musical favorite of youth. He shows — what charms the young — a full heart, bold thoughts, and rapid impulse. He tells them of pet fancies, romantic histories, loves, and adventures, and throws a dash of humor into the picture, but not so much as to disturb the gentleness and tenderness of his ideal; and, at the same time, he adds wings to the fancy of his interpreter in a way unknown to any other composer but Beethoven."

In his instrumental music Schubert was the true successor of his great model, Beethoven. He was not, however, a mere imitator; on the contrary, it is very remarkable how little we feel the influence of Beethoven's style in Schubert's motives and thematic features. His melodies are all his own, and bear the stamp of his peculiar character and individuality. He shows his affinity to his great prototype chiefly in the broad outlines of form, massive rhythmical effects, bold modulations, dramatic climax, emotional depth, and intensity of the slow movements, the fire and grandeur of the finales, the variety and effectiveness of the instrumentation. The most striking quality of Schubert's music is its wealth of lyric expression. What exquisite melody, pure, naïve, and refined, is bestowed lavishly everywhere, even to excess!

The charge has been made that many of his movements are diffuse and spun out. Yet Schumann well named his longest work "the symphony of divine length." His diffuseness was the result of his marvelous spontaneity. Whatever he wanted was at his fingers' ends; he never hesitated, and never seemed to aim at making innovations or doing things for mere effect. He rarely revised his music; in this he was very different from Beethoven, who worked over his themes again and again, transforming almost every measure. In improvisation Beethoven was bold and impassioned, but as soon as he took his pen in his hand he became all at once extremely cautious and hesitating. This is shown vividly in his remarkable notebooks, in which he jotted down his musical thoughts as they occurred to him. All was gradual and with him all was organic; his music grew like a plant or tree.

His method of work compared with that of Beethoven

Schubert's method was different; everything seemed to come to him at once, without effort. For this reason many of his early works do not fulfill the highest ideal, compared with the standard he afterwards reached. Schubert did not extend or modify the traditional form of the symphony, quartet, and sonata, but followed the general outlines marked out by Beethoven, just as Mendelssohn, Schumann, Brahms, and other recent composers have done. Is this not proof that musicians, like poets, may use forms that are centuries old and endow them with freshness and newness by virtue of their individuality, originality, and poetic gift ? The theory that Beethoven's "Ninth Symphony" is the last great work of pure instrumental music is disproved by the fact that the symphonies of Schubert, Schumann, Tschaikowsky, Brahms, Dvorak, and others are as eagerly listened to nowadays, with as much joy and delight, as the symphonic poems of Berlioz, Liszt, and Strauss, and the musical dramas of Wagner. Have these supplanted the cyclical instrumental forms? Assuredly not. The organic form of the symphony still remains the highest manifestation of pure music, though the future may give birth to something beyond it. Schubert, by virtue of his poetic gift, endowed this form, inherited from Beethoven, with a romance and a magic that have never been surpassed. Liszt called Schubert the most romantic and poetical of all composers.

Character-
ization of
his music

Here one may ask, What is the difference between the classical and the romantic in art ? The question is easier than the answer. I shall not attempt to solve the problem. Writers on music, especially certain Germans, use these two words arbitrarily in order to carry out a pet theory. Is it not true that what we call romantic to-day may, in the course of time, become classical ? These terms as applied to music do not bear the same clear interpretation as in literature, except in so far as the musical drama is concerned. The extravagant and imaginative tales and poems of the Middle Ages, in which the supernatural world of enchantment and magic mingled with real life, are called romantic, as opposed to the antique simplicity and harmony of design and the avoidance of extravagance that characterize Greek tragedy. The same standard does not apply to music. It may be said that all music is classical which reaches the highest standard of beauty, as expressed in symmetrical form and purity of feeling. According to this definition the music of Schubert, Schumann, and others of the so-called romantic school is truly classical. On the other hand, some of Bach's classical music is romantic. Music which seems strange at first may soon fascinate us by its beauty and charm, and may awaken associations that recall the past. Music full of surprises and undreamed-of effects, holding us spellbound and entranced, may well be termed romantic. And this is what characterizes Schubert's music.

"So careless of fame was Schubert," says John Fiske, "so suddenly did death seize him, and so little did the world suspect the untold wealth of music written upon musty sheets of paper tucked away in sundry old drawers and cupboards in Vienna, that much has remained unknown until the present day. As from time to time new songs, sonatas, trios, or symphonies were brought to light, a witty French journalist began to utter doubts of their genuineness and to scoff at the 'posthumous diligence of the song writer Schubert.'" The world owes a debt of gratitude to Sir George Grove for collecting and editing many of these long-neglected manuscripts. At the end of his exhaustive article on Schubert he gives a complete chronological catalogue of Schubert's works.

Discovery of un-known works

Time is a merciless critic and sifts the chaff from the wheat. It is the cruel fate of most composers, even the greatest, to have the larger part of their works ultimately shelved. Handel's forty operas are forgotten and more than half his oratorios are rarely performed. Out of Haydn's one hundred and twenty-five symphonies only a dozen or so are now heard in the concert hall; the same proportion holds for his string quartets. Not a third of Mozart's works can be said to live. Mendelssohn, Spohr, von Weber, Brahms, Rubinstein, Dvorak, Tschaikowsky, and all other modern masters are subject to the law of the "survival of the fittest." Beethoven alone has stood the test of time. Very few of his compositions are weak and insignificant; most of them are immortal, like Shakespeare's.

Works on which his fame rests Schubert's eleven hundred works share the common lot. The greater part are interesting only as the product of a genius who wrote too much in his short lifetime. Yet no composer has created so many beautiful and ideal songs as Schubert, and no one except Beethoven has surpassed him in the quality of a few of his last instrumental works, — the C major symphony, "Unfinished Symphony," the quartets in G and D minor, the quintet in C, and the octet in F. Other noble compositions are the piano trios in B♭ and E♭, the piano sonata in A minor, "Moments musicals," impromptus, fantasias, dances, marches for piano, overture and entr'acte music to "Rosamunde," overtures to "Fierabras" and "Alphonso und Estrella."

Before he died Schubert was attracted more and more to the large forms of instrumental music; if he had lived twenty years longer, no doubt he would have created symphonies and quartets that would have excelled all he had accomplished before. But alas! he was cut off untimely before he reached the climax of his artistic development. If he had lived to complete his full span of years, he would have more than fulfilled the glorious hopes expressed in the line chiseled on his tombstone: "Here lies buried a rich treasure but still more glorious hopes." Yet though this ideal destiny was not realized, let us be thankful for the rich treasure he left. As a song composer he is supreme, and as an inspired poet of the symphony there is only one who surpassed him. Within a few short years he created masterpieces which will never grow old, but will always live among the noblest works of art, and bloom in coming ages with perennial youth.

INDEX